The Politics of Marketing the Labour Party

Dominic Wring
Lecturer in Communication and Media Studies
Loughborough University

First published 2005 by
PALGRAVE MACMILLAN
Houndmills, Basingstoke, Hampshire RG21 6XS and
175 Fifth Avenue, New York, N. Y. 10010
Companies and representatives throughout the world

PALGRAVE MACMILLAN is the global academic imprint of the Palgrave Macmillan division of St. Martin's Press, LLC and of Palgrave Macmillan Ltd. Macmillan® is a registered trademark in the United States, United Kingdom and other countries. Palgrave is a registered trademark in the European Union and other countries.

ISBN 0–333–68952–6 hardback
ISBN 0–333–68953–4 paperback

This book is printed on paper suitable for recycling and made from fully managed and sustained forest sources.

A catalogue record for this book is available from the British Library.

Library of Congress Cataloging-in-Publication Data
Wring, Dominic, 1968–
    The politics of marketing the Labour Party / Dominic Wring.
        p. cm.
    Includes bibliographical references and index.
    ISBN 0–333–68952–6 (hardback) – ISBN 0–333–68953–4 (pbk.)
        1. Labour Party (Great Britain)–Public relations–History–20th century.
2. Communications in politics–Great Britain–History–20th century. I. Title.

JN1129.L32W75 2005
324.24107'09'04–dc22   2004051150

10   9   8   7   6   5   4   3   2   1
14   13   12   11   10   09   08   07   06   05

Printed and bound in Great Britain by
Antony Rowe Ltd, Chippenham and Eastbourne

For Claire, Margaret and Philip

'The issue of the campaign is can they fool you with their lies and get you to vote in their interests instead of your own'

Upton Sinclair, 1934

'(There is) a vocabulary of fact and knowing and memory, of wit and of everyday doubt, a vernacular that could not be extinguished no matter how it was cursed for "cynicism", a dialect that the focus group could never quite reflect, the resilient language of democracy'

Thomas Frank, 2001

Contents

Preface and Acknowledgements

In his 1968 novel *The Image Men*, JB Priestley explored the political impact of what he had previously castigated as 'admass culture'. The book featured an ambitious Shadow Home Secretary speaking of the need for 'New and Inspiring Leadership based on Our Sound Old Traditions and yet irresistibly Moving Forward into the Modern Age' and concluded with a fictional prime minister and leader of the opposition trying to outdo the other by reinventing their public selves with the help of the same dubious Institute of Social Imagistics consultancy.[1] The foresight of the tale was demonstrated thirty years later during the so-called 'lobbygate' story, an embarrassing episode that revealed the close relationship between the Prime Minister's office and a firm belonging to a former aide of Tony Blair. The consultancy documents of the lobbyists involved replicated the kind of verbose, self-serving corporate rhetoric Priestley had set out to satirise.[2] More importantly, the episode provided insights into the workings and culture of a highly elitist, so-called 'new' Labour project that 'owes more to market research (than) Marx or Methodism'.[3] As Blair's key lieutenant Peter Mandelson saw it the party won office because it understood its 'customer base, who they are, where they're coming from and what they want...' and by promoting an 'offering through all the components that make up a successful brand-product positioning, packaging, advertising and communications'.[4]

A key aim of this book is to place recent developments in context by exploring the development of Labour's political communication since its formation at the beginning of the twentieth century. Historically Labour had been the major party more resistant to using marketing and so its increasing acceptance of it over the course of the century led to a significant transformation of the wider political system as well as its own campaigning. Furthermore it is misleading to imply, as the key practitioner accounts do, that Labour's development as a professional, communications aware party began after the 1983 defeat.[5] Nor is it the case that the Conservatives were always the most innovative strategists.[6] Being a wealthy organisation enabled the Tories to experiment with different strategies but in many ways Labour's comparative poverty meant its organisers came up with all the more ingenious and novel approaches to electioneering.

Communication between politicians and the public has always played a crucial role in electoral politics. This relationship significantly changed with the introduction of universal suffrage and with it the need for mass propaganda campaigning. Labour strategists were not slow to respond to the new political environment and Sidney Webb made a significant practical and theoretical advance by developing the 'stratified electioneering' concept in 1922. Webb encouraged party organisers to think about differentiating between voters in order to better tailor appeals to specific sub-groups and evidently understood the potential benefits of stratification or what, in marketing terms, became popularly known as segmentation and targeting. Underpinning this analysis was a desire to appeal to the non-partisan or less committed Labour voters.

In assessing the strategic development of the party, consideration will be given to how campaigning has become increasingly professional and beholden to marketing specialists and techniques. Discussion will consider the continuities as well as the more publicised changes in electioneering. The second major theme deals with the party's philosophical approach to influencing public opinion. Early Labour edict developed a particular view of engagement that emphasised the value of didactic or 'educationalist' forms of political communication designed to convert and literally 'Make Socialists'. However, as Labour became the principal anti-Conservative force, some party organisers began to promote a more short-term, less intensive 'persuasionalist' approach committed to 'Selling Socialism'. These strategists drew on the parallels between campaigning and commercial marketing and, in certain cases, sought advice from professional consultants. More traditionally minded Labour organisers condemned the use of 'capitalist' methods. This tension and the resulting rivalry have formed a significant if comparatively neglected aspect of intra-party debate. Finally, and arguably of most importance, is the way in which the changing nature and organisation of campaigning have impacted on the balance of power within the party. Consideration will be given to how strategic deliberations have transformed the way the party is governed and who ultimately makes the key decisions. There is a wide consensus that power has been increasingly centralised in a seemingly omnipotent Labour leadership although there is less agreement as to when this occurred. Here the study will use marketing perspectives to help explain how and when the diminution of intra-party democracy and accountability took place.

I am grateful to everybody who was interviewed or has otherwise helped me in the completion of this study. During my time at Nottingham, Cambridge, Nottingham Trent and Loughborough Universities I have appreciated the benefit of numerous colleagues' views and comments. Peter Golding, Phil Harris, Bruce Newman, Dennis Kavanagh, John McClelland, Jim McGuigan, Neil Morgan, Peter Morris, Tony Mughan, Steve Peake, Maggie Scammell, Eric Shaw and my publisher Alison Howson have provided invaluable support and advice. I am especially grateful to David Deacon, Bob Franklin, Graham Murdock and Nicholas O'Shaughnessy for their wisdom and encouragement. I am indebted to John Rentoul of *The Independent*, formerly of BBC's *On the Record*, who kindly allowed me access to the research notes he used in making the 'Vote Race' television series during the 1992 general election. Sincere thanks are also due to Walter Burley, a long-standing member of the *Labour Organiser* editorial team, who generously gave me several old volumes of a journal that has proved invaluable to the completion of this work. I would also like to express my gratitude to Labour party members and ex-members who kindly discussed their views with me.

I would like to express my thanks and appreciation to all the friends and family who have helped and guided me for so long. My parents, Margaret and Philip Wring, have never ceased to aid and inspire me in all of the things I have chosen to do. Mary and Peter Lawrence have been the most hospitable friends and I will always cherish our interesting conversations. I would especially like to thank Claire for all her love and support and for being a constant source of creative inspiration and ideas; I now even understand why you don't want to see a copy of *Labour Organiser* ever again. Cheers for everything love. And Tilly, thanks to you for being so brilliant. Expressing my gratitude here is not sufficient thanks but I hope it is at least a start.

DW

List of Abbreviations

BMP	Boase Massimi Pollitt
CCD	Campaigns and Communications Directorate
CDS	Campaign for Democratic Socialism
CLP	Constituency Labour Party
CMT	Campaign Management Team
CPV	Colman Prentis Varley
CSC	Campaign Strategy Committee
CWS	Co-operative Wholesale Society
GLC	Greater London Council
GMB	General Municipal and Boilermakers' Union
ILP	Independent Labour Party
IPPR	Institute for Public Policy Research
ITN	Independent Television News
ITV	Independent Television
KMP	Kingsley Manton Palmer
LCC	London County Council (1930s)/Labour Co-ordinating Committee (1980s)
LPE	London Press Exchange
MORI	Market Opinion and Research International
NEC	National Executive Committee
NOP	National Opinion Polls
OMOV	One Member One Vote
ORC	Opinion Research Centre
PEB	Party Election Broadcast
PLP	Parliamentary Labour Party
PORD	Public Opinion Research Department
PPB	Party Political Broadcast
RSL	Research Services Limited
SCA	Shadow Communications Agency
SDP	Social Democratic Party
T&G/T&GWU	Transport and General Workers' Union
TUC	Trades Union Congress
WFA	Workers' Film Association

Introduction: Inside the Political Market

The study of Labour party strategy

Traditionally analysis of Labour party strategy combined a focus on major issues of political economy with an assessment of the role played by relevant actors, notably the trade unions.[1] By comparison contemporary accounts dealing with the same topic have tended to dwell on the activities of elite groups like the leadership's spin-doctors and their involvement in what the leading trade journal has termed the greatest public relations campaign of all time.[2] This change reflects an evolving representation of the party that has found expression in the dubious dichotomy of 'new' versus 'old' Labour popularised by Tony Blair and his chief strategist Philip Gould. Despite his own professed interest in historical rather than purely social scientific inquiry, the latter's influential memoirs caricatured the party's approach to communication prior to the mid-1980s thus: '(it) abhorred photo opportunities and still believed the way to address the public was to don a donkey jacket and harangue the party faithful at rallies...'.[3] In the relevant passages of his book, Gould is particularly dismissive of Harold Wilson although his discussion fails to acknowledge that leader's major contribution to overseeing Labour's strategic development not to mention his popularisation of images now more associated with Blair such as 'New Britain'. Nowhere either is there mention of the groundbreaking *Must Labour Lose?*, a study into 'people's aspirations' that greatly influenced party thought and practice at the beginning of the 1960s.[4] By contrast this book seeks to put recent events in proper historical context by tracing the development of the party as a campaigning organisation from its first decade onwards.

1

Labour's association with professional communications has led some of those most intimately involved to disavow many of the claims made of their work. It is noteworthy that Peter Mandelson, the influential public relations strategist, refutes the idea that the party was 'a creation of the spin doctors... that lacks real substance'.[5] Tony Blair has been similarly emphatic: 'I want to make one thing very, very clear indeed. New Labour is not some public relations exercise. It's not a marketing gimmick. It is a new and different changed Labour Party. It is changed in opposition and it will remain changed in government, and nobody should be in any doubt about that at all'.[6] The characterisation of political marketing as a superficial promotional exercise is replicated in other, more detached assessments of 'new' Labour that liken the former to 'a ploy' concerned with 'skin deep' changes.[7] The misunderstanding of what marketing is and does diminishes the role and significance of a process that has two main constituents: 'First, it is a philosophy, attitude and a perspective. Second, it is a set of activities used to implement that philosophy'.[8] Marketing then is as much concerned with the so-called substance as it is with the style of politics and has as a consequence become an entrenched feature shaping the democratic marketplace.

The electoral marketplace

Since its first recorded usage in Stanley Kelley's study of American electioneering, political marketing has become a commonplace term in modern electoral analysis. The idea of the market originated as a conceptual alternative to the notion of the campaign as a military, sporting, theatrical or religious spectacle.[9] This perspective was most clearly articulated in Anthony Downs' classic *An Economic Theory of Democracy* that conceived of voters as sovereign consumers. Downs' rational choice analysis also formulated a model of electoral competition based upon a now familiar political adage: a party can best mobilise the support of median voters by aligning itself more closely towards its principal opponent's position and, by extension, the ideological 'centre-ground'.[10] The subsequent popularisation of the study and practice of political marketing have been encouraged by developments in psephological and management theory as well as wider socio-economic change.[11]

In Britain and other advanced democracies the idea of a political marketplace consisting of discriminating electoral consumers began to attract increasing attention with the rise of so-called 'volatility' from the 1970s onwards. Previously psephologists had tended to emphasise the stability of partisan preferences but the downturn in the main parties' support led to a concerted examination of why increased numbers of people appeared to be changing their vote.[12] Consequently there was a move from explaining electoral behaviour in terms of demographics to a consideration of factors like image and issues. The increasing recognition of political choice rather than the stability of preference also attracted the interest of management theorists. In a groundbreaking essay on the need for a wider, more socially aware conception of marketing, Kotler and Levy included elections in their remit because: 'Political contests remind us that candidates are marketed as well as soap'. This perspective was reinforced by the rapid growth of American campaign consultancy and the production of strategic reports like *A New Concept in Political Marketing*.[13] The role of the marketing sector in British politics was most publicly demonstrated by the relationship between the Conservatives and advertisers Saatchi and Saatchi. This arrangement had far reaching consequences so that: 'By the end of the Eighties it was just impossible to talk about politics without talking about communication, about consuming policies...'.[14]

Due to the peculiar nature of the environment in which they operate politicians are more equipped to influence the deliberations of their market than commercial firms. This is because as Gamble observed:

> The actual workings of the mass democracy has divided the political market into two camps. There are those that compete for office and those that vote. Like the producers and consumers in economic markets it is a mistake to believe that these two functions are of equal importance. One is active, creative and continuous; the other is passive, receptive and intermittent.[15]

The realist conception of democracy offers an important corrective to the caricature of marketing as a process monopolised by the needs and wants of consumers. This is particularly true of politics where, as Webb argues, there are 'limits to the malleability of the product... party programmes can only retain credibility if they adapt within the bounds of enduring ideological reputations'.[16] Mindful of this Mauser provided a useful challenge to the Downsian assumption that informs much political marketing analysis, namely that floating voters are the sole or main target audience. Rather as so-called conviction politicians like Reagan, Thatcher and Mitterrand demonstrated, it was possible to appeal to potential electors without necessarily alienating core supporters through careful strategic positioning.

The electoral marketplace exists within a wider political environment that includes various factors notably economic trends such as unemployment levels and consumer confidence, events of domestic and international importance, pervasiveness and partisanship of the mass media, and their own and their opponents' organisational competence and resources. The latter are geared towards developing a campaign based on an appropriate 'mix' of marketing variables from the so-called 4Ps of product, promotion, place and price.[17] The political 'product' or offering consists of three core components: 'party image', 'leader image' and 'policy commitments', each of which can have a differential influence on specific types of voters.[18] Party image encompasses the organisation's previous record in office, recent history and its unity of purpose and in turn relates to the psephological theories that promote the view that most voters behave according to their partisan identification or on a retrospective evaluation of what the organisation has done. Consequently this construct acts as a means of evaluating the organisation as a potential 'service' provider in government.[19] Likewise the importance of leader image has been acknowledged in studies into the presidentialisation of British politics. Television coverage has extenuated this trend as Kotler noted: 'Voters rarely know or meet the candidates; they only have mediated images of them. They vote on the basis of their images'.[20] The popularisation of rational choice theories of voting and its idea of the discerning electoral consumer have promoted the importance of the other product dimension, the policy platform on which a campaign manifesto is based.[21]

The two principal promotional tools are 'controlled' or 'paid' and 'free' media. The term controlled covers advertising, direct marketing and other forms over which the producer maintains complete editorial control. Free media is the coverage politicians receive but do not buy and hence have less influence over. Given parties and public attach greater importance to this kind of exposure there has been a marked rise in the use and prominence of spin doctoring and other news management techniques.[22] Placement revolves around the regional and local party organisation responsible for co-ordinating regional visits by senior politicians and the voluntary efforts of canvassers at grassroots' level. Increasingly much of this work involves computers, direct mailings, phone banks and call centres.[23] Price, the least tangible P, relates to the interpretation of environmental phenomena by voters and involves their feelings of national, economic and psychological hope or insecurity.[24] Politicians seeking to capitalise on the latter have embraced the increasingly popular form of negative campaigning. In the economic sphere this has led to opponents being accused of proposing irresponsible tax raises or budget cuts. In times of international or domestic insecurity some politicians, particularly incumbents, have been prone to stressing their rivals' apparent lack of diplomacy or administrative competence. Other negative campaigners have attempted to exploit latent prejudices about an opponent because as O'Keefe recognised: '...in no other campaign situation are target audiences required to take into account not only ideas, issues, and policies, but also such human traits as honesty, professional expertise, and managerial style'.[25] Pricing strategy can also be about the promotion of positive themes such as the 'feelgood factor' or 'nation at ease with itself'.

Implementing a marketing mix involves the use of strategic tools such as market research, segmentation, targeting, positioning and branding. Historically polling consisted of quantitative based demographic studies of changes in partisanship and reactions to salient issues according to the voters' particular background. These studies began to be complimented by 'psychographic' forms of research devoted to different groups' value and attitudinal structures.[26] The resulting data and its analysis are central to the political marketing process because it allows strategists to segment the electorate in order to identify potential targets and position the brand in a way that is designed with 'floating' voters in mind.[27] Implicit in this and much of the previous discussion has been a focus on contemporary events. Later chapters will consider the role of marketing in modern British politics and, more specifically, Labour's affairs. This study is also concerned with understanding how the party developed as an organisation since it began competing in general elections at the beginning of the twentieth century. To this end an evolutionary model of marketing will be deployed to analyse the continuities as well as the changes in Labour as a campaigning party.

The evolution of campaigning

In an insightful study of US presidential elections, Avraham Shama used Keith's popular framework to argue that the history of American campaigning is analogous to that of commercial marketing in that it too has evolved through the key stages or 'orientations' of 'production', 'sales' and 'marketing'.[28] More recently political scientists have applied their own three phase models in analysing how electioneering has become increasingly 'post-modern'. But this term does not fit easily with the reality of highly mediated campaigns whose discourse is now completely driven by elite priorities. Rather this study prefers to define the key stages of electioneering as the eras of 'propaganda', 'media' and 'political marketing' and concentrates on understanding the evolving relationship between politicians and voter audiences rather than media or technological advancements (see Figure 1).[29]

The emergence of the first publicity advisers encouraged politicians to exploit the new promotional opportunities afforded them by mass communications and led to the development of a campaign similar to that of a commercial firm engaged in a production-led strategy. According to Shama success could be measured by the amount of publicity generated:

> The candidate was viewed as a product needing mass exposure, resulting in increased public awareness which was assumed to be positively connected to voter preference. Therefore, number of exposures and length of exposures were taken as the key for victory in the campaign.[30]

This strategic outlook meant cursory attention was paid to voter attitudes and so it somewhat resembled the Fordist nostrum 'the consumer will buy what we produce'. Campaigns were formulated on the basis of 'guess and intuition' although this did not preclude occasional experimentation with rudimentary forms of segmentation and other tools. The term propaganda is perhaps an appropriate one for this, the most elementary form of mass campaigning given Qualter's definition of it this largely unidirectional process as: 'The deliberate attempt by the few to influence the attitudes and behaviour of the many by the manipulation of symbolic communication'.[31]

In evolutionary terms the production-led approach is superseded by the more sophisticated selling orientation. Shama links the emergence of this phase to the routine usage of polling research by politicians eager to better understand how voters received, processed and responded to different political communications:

> (P)olitical campaigning was viewed and practised as the selling of candidates... Instead of promoting the product as it stood, it would be modified in the direction of greater voter appeal. It was not a

Commerce	Politics	Strategy	Target
Production	Propaganda	Exposure	Voters
Sales	Media	Market Research Market Segmentation Advertising & PR	Voters
Marketing	Political Marketing	Market Research Policy Development Positioning Market Segmentation Advertising & PR Direct Mail	Voters Members Affiliates Donors Mass Media Opinion Formers
			Adapted from Shama (1976)

Figure 1　Political Marketing Orientations

question, however, of actually finding candidates who best fitted the voters' desires, but rather remodelling existing candidates to appear more congruent with the voters' desires...(polling) studies were conducted concerning the effectiveness of different promotion appeals and media in reaching the voters.'[32]

Surveys of the electorate were used to help segment and target selected groups of potential supporters with relevant appeals as part of a highly media-centred operation designed to best represent the politician.

The third, most advanced form of campaigning was political marketing. Politicians' embrace of this strategic orientation led to the development of a more intensive relationship between the electorate and themselves. The 'marketing concept' involved campaigners taking account of the needs and wants of voters in order to maximise support in the hope of realising their aims. Electioneering became less concerned with short-term promotionalism and more about developing an effective strategic mix with the help of quantitative and qualitative opinion research. Feedback from voter analysis began playing a critical role and now informed every dimension of the political offering. Similarly positioning, segmentation, targeting and branding became more integral aspects of electioneering in a shift to professionalism that '... represents a qualitative change in the nature of "state of the art" campaigns: a move from tactics to strategy, from promotion to marketing, and from issues to agenda.'[33] The embrace of the marketing concept also involved the targeting of audiences other than the general electorate, namely key voter segments, sectional interest groups, party members, potential and actual donors, opinion formers and the agenda setting mass media.[34] Consequently strategic activity became increasingly concerned with managing these distinct constituencies and led to the empowerment of electoral professionals including strategists, aides and advisers or, as they increasingly became known, the image makers, spin doctors, pollsters and policy wonks.[35]

Plan of the book

The following chapters examine Labour's development as an electoral organisation and its gradual adoption and then use of marketing techniques, personnel and concepts over the course of the twentieth century. This is done in three sections, each relating to one of the evolutionary phases of campaigning discussed above, which collectively draw on the various literatures that inform the study of campaigning.[36] The first part looks at Labour's emergence as a propagandist party prior to the 1950s. Chapter One considers how the federal nature of the organisation and its dual leadership structures influenced its response to a massively enlarged electorate. Discussion focuses on the emerging debate between those strategists who believed in directly educating public opinion as the basis of emancipating society and others who favoured less didactic and mediated methods as a way of communicating to voters less interested in politics. Chapter Two examines the party's response to the challenge of symbolic politics and reviews campaigners' early experimentations with media and marketing techniques, particularly during the inter-war years. Here there were notable innovations using basic advertising, public relations and opinion research tools for publicity purposes.

Chapter Three opens the second part of the book with a discussion of Labour's strategic response to the emergence of 'admass society' and the ensuing internal debate over how the party should respond. In practical terms there was a fierce controversy as to whether Labour should employ and be seen to endorse commercial specialists and their practices. Chapter Four assesses the pivotal role of Harold Wilson in overseeing an ambitious programme of reforms to campaigning that greatly enhanced the influence of advertising, public relations and market research professionals. The centralisation of authority within the parliamentary hierarchy inspired by these changes also contributed to the internal tensions that engulfed Labour during the 1970s. Chapter Five analyses the organisational response to the 1983 landslide defeat and considers how Neil Kinnock was able to enhance his leadership by formalising the role and extending the influence of marketing professionals within the party. The strategy had important consequences, not least in stabilising Kinnock's position following the 1987 general election setback.

The final section of the book examines how marketing techniques, personnel and, most crucially, concepts combined to totally transform the Labour party. Chapter Six analyses how the market research conscious Policy Review challenged Labour orthodoxy and transformed its programme. Chapter Seven considers how Kinnock's 'modernising' acolytes on what is termed the party's new right defended and continued to support their former leader's reform project after the 1992 defeat had rendered it most vulnerable to criticism and attack. Sympathetic media coverage, particularly of highly selective opinion research findings, enabled the faction to promote its views as well as the leadership credentials of Tony Blair. Chapter Eight argues the contemporary party is primarily a legacy of the Policy Review in that the 'new model' Labour organisation created during the Kinnock era provided the conditions for Blair's succession rather than the other way around. The party's subsequent election victories and performance in government are explored.

Part I
The Propaganda Age

1

To Educate or Persuade?

The politics of organisation

The early twentieth century saw the formation of a party destined to challenge the Liberal and Conservative hegemony. It also heralded the trade union movement's most serious attempt to sustain an independent electoral force dedicated to workers' interests. Such a course of action was encouraged by the work of theorists like Graham Wallas because '(the party) represents the most vigorous attempt made to adopt the form of our institutions to the actual facts of human nature'.[1] Prior to the parliamentary Labour Representation Committee's formation in 1900, union involvement in elections had been limited to initiatives such as the Labour Representation League and Labour Electoral Association. The Labour Party was officially launched in 1906. Its ethos informed the democratically agreed manifesto produced for that year's election. This collective effort contrasted with the personalised statements issued by the Conservative and Liberal leaders.[2] By the following two elections of 1910 Labour's ruling National Executive Committee (NEC) and its Secretary, James Ramsay MacDonald, were co-ordinating the campaigning. An ad hoc NEC propaganda and literature sub-committee dominated by candidates and serviced by a meagre headquarters staff of ten managed to distribute six million items of literature. The party also published some memorable posters including classics like 'Stand Solid for Labour' and 'Labour Clears the Way', a depiction of workers attacking the House of Lords. Though these efforts were dwarfed by the rival campaigns, Labour still made steady political progress.[3] Subsequent elections were postponed because of the First World War but this did not hinder Labour's development and when the conflict ended it was in a position to capitalise on the 1918

13

Representation of the Peoples' Act, a law that trebled the electorate to 21 million and gave some women the vote. The advent of a truly mass democracy presented the party with, in the words of National Agent Egerton P. Wake, 'a formidable problem in political engineering'.[4] The Labour bureaucracy responded by undergoing a major reorganisation.

Labour's internal democracy provided two centres of authority: the parliamentary committee (later renamed the Shadow Cabinet) and NEC. The likelihood of serious internal conflict and misunderstanding was diminished because many key figures served on both bodies prior to 1930. Furthermore the party's steadily impressive progress and eventual winning of office in 1923 and 1929 helped ease tensions and provided the two committees with significant responsibilities. In 1918 a new constitution confirmed the NEC's control of organisational matters and led to its overseeing the major reform of headquarters between 1917 and 1919. Membership of the Executive was subsequently increased and a formal system of sub-committees introduced. The headquarters' staff also grew to thirty; prior to the war there had been only seven permanent employees. This rapid expansion of the bureaucracy was part of a wider attempt to shift Labour from its 'more or less exclusive working-class base'.[5] To this end the constitution abandoned the party's previous structure by allowing individual membership to compliment the existing system of collective socialist society and trade union affiliation. Labour launched its earliest recruitment drive in 1924 in the hope of bolstering its grassroots structure where previously it had been reliant on the regional presence of a trades council, Independent Labour Party branch or Member of Parliament.[6] This helped foster a burgeoning network of local constituencies and enabled Labour to increasingly rely on a formidable army of canvassers and leaflet distributors. It also meant significant responsibility for electioneering lay outside the central apparatus amongst a new base of activists keen to participate and make the party a more 'bottom-up' organisation.[7] The party's subsequent campaigning efforts also began to attract favourable comments from foreign observers, notably two experts from the US.[8]

Those working at Labour headquarters did not share the relative freedom of the growing numbers of locally-based agents supporting the expansion in grassroots' activity. However close political scrutiny and management of officials were made difficult given the first two party secretaries, Ramsay MacDonald and Arthur Henderson, were also leading and busy parliamentarians. Labour addressed this problem at the 1930 Annual Conference when it debated a motion to bar sitting

MPs from holding the most important organisational portfolios.[9] Reformers argued for a full-time chief executive with administrative experience rather than political skills and, after Henderson's retirement in 1934, the party appointed its longest serving employee J.S. Middleton as Secretary. Middleton refashioned his job description to resemble that of his Tory counterpart, the Director General, in order to devote more time to the organisation of politics rather than the politics of organisation.[10] In spite of this change there were the beginnings of a potentially serious rift between the NEC supported by headquarters and the parliamentary leadership ensconced in its 'gentlemen's club' at Westminster.[11] This partial divorce was then exacerbated by a serious political schism in 1931, when, in the run-up to that year's election, Labour was deserted by three key figures including leader Ramsay MacDonald. The party subsequently suffered a catastrophic electoral setback whilst MacDonald carried on as Prime Minister at the head of a Conservative supported coalition government. This episode undermined the relationship between Labour's extra-parliamentary wing and a now much diminished rump of MPs: the division was underlined by headquarters' relocation from Victoria to the T&G union's Smith Square offices in 1933. Those like 'Transport House Man' Hugh Dalton who did manage to forge partnerships with leading party officials and union supporters often did so to the detriment of their relationships with members of the Parliamentary Labour Party (PLP).[12]

The politics of propaganda

War propaganda, media growth and a greatly enlarged electorate awakened politicians to the campaigning possibilities of mass communications during the inter-war period. Hitherto, electioneering had largely consisted of canvassing, leafleting and platform oratory. Now Labour campaigners began to consider using film, broadcasting and professional advertisements. These initiatives were, however, dogged by bureaucratic inertia, internal rivalries and poor finances and reinforced by ideological objections from those who advocated 'making' socialism rather than 'selling' it. The latter position derived from a belief that the means were, as Herbert Morrison argued, indistinguishable from ends:

> We must have an efficient machine and glory in its efficiency, but winning elections at the cost of truth and of Labour and Socialist principles is wrong and ought not to be done. We have to be great

electioneers, not for the purpose of winning elections alone, but also for the humanity and the bringing of the new social order.[13]

Ironically Morrison would soon become a leading proponent of a less holistic approach in an ongoing debate within the Labour movement over the form as well as the ultimate aim of political communication.

The educationalists

Many inter-war Labour organisers believed campaigning was primarily about converting people to their cause. Their approach was informed by a philosophy dedicated to overcoming ignorance and emancipating the dispossessed and derived practical inspiration from the pioneering work of advocates like Robert Blatchford. Blatchford, founder of the *Clarion* journal, wrote of his mission to convert people in his acclaimed 1895 pamphlet *Merrie England*: 'I think that the best way to realise Socialism is to make Socialists. I have always maintained that if we can get once yet the people to understand how much they are wronged we may safely leave the remedy in their own hands. My work is to teach Socialism, to get recruits to the Socialist Army'. He attempted to do this through his 'calm, factual and closely documented' journal and the healthy network of *Clarion* clubs, choirs, scouts and speaker tours that were run 'with the smooth efficiency of a modern advertising campaign'.[14] Blatchford's evangelical style and participatory approach particularly appealed to early Labour activists because many of them had originally become politicised through their involvement in the Independent Labour Party or Nonconformist churches. This encouraged the development of what Independent Labour Party (ILP) orator Shaw Desmond called a 'spirit of religion' pervading what soon became 'essentially a "faith" rather than a "politic" movement' adhering to 'a rationalist equivalent of Christianity'.[15]

Early Labour evangelists like MP Cecil Wilson saw universal suffrage as an opportunity 'to create in the minds of the people a deep conviction that things were not as they should be'. Such a view drew inspiration from the classical works of Aristotle, Jeremy Bentham and J.S. Mill and their belief that democracy depended on reasoned debate amongst an informed citizenry rather than the populist appeals characteristic of mob rule. Many Labour members also believed didactic methods offered the most effective means of realising their goal of transforming society because, as one activist argued: 'the revealed weaknesses of Democracy can be overcome only by persistent education and propaganda... until socialist propaganda influences public opinion, and until socialists are chosen as representatives on public bodies, no secure basis for the socialist state can be laid'.[16] The resulting theory and practice of what Barker terms 'educational socialism' was thus willingly embraced in a party 'thoroughly persuaded (of the) crucial relationship between policies, propaganda and the process of building a new kind of... Intelligent democracy... in which citizens could participate in creating their own freedom'. According to leading figure Fred Jowett, Labour would be well placed to win battle for popular opinion because: 'Our chief weapons are education, agitation and organisation'.[17]

The 'educationalist' approach to politics was central to the work of a number of organisations associated with the early Labour party including the Socialist Sunday schools, Workers' Educational Association, National Council of Labour Colleges, radical elements in the free churches and, of course, the ILP. These groups' overlapping memberships helped reinforce their activists' conviction that direct, fact to face instruction was the best means of inculcating one's cause. Furthermore, and despite their characteristically evangelical tone, these campaigners believed rational, fact-filled discourse offered a way of countering opponents' perceived reliance on fear and fiction.[18] Most were also highly optimistic about the challenge before them although the cautious Arthur Ponsonby warned public opinion could quickly fall prey to 'emotionally' charged propaganda before degenerating into 'collective hysteria'. Ponsonby's fears reflected a widespread concern about the possible contribution of 'image politics' to political distortion and subterfuge.[19] Some educationalists responded by arguing the party needed to increase its propagandistic efforts and engage in what organiser Fred Kettle termed 'perpetual electioneering' whereby politics became 'essentially one continuous campaign and not an intermittent effort' because, as he saw it: 'Propaganda can be effective both psychologically and intellectually. Our propaganda is designed to convert and convince, Tory propaganda to influence and sway. So Tory propaganda is more rapid in action but less lasting in effect'.[20]

The persuasionalists

Those critical of educational socialism favoured more 'persuasional' forms of campaigning. This approach, couched in symbolism, was primarily designed to provoke more of a short-term emotional response and drew on Plato's contention that the Aristotelian ideal of democracy was an imperfection vulnerable to the tyranny of the suggestible mob. Many campaigners adopted a similar view of the political process, notably Lord Russell who, soon after the Great

Reform Act had laid the basis for the modern political system in Britain, was being advised by strategist Joseph Parkes to act on the assumption that a discerning electorate did not exist. Parkes' contention was later promoted in Graham Wallas' *Human Nature in Politics*, a 1908 book that challenged the long held 'intellectualist assumption' of much democratic theory.[21] The text explored the 'progressive elitism' of another prominent Fabian, George Bernard Shaw, and his criticism of the way 'proletarian democracy' encouraged vote-seeking politicians to, in his words, 'learn how to fascinate, amuse, coax, humbug, frighten, or otherwise strike the fancy of the electorate'.[22] Wallas used less provocative terms to outline why he believed mass propaganda activities made it unlikely that universal suffrage would stimulate informed public debate. Politicians, he argued, would inevitably use 'image' based appeals to win over the electorate: 'It is the business of the party managers to secure that these automatic associations be as clear as possible, shall be shared by as large a number as possible, and shall call up as many and as strong emotions as possible'.[23]

Despite the absence of confirmatory evidence, some early Labour agents suspected public opinion to be less homogenous than was commonly supposed. They shared Wallas' view and argued the party needed to dilute its earnest appeals and adopt more short-term propagandist goals because a critical mass of the public were perceived to be fluid in outlook and disinterested in politics, particularly of the religious, intensely educative kind. As one 'persuasionalist' put it, Labour needed to face a harsh electoral reality: 'I infinitely prefer a convinced and thoughtful voter, but we must face the fact that many voters do not think very much, and many years will elapse before they cease to allow others to do their thinking for them'.[24] A sympathetic advertiser estimated 80–90% of people, the 'great ill-informed, uninterested, simple-minded majority' were 'fairly indifferent' to politics.[25] Material in the agents' journal *Labour Organiser* entitled 'Publicity' also challenged the received educationalist wisdom:

> ... political conversion is being attempted by the Labour Party largely with mid-Victorian weapons- the heavy serious speech, the equally heavy and serious tract, and an assumption that life is lived to-day as it was in the 'nineties'... Labour has not caught the spirit of the times and our publicity has hardly begun to change to modern methods.

The article continued by discussing the possibility of change: 'Yet light is coming... We too may practise that artistry which pulls the population and gives them impulse or inclination one way or the other'.[26] The author was one of a group of persuasionalists who encouraged the party to become 'as much electorally as educationally orientated' and target what was widely believed to be a largely apolitical audience with carefully planned promotions.[27] This was not an easy task and demanded a major change of emphasis as propaganda officer Maurice Webb acknowledged during a 1937 conference on 'Selling Socialism':

> It (publicity) was too diffuse and lacking in simple central ideas; tended to be gloomy and out of touch with human interests, was too obviously propaganda and often directed to the politically interested section of the population only: it lacked a patriotic note.[28]

The politics of the media

The turn of the century heralded the emergence of a so-called 'mass society' where public attitudes and behaviour ceased to be largely governed by inter-personal relationships and experiences.[29] In the electoral sphere this change manifested itself with the introduction of near universal suffrage in 1918 and forced politicians to reconsider their approach towards a newly enlarged 'market' comprising millions of voters. Organisers at Conservative and Labour headquarters took particular interest in evaluating the best means of communicating their cases and became increasingly interested in using the mass media for this purpose.

'The Best Propaganda is Unorganised': the Conservative nation

Although Labour welcomed the massive extension of the franchise some in the party worried that millions of new voters might be subjected to questionable propaganda because, as one agent put it: 'the average elector is still swayed by the emotion of fear'.[30] Ramsay MacDonald was in little doubt as to where the main threat to rational debate came from:

> Conservatism no longer resists but welcomes a democratic franchise, because experience has shown it that it can manipulate that franchise and owing to its control of the press and the influences that make opinion, it can get from a wide electorate- especially from the

broad margin of electors who take no rational or abiding interest in politics or in their national affairs- mandates which suit itself. The democracy has become its tool, and it finds renewed strength in masses of newly enfranchised people. In awakened subordinate minds it finds both its strength and its justification.[31]

A similar perspective informed a penetrating *Labour Organiser* series on 'The Psychology of Political Parties' that concluded the Conservatives' appeal lay in regressive social forces like jingoism, patronage and the hereditary principle. Herbert Morrison extended this analysis and identified other important Tory attributes such as deference, prejudice, conviction and newspaper readership. Both reviews supported Jennings' telling observation that 'the best propaganda is completely unorganised'.[32] Central Office was, however, far from complacent and became the first party to employ a full-time publicity official in 1910. Sir Malcolm Fraser took the posting and the following year saw a Press Bureau established. Its work was significantly eased by a newspaper industry overwhelmingly committed to creating what an opponent described as 'a mass psychology' favourable to the Conservatives.[33]

More fundamental Conservative reorganisation came in 1926 following the appointment of J.C.C. Davidson as Party Chairman. His reforms followed the logic of a then popular campaign guide: 'Winning elections is really a question of salesmanship, little different from marketing any branded article'.[34] The following year saw former MI5 operative Joseph Ball appointed Director of Publicity and, together with Davidson, he revolutionised the party's propaganda machinery. Their image-conscious approach was preoccupied with mobilising popular opinion, winning votes and retaining power rather than converting people to Conservatism.[35] Consequently the Press Bureau was expanded and specialist sub-sections formed to target stories at the media. Furthermore the party set up Bonar Law College as a training centre for candidates and began coaching spokespeople prior to their participation in Party Election Broadcasts (PEB). Evidence of innovative approaches at grassroots' level came with the first ever telephone canvass by the Streatham Association in 1927.[36] Central Office also courted particular target groups, notably women, and began commissioning work from filmmakers and advertising agencies. The 1930s saw the party and its coalition allies set up the innovative National Publicity Bureau with much professional input and a generous budget.[37]

'Discreetness' at work: Labour's first full-time publicists

Labour formed its first Press and Publicity Department in October 1917 as part of the wholesale organisational and constitutional review undertaken at the end of the Great War. 33-year-old Herbert Tracey was appointed head of the new three strong section and became the first national official responsible for party presentation. It was something of a departure for Tracey who, following four years in a Welsh elementary school, had initially worked as an errand boy and then assistant foreman in a flourmill. His faith led him into the Methodist ministry and he served as a preacher for six years. In 1910 Tracey became assistant editor of the *Christian Commonwealth*, 'an organ of liberal theology and social ethics'.[38] His subsequent work for Labour helped improve the effectiveness of headquarters' propaganda during the party's acclaimed 1918 election campaign.[39] Tracey's department was characterised by its 'discreetness of approach' towards the 'capitalist press' in answering journalists' queries, producing press releases and running the weekly Labour Press Service. It was not long however before the burden of dealing with agencies such as Reuters, Central News and the Press Association prompted a former official to complain about the section's limited resources.[40]

Like Tracey many of his colleagues had worked in the religious press though some also came to Publicity from the Labour supporting *Daily Herald* and even right wing titles newspapers including the *Daily Mail* and *Daily Express*. In 1919 William ('W.W') Henderson, the 28-year-old son of the party's Secretary Arthur, joined a now ten strong department. Henderson junior, a former *Daily Herald* lobby correspondent and ex-*Daily Citizen* reporter, eventually took charge in 1921 when Tracey left to work in the United States and then at the Trades Union Congress (TUC). The two rekindled their partnership following the merger of party and TUC functions between 1922 and 1926. Tracey went on to manage Congress' publicity during the General Strike and became an author whilst his successor continued as head of publicity and twice served as MP for Enfield before entering the House of Lords in 1945.[41] Throughout his tenure Henderson limited his contributions to the debate over Labour campaigning though his department was dominated by educationalist inclined officials resentful towards the 'cleverness' of 'outside volunteers' who, according to G.D.H. Cole, 'were quite often given as many kicks as thanks in return for their trouble'.[42] These organisers' distrust of professional advisers was matched by their antipathy for the mainstream press.

A 'Polluted Stream of Misinformation': the newspaper industry

The study of political communication has been dominated by debates about the role and impact of mass media. This discussion has tended to focus on the involvement of broadcasters and the highly partisan newspaper coverage.[43] Commenting on developments in the late 19th century, Matthews identified a trend towards more biased interpretations in the then dominant print media with the result that: 'politics began to be more packaged for consumption by the readership of the newspaper'. After the 1890s the variety of editorial opinions decreased because many smaller family concerns were unable to continue publishing their advertising deprived titles and, of the 2000 privately owned newspapers that did survive, many regularly made Labour a target of vitriolic criticism.[44] Practical evidence of the anti-party press ferocity came during the 1909 Bermondsey by-election and though the 1918 election saw more objective coverage such treatment was relatively short-lived.[45] In the most infamous example of newspaper bias, the *Daily Mail* published the so-called Zinoviev letter just before the 1924 election. The story featured a message purporting to come from the Bolshevik foreign affairs spokesman in support of the 'pro-Moscow' Labour government. The letter was later revealed to have been a concoction of Conservative Central Office and the security services but the minority administration was compromised by the affair and lost the election.[46] Unsurprisingly many in the party continued to be contemptuous of what one Labour organiser denounced as the 'capitalist press' with its 'polluted stream of misinformation'.[47]

Few Labour partisans had much interest in the privately owned media but some were aware of the need to engage with those writing and reporting about political events. Herbert Morrison, an increasingly influential figure within the party, drew on his past experience working in the industry to encourage colleagues to take a greater interest:

> Discretion is always desirable, but generally speaking it is best to assume that newspapermen are your friends, and to send party publications to the Press, treating all papers equally. Newspapermen often write things we do not like and capitalism is as bad for journalism as it is for other occupations, but it is no more a reason for treating journalists with personal discourtesy than the need for housing would justify a housing reformer abusing a building trades operative engaged in the erection of a cinema.[48]

Morrison recognised a politically active media was a potentially serious barrier to the effective promotion of Labour policy. Others agreed but were still uncertain about the wisdom of liasing with print journalists and this led them to evaluate alternative means of communication. Many saw broadcasting, in particular, as an exciting opportunity to directly publicise the Labour message to a wide audience.

'The Modern Magic Box': the arrival of broadcasting

Radio became a key vehicle for political communications between the mid-1920s and early 1950s when it enjoyed a virtual monopoly in broadcasting terms. Initially a private company, the British Broadcasting Company was soon brought under supervision by a government eager to regulate this new and popular medium. In 1924 Vernon Hartsthorn, Postmaster General in the first Labour administration, relaxed restrictions on radio content and introduced PEBs so that each major party received one PEB in the campaign that year. The following election of 1929 saw an increase in the number of Broadcasts although Labour strategists doubted the value of airtime in a campaign still dominated by the partisan print media.[49] Initial party distrust of broadcasters turned to hostility in 1931 with one organiser condemning the allocation of PEBs as evidence that 'the BBC became virtually a Tory platform'.[50] During the election party fears that radio might be used in an emotive way were realised with the airing of what amounted to the first ever 'negative' Broadcast. Philip Snowden's notorious PEB featured the ex-Labour Chancellor's denunciation of his former party's plans as 'Bolshevism run mad'. The Soviet theme also motivated Labour criticisms of the BBC's allegedly anti-Russian coverage and one organiser went as far as to suggest the party use foreign stations including Luxembourg to communicate propaganda and thereby bypass the Corporation's monopoly.[51]

The 1930s saw a rapid growth in radio ownership and by the 1935 election an estimated 40% of the electorate heard Conservative leader Stanley Baldwin's broadcast. The 1945 election confirmed the growing importance of radio when Winston Churchill used his PEB to attack the 'Gestapo' tactics of Labour. In contrast party leader Clement Attlee spent his airtime promoting what he believed was a sense of 'thoughtful and solid reasoning' amongst the electorate.[52] Similarly Patrick Gordon-Walker, appointed Labour's first broadcasting officer in 1946, saw the benefits of this 'refined' means of communication. By the 1950 and 1951 general election campaigns radio was serving 12 million licence holders with both main parties using 'personalities' to make their case: Labour employed writer J.B. Priestley and businessman Richard Stokes whilst the Tories relied on British Medical Association representative and 'Radio Doctor' Charles Hill.[53] Inventive propagandists like these and the success of other broadcast campaigners, notably the Danish Socialists led one strategist to conclude: '(the) soap box has given way to the modern magic box, we must learn to master its tricks'.[54] Within a few years, however, television would supersede radio as the most popular news medium.

Forward with Labour: the Left press

Labour hostility towards the mass media led party strategists to seek more direct ways of communicating their message to new audiences of potential supporters. Much of this took a printed format and, as a consequence, involved a formidable cadre of pamphleteers that included the activist journalist and first leader Keir Hardie.[55] The resulting material was characteristically economical, colourful, well written and filled with photography. Labour could also rely on a healthy distribution network of volunteers working for a range of local party newspapers as well as national titles including *Clarion, Labour Leader, Labour Women, New Leader, New Statesman, Tribune, The Nation, Co-op Citizen*, and *Forward*.[56] Other organisations like the National Council of Labour Colleges produced sympathetic journals such as *Plebs*. Party agents were served by their own publication, *Labour Organiser*, a title founded by West Midlands regional organiser Herbert Drinkwater in 1920 to be 'the only Labour journal devoted to Organisation, Electioneering and Business matters'. With a circulation of 1500 '*LO*' featured material on electoral law, news for agents, correspondence, campaign tips, columnists and adverts for groups such as the 'Labour Propaganda and Publicity Service'. In 1924 the journal introduced an advice column written by the 'Campaign Doctor' re-titled 'The Consultant' a couple of years later and even briefly ran a telephone query service.[57] Among the mass circulation press titles the short-lived *Daily* Citizen, *Daily Herald* and weekly *Reynolds' News* stood alone as committed Labour supporters. Founded in 1912 and briefly owned by the party during the 1920s, the *Herald* became the largest selling paper in Britain in 1933 but was dogged by financial problems arising from poor advertising revenues. It survived as a pro-Labour daily into the 1960s only to be taken over and relaunched as the *Sun* by Rupert Murdoch.[58]

2
The Challenge of Symbolic Communication

'The Trilogy of Electoral Action': traditional forms of campaigning

The rise of mass communication and overhaul of Labour's publicity machinery in 1917–18 did not result in the abandonment of more traditional electioneering practices and indeed these continued to dominate inter-war campaign efforts. In discussing the 'Organisation of Propaganda', *Labour Organiser* editor Herbert Drinkwater considered new developments such as cinema before concluding that the key tools were still the meeting, doorstep visits and leaflet rounds. Such approaches were the direct equivalents of Ostrogorski's earlier 'trilogy of electoral action' that identified 'the stump', 'the canvass' and 'political advertising' as the main elements in nineteenth century electioneering.[1] Drinkwater's attitude was understandable given the relative abundance of volunteers for this kind of work constituted one of the few ample resources Labour could rely on. The commitment to maintain direct-voter contact characterised the party's approach well into the twentieth century as Butler observed of the 1951 election: 'Its very amateurishness helps the Labour organisation to breathe the same air as the people to whom it is appealing'.[2]

William Gladstone famously highlighted the power of oratory in his 1880 Midlothian campaign. Speechmaking continued to be an important aspect of electioneering after 1918 although some began to argue that mass suffrage heralded the end of 'the golden age of the political meeting'.[3] Labour politicians in particular continued to promote the value of this kind of event to the extent that party campaigns 'groaned under the weight' of them.[4] Some agents became increasingly concerned about the political appeal and effectiveness of their meetings and encouraged colleagues to think more carefully about how they should promote their speakers. Harold Croft, the author of the official party campaign guide, counselled fellow organisers thus:

> Consider– is it enough to announce that John Smith MP will address a meeting? People will not particularly concern themselves about a Mr John Smith but get it across to them that John Smith MP has done something in his life, or that he is one of the few men who can talk on such and such a topic, and people become curious and want to hear him.

During the 1924 election Labour demonstrated its commitment to oratory by investing in an expensive loudspeaker system to accompany Ramsay MacDonald on his tour of the country.[5] Party headquarters also retained several full-time propagandists who visited local parties and delivered speeches on requested themes. In 1931 this service incorporated several recently defeated MPs and their efforts were coordinated by full-time Propaganda Officer Maurice Webb. Other speaker initiatives included the *Clarion* van tours and an assortment of freelance orators who advertised through sympathetic publications.[6] During the 1922 election Jessie Stephen attracted the interest of working-class women in Wakefield with a series of impromptu back-street meetings. The efforts of Stephen and others formed an important part of a wider, 'extremely creditable' effort: 'Indeed the particular emphasis of Labour campaigning- its constant public meetings and demonstrations- led to much admiration and fear amongst opponents'.[7]

Like oratory, canvassing played an important role in party culture and campaigns. One influential organiser urged agents to concentrate on their doorstep work rather than holding meetings that he estimated only an eighth of the electorate attended. Canvassing remained a significant and obvious part of Labour campaigning despite arguments over its efficacy.[8] The same activists who called on voters invariably leafleted them as well and the dissemination of Labour literature became important because of the virulent opposition from most of the press. The party's first major publicity effort in 1910 election involved the distribution of 5 million leaflets, 800,000 manifestoes and 50,000 posters. This considerable undertaking was, however, still dwarfed by the Conservatives' 50 and Liberals' 41 million items. By the 1920s this gap had narrowed. During the

1923 campaign, leaflets were designed to appeal to voters as mothers, agricultural workers, ex-servicemen, teachers and white-collar 'brain-workers'.[9] At least one candidate, Margaret Bondfield, used a direct mail style address in the form of a hand-written letter to prospective constituents. By 1929 Labour was producing 43 million pamphlets, posters and leaflets. To finance this ambitious activity the party launched the 'Call to Action' (1932–33), 'Victory for Socialism' (1934–35) and 'Great Betrayal' (1935–36) fundraising campaigns. The 'Victory' initiative on its own raised £8,641 and greatly helped the subsequent general election effort.[10]

Assorted gimmicks and ephemera occasionally played a role in party promotional activities. One fund-raising venture involved selling postal-stamp-sized lottery tickets. The most memorable was the Social Democratic Federation's offering of 'penny nails in the corpse of capitalism'. Various mottos appeared on official party tickets including 'Labour's Bid for Power Fund' in 1929. Several agents devised stunts involving bell ringers, sandwich-board walkers and horseback riders to appeal to the less interested while groups like the *Clarion* Cycling Clubs and Fellowships catered for the more partisan. Labour publicists also looked to sympathetic organisations abroad for campaign ideas. In a twist on the 'selling politics like detergent' theme, the German SPD encouraged its British sister to distribute bars of soap and balloons to voters.[11] It was a tragic irony that Labour's ally also urged it to drop leaflets from planes, a practice that would later become widespread during the war.

Images of Labour

Labour's widespread use of 'traditional', educationalist methods of electioneering formed a barrier to those seeking to refashion campaigns and embrace 'image' politics. Yet the growing interest in ephemera also underlined the potency of symbolism as did the widespread use of banners and iconography by the trades unions and socialist societies that formed the party. Conservative Chairman Lord Woolton later praised these founders for their inspirational choice of name:

> The word 'Conservative' was certainly not a political asset when compared with the Socialist word 'Labour'. The man who first called the Socialist Party the 'Labour Party' was a political genius, for indeed the word 'Labour' implied the party that would look after the best interests of 'Labour'.[12]

The 'Labour' name was the most elementary part of attempts to develop a distinctive identity. Other initiatives followed including a 1924 competition that invited supporters to design a logo. The winner was a torch, shovel and quill symbol emblazoned with the word 'Liberty'.[13] The emblem did not become an integral feature of propaganda in the way its rose successor would but was popularised through its sale, in badge form, for 1/-d each. Other merchandise suggested organisers appreciated the benefits of a personalised appeal. A badge that depicted leader MacDonald bore out Jennings' argument that: 'the image is not devised only out of policy: it is in large measure produced by personality'.[14] The leader himself made a prophetic move when, in 1925, he attempted to update an important part of party culture by announcing a competition to a replace the traditional song, Jim Connell's 1889 socialist anthem 'The Red Flag'. The contest, co-sponsored by the *Daily Herald*, fielded 300 entries and was judged by conductor of the Glasgow Orpheus Choir Hugh Robertson and the Irish tenor John McCormack. Connell's song survived despite the tough competition.[15] By contrast, MacDonald defected from Labour six years later. The *Herald* competition highlighted the leadership's interest in image as well as the difficulty of making changes. Reforms were routinely blocked from within the organisation and especially at local level. An obvious of the independence regional parties enjoyed was their employment of non-standard colours. Several county organisers adopted shades not commonly associated with the national party. For instance in Warwickshire the Liberals used blue, the Conservatives red and Labour a more orthodox red and gold.[16] Despite the innate conservatism of many in the party, senior figures still encouraged organisers and candidates to think about using imagery in their verbal as well as visual appeals. In a 1922 article 'Facts and How to Use Them', Philip Snowden urged them to prioritise 'very matter-of-fact people' over the 'higher intellectual':

> It is so very easy to bore an audience with facts and figures and statistics. The person who uses facts in speaking or writing should remember that the way to impress is to give a mental picture of 'relativity'. That is an awful word, but what I mean to say is this: to say that we have 1,423,819 persons unemployed gives no striking and impressive mental picture. But if you say that the number of unemployed could be formed into a procession, four abreast, which would reach from London to Liverpool, you leave a permanent impression on your hearers' minds.[17]

The following decade 'a prominent advertising expert' acknowledged the propagandistic techniques of dictatorships and American presidential candidates in an article subtitled the 'importance of "human appeal" in printing, the psychology of attention and interest'. The piece suggested Labour publicity ideally 'avoids detail and concentrates on very broad simple human issues, which means something at a glance to everybody, including the harassed preoccupied housewife and mother; uses colour, both literally and metaphorically; and uses pictures'.[18]

The professionalisation of political advertising

At the outset of the twentieth century Wallas argued that 'advertising and party politics are becoming more and more closely assimilated in method'.[19] The inter-war years would vindicate his observation. The Conservatives first considered employing advertisers in the 1923 campaign but it wasn't until 1929 that Central Office acquired the services of the Holford-Bottomley and S.H. Benson agencies. Benson's, soon to gain recognition for their celebrated 'Guinness is Good for You' advertisements, fared less well their initial foray into politics with the ultimately unsuccessful 'Safety First' campaign. Benson's contract was nevertheless renewed for the two further pre-war contests and their efforts contributed to making 1935 one of the most expensive elections of all time.[20] Cumulatively these innovative Conservative campaign practices put 'psychological pressure' on Labour organisers to think about how they might better cope with the 'scientific problem' of publicity. Those advocating change were, however, careful to avoid mentioning the Tories and promoted the merchandising of 'Smith's Salts' and 'Bovril' as their role model.[21]

Having established itself as a £100 million sector during the 1920s, the industry understandably interested increasing numbers of Labour agents. In a far-sighted commentary, *Labour Organiser* contributor Gordon Hosking noted:

> Originally advertising was almost entirely of a commercial character, and was defined in many text-books as 'printed salesmanship'; but this definition is no longer adequate, for in recent years a form of advertising which has little to do with the selling of commodities has been developed extensively. For want of a better title we shall call it 'Social Advertising', since it is concerned with arousing public interest in undertakings of a social character.[22]

Other party supporters pointed to the apparent parallels between the work of a party and an advertising agency. In a timely piece on 'The Psychology of Political Advertising', George Horwill noted:

> The advertising side of elections, directly or indirectly, constitutes nine-tenths of an election organisation. Canvassing, printing, lecturing are methods used to influence the emotions and intelligence of electors; and these form part of what would be the advertising department of a commercial business.[23]

Horwill conceded that, though advertising could foster 'primitive emotions', the party should further investigate the medium because according to another strategist it was: 'An art we must understand and learn to apply... (A)dvertisement value is a subtle and almost immeasurable thing. It is certainly not intrinsic to its cost'.[24] The Labour leadership considered employing an advertising firm for the 1935 election but abandoned the idea on the grounds of cost although financial considerations were not the only factor. Educationalists within the party and at headquarters continued to thwart the use of a commercial agency and a tool they associated with non-socialist values such as acquisitiveness, combativeness and primitive emotions. In 1936 there were discussions about forming an advisory committee of 'experts' but the proposals were in effect sidelined and remitted back to the NEC for further debate.[25]

'Labour is Building Better Britons': the London experiment

The predominance of educationalism within the party did not prevent one senior politician experimenting with persuasionalist methods. Herbert Morrison became a key party figure of the mid-twentieth century and its most important advocate of professional publicity: as early as 1920 he was castigating Labour's promotional material for being 'dull, heavy and badly displayed'. Evidently people took him seriously and Morrison was elected to the National Executive Committee the same year, becoming an industrious member of its Literacy and Publicity Sub-committee. In 1921 he demonstrated his publicity skills with *The Citizen's Charter*, a lively pamphlet supporting his parliamentary bill to protect against local business monopolies.[26] Morrison took great personal interest in promoting London County Council (LCC) on becoming its first Labour leader in 1934. He subsequently became instrumental in reforming the authority's media relations and issued handouts for journalists and held press conferences at which sherry was served. Morrison also used off the record briefings, feeding favourable stories to sympathetic contacts like Preston Benson of the *Star*, a paper that became known as 'Herbert's anchor'. Other image-conscious work included the floodlighting of County Hall. Morrison significantly expanded the LCC publicity department and closely involved himself in its work: 'Presentation sometimes became more important than content, and he would judge an official's memorandum by its usefulness for reporters'.[27]

Morrison's interest in publicity set him apart from other Labour politicians. His preoccupation with presentation did not, however, stem from his LCC career. In 1912 he had started working for the *Daily Citizen* as a circulation traveller before becoming deputy section manager. The job proved useful to his political career because Morrison gained insights into layout, advertising and the wider role of the press: 'With his experience which, though small, had been intensive he saw the value of what later came to be known as public relations but which was then known quite bluntly as propaganda'. Later, as Mayor of Hackney Council in the 1920s, he would regularly provide local journalists with stories about himself.[28] On becoming leader of the LCC he continued with this practice and used it to great effect on one memorable occasion when the authority's Auxiliary Fire Service launched an appeal for volunteers. Morrison added his support by employing an advertising agency and organising a press conference at County Hall where he exited a window and climbed down a ladder onto a fire appliance to make his statement. This early example of a 'photo-opportunity' was a public relations coup.[29]

The re-organisation of LCC publicity led Morrison into forging working relationships with several sympathetic professionals and his eventual recruitment of some of them to help him with his 1937 re-election campaign. Those volunteering their services included executives from the London Press Exchange and other agencies such as Robert Fraser, George Wansborough and Clem Leslie who acted as chairman. The strategists promoted the key themes of housing, education and the leader's persona because the advisers' 'unanimous recommendation was to personalise it (the campaign) in Morrison'. They were were backed by generous donations from the T&GWU and NUGMW unions.[30] Leslie was greatly impressed by his client: 'We were responsible for the strategy of the publicity, the writing, the layout and some of the ideas. Herbert was a good client. He didn't interfere. He told us the message and I could see that housing offered a good theme'. The thrust of the campaign was conveyed in a poster of

Morrison with children alongside the slogan 'Labour is Building Better Britons'. Other copy, some of it designed by the popular railway advertising illustrator Tom Purvis included: 'Labour Gets Things Done in London', 'Let Labour Build the New London' and 'Labour Puts Human Happiness First'. The team devised adverts for hostile newspapers like the *Daily Express* featuring wavering Conservatives declaring their support for Morrison. The campaign was also popular with the Labour press and the *Daily Herald* reproduced key manifesto themes together with the 'Building Britons' poster.[31]

Morrison's approach appeared to be vindicated following the party's victory on an improved 51% share of the vote and near doubling of its majority. The trade journal *Advertising Monthly* praised the strategy claiming it had 'set the standard' for commercial operatives whilst the leader's biographers described the campaign as 'the most professional ever fought in Britain'. Ralph Casey, a colleague of Harold Lasswell, argued the election offered valuable lessons to others not least his fellow Americans given the use of 'young liberal-minded advertising men and public relations specialists... marked a departure from the usual labour-movement tradition of relying on a staff of journalists for propaganda services'.[32] The victory again highlighted the internal party tensions over communication strategies. Morrison was nominally accountable to the London Labour Party executive but in practice kept his strategic formulations largely secret because he feared a backlash from committee members. Educationalists in the LLP hierarchy like Joan Bourne objected to professional advertising because of its capitalist associations and the way it led to a personification of party campaigning with its uncomfortable echoes of the 'Fuhrer' principle.[33] Committee members also feared such an approach would strengthen the leadership's control over the party and was one reason why the successful London experiment did not revolutionise Labour campaigning. Nor did the potential expense and imposing personality of Morrison recommend the new approach to an organisation that contained a number of influential people hostile to him. The London leader's image as a 'Tammany right-winger' and 'professional machine man' alienated potential allies including formidable bureaucrats such as Morgan Philips.[34]

'An Electoral Howitzer': poster propaganda

Posters provided local Labour parties with a relatively inexpensive form of publicity. They also provided the party with some extraordinary promotional imagery. An example of this was the first classic poster,

'Hope for Labour', produced for the 1906 election. During the 1910 elections the party commissioned artist Gerald Spenser Pryse and cartoonists Will Dyson of the *Herald* and Low of the *Star* to design masterpieces like 'Stand Solid for Labour' and the anti-House of Lords' advert 'Labour Clears the Way'. More memorable images followed including the striking 1923 picture 'Greet the Dawn: Give Labour it's Chance'. As an enthusiastic *Labour* Organiser contributor put it, the party needed to ensure that every poster opportunity should be 'an electoral howitzer'.[35] By 1929 the party was producing posters in quantity as well as quality and distributing 311,000 bills.[36] During the 1935 campaign Labour adopted the larger outdoor poster format popularised by the Conservatives for a series of emotive designs including 'Election crosses or wooden crosses', a reference to the Tories' alleged warmongering. Another image, 'Stop War', depicted a baby in a gas mask and attracted considerable controversy on grounds of taste and accuracy. The poster was somewhat vindicated later when the wartime government began issuing breathing equipment to infants.[37] Most Labour publicity did not, however, resort to making negative appeals. This point would be amply demonstrated in the party's historic 1945 campaign.

The 1945 election resulted in a political earthquake. Labour's victory came a decade and a half after a schism had left the party divided and leaderless. The scale of the win stunned commentators and followed a characteristically modest campaign whose approach was typified by travel arrangements involving Clement Attlee and *Daily Herald* journalist HRS Philpott being driven around the country by the leader's wife.[38] Where Winston Churchill attacked Labour's 'Gestapo' tactics, Attlee offered a considered response and left the anti-Tory sloganeering to his Fleet Street allies. Party head of publicity W.W. Henderson helped this process by maintaining 'discreet' contacts with selected journalists.[39] The most vocal Labour supporter, the *Daily Mirror*, declared 'Don't Let It Happen Again' in a bid to remind soldiers and their families of the broken promises made after the Great War. The paper described how an intention to build a country 'fit for Heroes' had turned into the nightmare of the 'Hungry Thirties'.[40] Memories of the widespread poverty during that decade were confronted in the Labour manifesto, 'Let Us Face the Future', which promised a peacetime dividend based on a welfare state giving all citizens access to decent healthcare, education and other benefits. The results of the election appeared to justify the party's ambitious programme.

Practical planning for the campaign began in 1944 with a meeting of the NEC Elections and Organisation Sub-committee. Members discussed ways of cultivating the votes of wavering Liberals and disillusioned Conservatives; these 'floating' electors were regarded as more important than potential supporters aligned with left groups such as Commonwealth or the Communists. Furthermore Attlee's aide Evan Durbin monitored Ministry of Information sanctioned opinion surveys and would have probably been aware that the British Institute of Public Opinion polls were suggesting a major swing towards Labour in the country. This evidence may have influenced a manifesto whose 'main strength lay in the balance found between a distinctive socialist alternative and a reasonable appeal to the middle ground'.[41] In February 1945 the NEC convened a Campaign Sub-committee that included Percy Cudlipp, Harold Laski, Ellen Wilkinson, Michael Young and Herbert Morrison in the chair with W.W. Henderson as secretary. Morrison was the obvious choice to oversee affairs given his past experience. He was not, however, the only Labour figure with communications' expertise as many of those now returning to active politics had served in the government's psychological warfare service. This group of propagandists included senior candidates like Hugh Dalton and Richard Crossman.[42]

Morrison's committee took advice from professional designers, the Co-operative press, Odhams, the TUC and trade unionists in the print industries before supervising the distribution of 400,000 posters, 500,000 manifestos and millions of pamphlets, leaflets, booklets and assorted election ephemera. Artists Philip Zec of the *Mirror* and John Armstrong created memorable propaganda images like the latter's 'And Now- Win the Peace' graphic.[43] Another poster developed into a series that encouraged voters to think of others by using the slogan 'Vote for Them/Him/Her' alongside images of old and young women, a worker, manager, boy and victorious soldier. Despite the party's impressive range of posters most practical Labour campaigning revolved around the grassroots' work. Preparations for the coming election were debated in the party agents' journal *Labour Organiser* throughout the war. These discussions intensified with the realisation of peace and helped unite a disparate community of activists. Future Prime Minister and candidate James Callaghan recalled his sense of detachment during his first campaign: 'I was not conscious of any interference from Transport House. We fought our own election. We were isolated'.[44] Ultimately his and the many other Labour candidates' victories helped vindicate those committed to pursuing educationalist methods of electioneering. Many party activists believed 1945 demonstrated the benefits and indeed the necessity of a didactic, inter-personal approach in building a cohesive majority for the left.[45]

Reel images: the development of film propaganda

The early twentieth century saw the rapid development of the film industry. By 1934 there were 957 million cinema admissions to watch what became 'the medium of the working-class'.[46] Up until this time propaganda had been largely conceived of in print terms. Subsequently parties began to investigate the campaigning potential of cinema. Labour received offers of support from sympathisers involved with film projects including a Mr Greenwood who alerted headquarters to the availability of his 'daylight cinema van'. In 1919 the party convened a Film Propaganda Sub-committee with Sidney Webb in the chair and an illustrious membership that included Bernard Shaw, J.S. Middleton, Rebecca West, Francis Meynell and Arthur Henderson. Reporting in 1920, Webb wrote:

> During the War the Cinematograph became a powerful instrument of propaganda in the hands of the Government. The experience gained in this attractive and striking method of publicity is now being used by capitalist interests in various ways to undermine and check the progress of Labour throughout the country...[47]

Webb suggested the party show films such as 'Les Miserables', 'Jo, the Crossing Sweep' and 'The Melting Pot' and emulate schemes pioneered by labour movement bodies from a Seattle based union to the Scottish Miners' Federation. Unfortunately for Webb financial pressures limited the party's investment in film and critics argued its scarce resources should be concentrated on cheaper member activities like drama and music groups. There were, however, several enterprising grassroots' initiatives including the ILP Masses Stage and Film Guild, Daisy and Raymond Postgate's Socialist Film Council and the efforts of individuals like Rudolph Messel.[48] A party branch in Nottingham even made *Love and Labour*, an unlikely feature about a young man finding socialism and a sweetheart on a day trip to Southend.[49] Sympathetic local authorities also showed how film could be used for public information campaigns but it was the Socialist Film Council's liaisons with publicity chief W.W. Henderson that probably did most to renew leadership interest in film.[50]

During the 1929, 1931 and 1935 general elections Labour film propaganda was conspicuous by its absence. This happened despite warnings about the value of cinema vans from journalist William Mellor and the party's SPD allies in Germany. The Conservatives' deployment of such vehicles proved a success. During the 1931 campaign 22 vans visited 79 towns on 549 separate occasions and enabled the Tories to by-pass the major newsreel producers whose fear of the British Board of Film Censors meant they provided little meaningful political coverage.[51] The initiative left an impression on some in the Labour movement. Writing on 'Film and Television', one party commentator recognised that: '(these media) have entered into political propaganda... A new and devastating form of propaganda is with us'. The article also provided an early acknowledgement of the potential future importance of television, then a fledgling alternative to cinema.[52] Few could have predicted that the medium would radically reconfigure politics within the space of a generation.

Following the 1935 defeat, Labour strategists revitalised party interest in cinema with the help of directors like Paul Rotha and Donald Taylor. Rotha, a collaborator of John Grierson in the documentary movement, was instrumental in organising film displays before the Annual Conference. A more ambitious meeting on the subject held the following year greatly impressed General Secretary J.S. Middleton and featured *Daily Herald* journalist Ritchie Calder extolling the cinema propaganda work of the Swedish Social Democrats. Rotha kept up the momentum with a pamphlet explaining the benefits of film. The TUC and Labour leadership responded by issuing an update of Webb's circular on cinema:

> During the war the cinematograph became a powerful instrument of propaganda in the hands of the government. Since then, with the development of talking films and the immense improvement in cinema technique, film production has become nothing short of a fine art, the propaganda value of which has been multiplied a hundredfold.[53]

Serious Labour interest in cinema did not last and led the disillusioned Paul Rotha to resign as an adviser. His colleague Ralph Bond accused party officials of being 'apathetic and indifferent' to film. The leadership's increasingly lukewarm response was partly motivated by the perennial concern over finance as well as a fear of working with Communist inclined filmmakers. Some educationalist also dismissed cinema as a trivial, diversionary pursuit unsuited to the purpose of socialist instruction. Furthermore the medium was not seen as a natural party ally because of the widespread perception that 'English and American feature films share an anti-Labour bias'.[54]

The problems over cinema encountered at national level did not prevent local organisers such as J.W. French from distributing political education films. At the 1937 Conference MP George Ridley attempted to reinvigorate interest in cinema and the party joined with the union and Co-operative movements in convening a new committee on film. The membership brought their considerable expertise to the venture and it resulted in the Co-operative Wholesale Society donating cinema vans to Labour. Cost, however, prevented the party from using the vehicles.[55] In 1938 the committee launched the Workers' Film Association based in Wardour Street, the geographical centre of the British cinema industry. The WFA's intention to produce electoral propaganda was relegated as the Association became increasingly involved in encouraging anti-fascists in Spain and elsewhere with classics like Ralph Bond's acclaimed *Advance Democracy*. Following the outbreak of war the WFA continued to distribute this kind of material all over Europe. After the conflict the Association merged with the CWS Film Unit to form the National Film Association. The incoming Labour government of 1945 demonstrated a commitment to film by making it part of its new Central Office of Information's operation. Similarly the party continued to experiment, albeit in a limited way, by producing the half hour feature *Their Great Adventure* about the flourishing of a cross-class romance in Attlee's Britain.[56]

Countering the 'Dialogue of the Deaf': understanding electoral 'psychology'

The inter-war period was characterised by a 'Dialogue of the Deaf' in which the political class, lacking access to polling data, gauged opinion through personal experience, intuition or election outcomes.[57] It was of little surprise when different politicians offered alternative interpretations of voter attitudes. Some organisers sought to overcome this lack of reliable electoral feedback by advocating the employment of more 'scientific' methods designed to improve communication and resonate with the electorate's 'human chord'.[58] This kind of analysis found willing adherents, most notably in a 1922 *Labour Organiser* series entitled 'The Psychology of Political Parties' which warned of the prime minister's ability as 'a past master of the psychology of the British people', and further counselled: 'Once we understand these psychological appeals and the hold they give on this or that strata of society we can understand better the lines upon which political policy, strategy, warfare, organisation and propaganda may best proceed'.[59]

Labour agents began to use more precise and sometimes scientific terminologies in their routine voter analyses. One organiser wrote about the benefits of winning over the non-aligned or 'outsiders' whilst another introduced and discussed concepts such as electoral 'swing' and the 'barometer' of public opinion.[60] Another agent with rural campaign experience urged the virtual abandonment of areas dominated by 'Tory landowners' where 'the farmer plays on the political psychology of the labourer'. A more optimistic colleague believed this kind of targeting would enable the party to locate rather than dismiss groups of voters: 'Though it be true that there are dozens of constituencies wherein it is only necessary to ring a bell to bring voters to the polls, the psychology of the rest of them is altogether different'.[61] Labour's massive setback in the 1931 election led to further calls for a better understanding of the electorate. As Woolwich agent W. Barefoot argued:

> ...mass psychology must be scientifically studied. Sentiment is not unworthy. Labour's job is to make it a Socialist sentiment. Our opponents have made a study of mass psychology and play it on the lowest plane. Labour must win mass support on the highest plane... Labour's task is to evolve a technique of mass attack on the capitalist system, which can be understood by the elector who never heard of Karl Marx... We want the substance of Socialism to be understood. The meticulous wording of resolutions after much cogitation at Annual Conference cuts no ice. It is mere shadow-hunting.[62]

Stratified electioneering

The single most important inter-war evaluation of public opinion by a Labour politician appeared in December 1922. Its author Sidney Webb, a leading intellectual and co-creator of Labour's 1918 constitution, is less remembered for his work as a strategist yet his paper, 'What is Stratified Electioneering', constitutes the earliest known attempt to segment the electorate: 'It has occurred to me, in watching the process of combined propaganda and advertising that we call electioneering, that one refinement of which it is capable is a certain amount of stratification'.[63] Webb further contended there was a need to target different people with alternative messages:

> ...it was an acute remark of H.G. Wells, twenty years ago, that modern Democracy was characteristically grey, not because any one

of the units making up the mass was itself grey, but because the mixing of them together produced a dirty and unattractive grey. He looked forward to a time when we might be able to see Democracy, not as grey but as very highly coloured indeed, the units being all allowed their separate individuality of hue.

He continued:

Now, I should like to see a little variegated colour in electioneering, in addition to the common grey. Every elector has his own 'colour', if we could only discover it. He differs in character and circumstances, temperament and vocation, religion and recreation- and in a thousand other ways from his fellow men. At present we tend to address them all in the same way, with the result of achieving everywhere a certain amount of 'misfit'.

These 'colours' or 'strata' could be isolated in different ways including occupational classifications like liberal professional, shopkeeper and insurance agent. Webb contended that 'stratified electioneering' could also help distinguish voters by their trades union, co-operative or religious affiliations. At least one Labour MP developed a register of his constituents' various denominations. Webb summarised the value of his analysis:

...we should, as far as possible, 'stratify' our electioneering; appealing to each section of the electorate in the language which that section understands; emphasising just the points in which that section is interested; subordinating the questions that each section finds dull or unpleasant; addressing to each section the literature most appropriate to it; and generally seeking to substitute, for the 'greyness' of mass propaganda, the warmer and more individual colours of each man's speciality.

The call for stratified electioneering excited others and the article earned the rare honour of a reprint in *Labour Organiser*. The analysis was endorsed by some influential figures in the party hierarchy including General Secretary Arthur Henderson who extolled the virtues of Webb's method in an address to agents in the key electoral battleground of Lancashire during their preparations for the 1929 election.[64] Labour's *The Conduct of Elections*, first published in 1931, also gave prominence to the concept. The guide's author Harold Croft believed the stratified approach would help agents cope with their diverse audiences:

> The vastness of the modern electorate has on occasion excited concern and raised doubts as to the efficacy of mass opinion in choosing and maintaining effective government. But the problem of ascertaining and fulfilling the desire of 30 million people is in essence no different from that of canvassing and implementing the opinion of a hundred villagers.

Croft suggested his colleagues should segment the electorate using behavioural categories like 'reliable', 'sympathisers', 'hesitants', 'opponents' and 'inert'.[65] Fellow agent Frank Edwards adopted more conventional demographic criteria in arguing for publicity efforts to be focused on the less discerning or non-partisan among the target groups of weak Conservatives, Liberals, workmen, women and selected religious observers. What made his comments on working-class male voters particularly novel was his insistence that they be regarded as the basis for the building of a coalition of support in marginal seats. Edwards gave the example of one southern English constituency of 35,000 voters where the party had first concentrated on mobilising the votes amongst the traditionally more sympathetic 13,750 strong manual workforce.[66] Occasionally very specific occupational groups were identified such as teachers, a group attacked by right-wing newspapers such as the *Daily Mail* for implementing 'progressive education policies'.[67]

The female or so-called 'flapper' vote understandably interested the pioneering Labour Women's Officer Marion Philips. Philips and her fellow organisers believed there was a justified need to appeal to these new voters to vote for them with specially designed communications.[68] Consequently the targeting of women played a useful role in the party's successful 1923 campaign. In his reflective 'Organisation of Propaganda' series, *Labour Organiser* editor Herbert Drinkwater pointed to the growing electoral importance of wives and those belonging to working-class households in particular. Drinkwater urged agents to counter the Tories' pervasive 'At Home' initiative with their own invite-only 'cottage' meetings for women. The official guide also recommended that local parties should produce an address from the 'candidate's wife' as a way of targeting the female vote.[69]

In 1937 polling techniques were formally introduced to British politics by the new Mass Observation organisation and when Gallup's first office was established in London. The latter gained credibility when it successfully predicted the landslide Labour victory in 1945.[70] This more obviously scientific form of public opinion research did not however end the interest in stratified electioneering and, following the war, *Labour* Organiser founder Harold Drinkwater continued to promote its 'ingenuity': 'It is Webb's methods that will bring home the bacon'. When the party did formally embrace conventional polling techniques these were used by strategists to support an updated and more scientific version of the original stratified concept in order to better refine and target the campaign message.[71]

The elusive strata: Labour and the middle-class

A recurrent theme of the debate over Labour's electoral fortunes is the perceived inability of the party to win over affluent voters. However the recognition of class as an electoral factor predates the Second World War and played a role in an inter-war era dominated by convention. A deferential society provided an unfavourable environment for a radical cause like Labour and this problem was reinforced by many workers' self-identification of themselves as 'middle-class' despite their recent experience of the 'hungry thirties'. Following the war a British Institute of Public Opinion survey confirmed this trend when it found that 50% of the population still thought this way whereas only 46% responded that they were working-class.[72] Voter reluctance to be so identified led some to question whether the party should continue to be known as 'Labour'.

Serious Labour interest in the middle-class vote does, however, predate the internal debates over social change that took place in the 1950s and after. Following the Great War, for instance, the party issued a pamphlet on *Why Brainworkers Should Join the Labour Party* and an agent warned colleagues not to 'slag off non-manual working-class people'. During the 1920s the *Daily Herald* encouraged the labour movement to take a greater interest in winning the support of middle-class people.[73] But it was Herbert Morrison who produced one of the most detailed assessments of the new electoral arithmetic in 1923 when he asked 'Can Labour win London without the Middle-classes?'. Morrison emphatically answered in the negative and encouraged activists to target white-collar professionals or 'brainworkers'.[74] In doing so, he used 1921 census data to estimate the capital was home to 2.32 million working and 1.23 million middle-class voters and argued the concentration of the former in safe parliamentary and council seats made it necessary for Labour to pursue the more affluent. This was, Morrison acknowledged, a group largely regarded by the party as a 'psychological problem'. Furthermore he noted how, besides their size, concentration in marginal constituencies and relationship to the 'balance of power', middle-class voters were also needed to compensate for the estimated quarter to a third of workers who supported the Conservatives. For Morrison Labour had no choice but to broaden its appeal to professional and self-employed people:

> ...by careful propaganda, by talking to them in a language which they understand rather than in some of our classic phrases which may be unintelligible or repugnant to them, there is no insurmountable difficulty which prevents us in due course securing a considerable number of supporters from among the middle classes and those who are 'workers on their own account.'

During the early 1940s Morrison returned to the theme of class when he warned Labour against using the kind of 'prefabricated slogans' that might alienate non-manual workers. In 1945 he underlined his personal commitment to winning over non-traditional supporters rather than the 'sectional interest' by moving from his safe seat in Hackney to the more prosperous East Lewisham constituency. Significantly Morrison was now chair of Labour's campaign committee and well placed to argue his case. Mass Observation executive Charles Madge noted the party's sincere attempts to cultivate the middle-class in tandem with the maintenance of its 'workerist' appeal.[75] The subsequent landslide victory was, in part, built on 'blackcoated' voters' support and excellent results in areas such as Lewisham. This lesson was not lost on those responsible for organising the following campaign in 1950 and there was a concerted attempt to win over non-traditional supporters among the middle-classes, rural dwellers and Liberals.[76] Morrison was again instrumental in formulating this strategy and his plan for the NEC urged the party to also develop 'propaganda for the consumer and the housewife'. When the 1950 election saw Labour's massive 1945 majority reduced to only five he was unrepentant and his diagnosis for renewed electoral success was for the party to 'modernise'.[77] Implicit in this proposition was the downgrading of overt class politics. Some more traditional organisers were sympathetic but saw the need to distinguish between the professional, a respectable strata in society worth cultivating, and the 'parasitic rentier rash' who did not work for a living and ought to be actively challenged. Labour's opponents in parliament and the mass media were nevertheless keen to suggest the party's language of class antagonism was aimed well beyond the latter, relatively small grouping.[78] This discussion would come to dominate internal debates following the electoral setbacks of the 1950s.

Part II
The Media Age

3
Admass Politics

From mass propaganda to mediated campaigning

The arrival of mass television helped transform the relationship between citizens, politicians and the media. For cultural commentator Marshall McLuhan it meant 'the medium is the message' in that form mattered as much if not more than content. The study of television soon became integral to political communication scholarship.[1] Critics like Habermas and Qualter argued that, far from being a source of enlightenment, the medium might be used to manipulate, trivialise or otherwise subvert debate.[2] Many on the left linked this concern to the commercially driven nature of the new broadcast services that rapidly developed during the 1950s. Writing in 1955 J.B. Priestley contended the power of advertising lay in its combining with mass television in the creation of a pervasive 'admass' society.[3] This process was enabled and its importance augmented by a major period of sustained economic growth and the creation of a so-called 'consumer society'. Advertising's twin role as a form of persuasive communication and economic process made it the target of sustained ethical and ideological critiques. Williams described the medium as 'the official art of modern capitalist society' in revisiting concepts such as members of the alienation originally popularised by the Frankfurt School.[4] Non-Marxist scholars also made telling observations. In *The Affluent Society* economist J.K. Galbraith challenged the advertising industry's assertion that it was responding to existing consumer needs rather than creating new wants.[5]

The launch of commercially funded television networks had a profound impact on politics as a more image conscious style of electioneering began to replace the propagandist approach. This change fostered a more impersonal 'media campaign' whereby parties began investing considerable resources in polling in order to refine and target their ever more professional advertising messages. Strategists began to increasingly appeal to voters as individuals rather than as members of social groups with a shared sense of identity. Kirchheimer likened the resulting campaigns to commercial enterprises: 'fulfilling in politics a role analogous to that of a major brand in the marketing of a universally needed and highly standardised article of mass consumption'.[6] This change had profound consequences for party organisations because the new tier of specialist advisers, termed a 'contagion from the right' by Epstein, invariably helped to further centralise power within the leadership.[7] In the British context this encouraged a 'nationalising tendency' whereby the London based headquarters were increasingly able to direct campaigns and other organisational resources.[8] One consequence of this trend was the beginning of a marked decline in individual membership and local agents.

For Labour any embrace of media campaigning required the negotiation of important organisational and ideological considerations. Most obviously the centralisation of power implicit within such a process challenged the federal basis of the party's internal democratic arrangements. Furthermore many Labour partisans were still committed to educationalist methods and opposed to employing professional communications methods and advisers who they believed were tainted by their associations with the most conspicuous forms of capitalism.

'The Penny Farthing Machine': Labour in the fifties

The Attlee government's collectivist ethos informed its approach to communication and, more particularly, the work of the Central Office of Information it established following the war. The new agency shared the party's educationalist ethos and used documentary film techniques rather than commercial style promotions to publicise its ambitious programmes. Some Labour activists went further and argued for advertising to be banned.[9] Predictably the party conference attacked the arrival of commercial television for forcing the 'values (of)... advertising agencies upon us'. It was then of little surprise when, in the aftermath of the 1955 election defeat, a conference proposal to set up a 'PR branch at HQ' was firmly rejected.[10] Significantly leading MP Harold Wilson, chair of the inquiry into the setback, partly blamed the result on the party's neglected 'penny farthing' organisation and the lack of local agents. Adopting an educationalist stance Wilson concluded that image conscious campaigning was not the solution because 'a professional machine would be offensive alike to our traditions and our principles'. This view prevailed at the conferences held before the subsequent election in 1959 and at one meeting 'delegate after delegate' queued up to join the attacks on advertising and associated methods.[11] This vocal lobby against media campaigning was compounded by an organisational structure and factional dispute that discouraged change.

Unlike the Conservatives Labour's internal democracy encouraged a committee rather than project management based approach to decision-making. Consequently responsibility for campaigning lay with several bodies including the leader, the Shadow Cabinet, the National Executive, various National Executive Committee (NEC) subcommittees, political (the Senior) and advisory (Junior) Broadcasting Committees and an organisational tier of the General Secretary, full-time staff and voluntary grassroots network. The existence of so many different stakeholders constituted a formidable barrier to change. This was further complicated by the workings of the committees given they were: 'made up of several different types of opinion, any of which may win the day when a decision is made'.[12] That said earnest debate over the nature of party political communications in the four campaigns held between 1945 and 1955 was muted because most candidates were largely left to their own devices to fight elections either called at relatively short notice or poorly resourced. Preparations for the 1959 poll would be very different.

If Labour's federal system of decision-making facilitated organisational tensions it also fostered factional rivalry between the party's highly motivated left and right-wing groupings.[13] This ideological dispute intensified following Hugh Gaitskell's replacement of Attlee as leader in 1955. After a third Labour defeat in 1959, Gaitskell attempt's to reformulate policy triggered acrimonious scenes at successive Conferences. So-called 'revisionists' on the party's right supported the leader's attempts to change the party's image and its standing through the abandonment of the policy advocating public ownership of industry enshrined in the revered Clause Four of the Labour constitution. Gaitskell's subsequent defeat over this issue buoyed his opponents on the left and intensified the debate over the party's direction.[14] In the context of party affairs, Epstein's 'contagion from the right' concept had added significance given that many of those who most wanted to renew Labour's image through media campaigning were younger, radical revisionists supportive of Gaitskell. The leader's supporters were able to articulate their ambitions through a range of well resourced publications and groups including *Socialist Commentary*, the Young Fabians, the Campaign for Democratic Socialism (CDS) and *Encounter*, the Atlanticist journal covertly funded by the CIA.[15] Leading the opposition to the revisionists were the Bevanites, a formidable group of left inclined educationalists like Barbara Castle, Michael Foot and Harold Wilson who derived their name from their mentor Nye Bevan. They suspected those interested in reforming the party's presentation were committed to promoting changes designed to reinforce their revisionist ideology and position. Speaking after the 1959 defeat, Wilson articulated the left's resentments:

> There is a lot of talk about the image of the Labour Party. I cannot think it would be improved if we were to win, and indeed deserve, a reputation for cynicism and opportunism by throwing out essential and fundamental parts of a creed for electoral purposes.[16]

The persuasionalist challenge

Former Cabinet minister and leading left-winger Harold Wilson had taken a particular interest in organisation and his 'penny farthing' report had demonstrated his ability to influence debate. One practical consequence of his inquiry was the formation of a new NEC Publicity Sub-committee and appointment of MP Alice Bacon as chair.[17] This body would eventually become an important forum for debate over the party's electioneering following the 1959 general election. Initially, at least, senior Gaitskellites including Bacon were opposed to adopting the more media-centred approach to campaigning advocated by persuasionalists during the inter-war period. This did not deter a group of mainly younger revisionists from arguing for a radical overhaul of Labour's political communications involving the use of professional advertising, public relations and market research expertise and techniques. In doing so they cited the perceived successes of the party's recent series of Party Election Broadcasts (PEBs) and, more contentiously, the Conservatives' groundbreaking campaign.

'Life's Better with the Conservatives': the work of Colman Prentis Varley

The Conservatives' embrace of media campaigning following their shock 1945 defeat was guided by grandees Lord Woolton, Lord Poole and R.A. Butler. A major turning point came in 1948 with the appointment of leading agency Colman Prentis Varley (CPV) as the party's advertisers. It was the beginning of a mutually profitable relationship and its political work became the subject of particular interest during the 1959 campaign that secured the party a third term in office. During two years of preparation CPV worked closely with a powerful Liaison Committee headed by Poole. This ensured the agency fully participated and played a significant role in campaign planning. Consequently CPV executives were the inspiration behind various initiatives including the celebrated copy 'Life's better with the Conservatives- don't let Labour ruin it'. The slogan was based on 'You've never had it so good', a paraphrase of prime minister Harold Macmillan's critical comment on the post-war austerity under Labour. Another memorable advert appealed to the working-class by depicting a manual worker under the slogan 'You're Looking at a Conservative'.[18] Labour frontbencher Richard Crossman attacked the agency for selling Macmillan 'as though he were a detergent'. But it appeared to help the Tories claim a historic third victory and few in the party had much reticence about using professional methods: 'Since the Conservatives accepted advertising as an integral part of the economy, they did not question the propriety of using it for political ends'.[19] In the aftermath of a further Labour defeat influential frontbenchers like Tony Crosland identified the party's publicity as a major weakness and were prepared to use their opponents' example as a means to challenge educationalist thinking that had long dominated strategic discussions:

> It is too late to maintain an ideological objection to these techniques... the leadership should... institute a thorough investigation into the party's methods and organisation of public relations, which now appear hopelessly amateur and old-fashioned compared with those of the Tories.[20]

A less publicised aspect of CPV's work involved the formation of the Public Opinion Research Department (PORD). The PORD was the first sustained attempt by a British party to incorporate polling into campaigning and it provided briefings for Central Office and the parliamentary leadership. The Department commissioned CPV subsidiary Market and Information Services Ltd to undertake an ambitious study of 5,000 electors at a cost of £1180. The 1949 report, entitled *The Floating Vote*, analysed the newspaper reading habits, occupation, recreations, age and gender of uncommitted electors and encouraged strategists to focus on women, young people, small shopkeepers and Liberal voters.[21] The PORD initiative came during a major repositioning of the

Conservatives that ended with them regaining office in 1951 having accepted some of the Labour government's reforming programme. According to Gamble the Tories demonstrated an anxiety to understand and align themselves with public opinion: 'If its power has grown since 1945 that is because the (Conservative) party has been busy adapting itself more and more to the special requirements and techniques of the politics of support in a political market'.[22] It would be simplistic to view this policy shift as the consequence of survey research but it is noteworthy that R.A. Butler, a leading figure in the Conservatives' rejuvenation, was the PORD's patron, keen student of psephological trends and one of the politicians who made opinion research an indispensable part of electoral politics. This led Butler's colleague Woolton to conclude that 'the voter is also the consumer'.[23]

'Britain Belongs to You': Labour on television

The 1959 election saw major innovations in at least one area of party publicity. The first televised Labour PEB in 1951 had seen propaganda expert Christopher Mayhew using graphics to claim: 'just as Crippen was the first crook to be caught by wireless, the Tories are the first political crooks to be caught by television'. This rehearsed performance also featured Mayhew's 'well off' colleague Hartley Shawcross whose presence was designed to reassure the 10% of the population rich enough to own sets.[24] During the ensuing decade 70% of households obtained televisions and it became a truly mass medium. Politicians responded by deviating from the 'talking heads' formula and experimenting with more sophisticated, dynamic kinds of film like the 1954 Party Political Broadcast (PPB) *Meet the Labour Party* featuring interviews with party members from different backgrounds.[25] One of those responsible for this change was MP Tony Benn, a former producer with the BBC North American service originally recruited in 1951 by the Herbert Morrison and his NEC Broadcasting Committee to advise them on radio. By the 1955 election Benn had become involved in making PEBs with the help of professionals like Donald Baverstock and Huw Wheldon.[26]

Following the 1955 campaign, Benn concluded television 'emerged as a major propaganda weapon' and argued Labour should emulate the 'Eden standard', a reference to the prime minister's media persona. He revisited this theme a few years later with a characteristically vivid metaphor:

> Just as one hydrogen bomb packs more power than the total load dropped in World War Two, so one television broadcast more

than equals a lifetime of mass rallies and street-corner oratory. Old methods of campaigning are as obsolete as conventional weapons.[27]

Benn had the opportunity to pursue his ideas through Labour's Broadcasting Advisory Committee. He was, for instance, insistent about countering 'The Buffer' that announces a PEB and encourages possible viewer desertion. Benn recognised that television might 'encourage false values and weaken the basic integrity of British politics' but still believed it to be the 'greatest, best and most important thing'.[28] The importance of the medium increased when the newly formed Independent Television News (ITN) news service reported on the 1958 Rochdale by-election campaign and thereby challenged a legal framework that was believed to prohibit this 'intrusive' kind of broadcasting.[29] Tony Benn's enthusiasm for television gained valuable NEC support and found a practical outlet during the 1959 election. This enabled Benn, his fellow politicians Christopher Mayhew and Woodrow Wyatt and BBC current affairs producer Alisdair Milne to make a memorable series of PEBs entitled 'Britain Belongs to You'. The Broadcast's format drew on the 'Tonight' programme, a popular format with which Milne had pioneered the use of a more informal, 'magazine' style approach. The programmes' 'brilliantly flexible formula' used music from Holst's Planet Suite, the graphics of designer FHK Henrion and film material supervised by Stephen Peet under the guidance of 'impressario' Benn. Gaitskell featured prominently but so did others including representatives of the kinds of voter the party was trying to win. The Broadcasts won widespread praise and even Conservative Chairman Lord Hailsham felt obliged to attack them for being 'glossier than thou'.[30]

Promotionalism in politics: advertising the party

Labour's conventional publicity efforts for the 1959 election did not attract anything like the attention afforded its Party Election Broadcasting. The NEC had resisted employing a professional agency despite the availability of sympathetic professionals like Michael Barnes and David Kingsley able and keen to advise the party on its presentation.[31] Labour preferred to continue to use sympathetic designers like FHK Henrion on an ad hoc basis. Publicity official William Timms also used the work of experts like Alec Davis to justify the need for a generic style in all party promotional materials.[32] This approach informed the 1958 'Into Action' campaign and its centrepiece *The Future that Labour Offers YOU* brochure produced by Richard Crossman and journalists Hugh Cudlipp and Sidney Jacobson. Labour distributed 1.4 million copies of the pamphlet and followed this up by circulating another glossy publication, *The Tory Swindle*, during the actual election. Henrion was commissioned to devise the first in a series of posters for a £22,500 campaign launched in spring 1959. The most memorable of these quaint images featured Gaitskell as 'The Man with a Plan' and promised that 'Labour will never forget the old folk'.[33]

Labour's third consecutive defeat in 1959 led to a major debate over the party's future. Several supporters complained headquarters had failed to make the most of modern advertising methods. The leader himself was convinced of the need for change and used his first post-election Conference address to challenge the educationalist assumption that policy based statements provide the best publicity material because, as one colleague put it: 'Nobody bothers to read or study political pamphlets these days. They just can't be bothered'.[34] In a *Political Quarterly* specially devoted to Labour's predicament, the editorial explicitly identified the party's lack of strategic coherence with the absence of a professional media campaign:

> It (Labour) retained an archaic, rambling structure in which so many conflicting views had to be taken into account, so many centres of power placated, that it was impossible for any decision on policy to be taken except on a compromise basis after an unedifying period of internal wrangling. It failed to adapt its means of propaganda and publicity to the age of television and 'admass'.[35]

Younger Gaitksellites such as Bernard Donoughue were the most vocal in calling on Labour to use advertising techniques. For Donoughue a key turning point was his experience as a volunteer helping J.F. Kennedy's 1960 campaign for the US presidency: 'that did have quite an effect on me. When you came back from America the Labour party really did look like something out of a museum'. Tony Crosland also saw the potential benefit in emulating Kennedy and his 'new frontier' theme.[36] In one of the first major essays on 'Labour Publicity' for the *Political Quarterly* special another Gaitskellite activist, Christopher Rowland, acknowledged the cultural challenge of 'Americanisation' and argued it justified a more image-conscious approach to campaigning given, for example: 'One photograph of Mr Macmillan pruning his rose garden with a pair of non-sequiters is worth half a dozen solid speeches by Mr Gaitskell'. The presidentialisation implicit in this process was welcomed by a Young Fabian Group report that noted how a media culture meant the leader was increasingly 'the party in camera'. The Group also called for the wider personalisation of political communication through the appointment of a new Director of Information who would take a personal and strategic responsibility for promoting the party.[37]

For campaign reformers like Christopher Rowland the key issue for Labour was the need to overcome its 'amateurism'. His practical solution was the party's establishment of a voluntary panel of sympathetic advisers in time for the next election. Rowland gained support from a vocal lobby that included MPs Sydney Irving, Fred Mulley and others associated with the influential revisionist journal *Socialist Commentary*.[38] Their position was strengthened by the existence of a group of supporters within the industry willing to work for the party. They included advertising executives like Michael Barnes, Prospective Parliamentary Candidate for Wycombe, who recognised that before marketers had the chance to convince the electorate they would need to win over a sceptical party by reassuring traditionalists that '...modern advertising is scientific... (and) not by itself either good or evil' and that they would not promote Labour 'like a soap powder'.[39] The Young Fabians went further and argued professional consultants were needed to overhaul party publicity and take account of changes in 'management methods' and the emergence of the 'permanent campaign' in the belief that this would create a 'powerful and expert press and broadcasting department which can give authoritative advice, even on minutiae which might subconsciously influence the voter, to all the people who appear in public on behalf of the party'.[40] Those advocating professional methods were in effect supporting the greater centralisation of authority within the parliamentary leadership and London headquarters because, as Rowland candidly recognised:

> The nationalisation of politics – the move from the doorstep and local meeting to the television screen and large advertisement has reduced the value of Labour's traditional weapon of free labour of the constituency member and placed a premium on the expensive weapons of broadcasting and advertising.[41]

Prototype 'Spin Doctors': the Campaign for Democratic Socialism

During the late 1950s educationalists on the NEC effectively discouraged the embrace of professional communications techniques despite the ongoing commissioning of reports from public relations consultant Peter Davis during this period. Official Percy Clark believed the Executive's reticence stemmed from fear and their being 'terrified of anybody who knew anything about the job'.[42] During the 1959 campaign there had been attempts to develop a strategy to deal with journalists, notably through the first ever election press conferences presided over by General Secretary Morgan Philips. The party had also retained A.J. McWhinnie of the *Daily Herald* as a media adviser yet overall there was no real attempt to use public relations practices and personnel in a systematic way during the election; indeed professional offers of such help were 'coldly rebuffed'.[43] Following the defeat it was once again younger Gaitskellites belonging to a new grouping called the Campaign for Democratic Socialism who were most keen to remedy this situation. The CDS would be instrumental in not only advocating the use of public relations in politics but in demonstrating the potential benefits of this approach.

The CDS had come into being to support Hugh Gaitskell, particularly over his controversial stances on Clause Four and unilateralism. Founder member Brian Magee described the grouping as the 'modernisers' of their day committed to mobilising the 'quiet majority' of Labour members in support of the leadership.[44] The Campaign was relatively successful in raising money, notably through a 1961 fundraising dinner organised by Jack Diamond and hosted by businessman Charles Forte. The CDS also excelled in its ability to pursue a public relations' strategy through quality and popular newspapers because, according to the group's Steering Committee objectives, it was committed to: 'Encouraging sufficient press publicity to keep the Campaign in the news and to raise the morale of those supporters with whom we shall have little personal contact – and of other well disposed people'.[45] PR consultant Denis Howell and political journalist Ivan Yates directed most of this work and, like latter day 'spin doctors', targeted news correspondents and editors with copy. Consequently the CDS built up an impressive network of media contacts:

> It got a consistently favourable press in many of the more influential opinion-forming newspapers and periodicals. *The Times*, *The Guardian*, *The Observer* and *The Economist*, whilst by no means unquestioning admirers of the Labour Party, were nevertheless plainly sympathetic towards Gaitskellite activity in the party and likely to accord it friendly attention.[46]

By contrast other Labour factions, especially on the left, had few allies in the media industry and relied on small circulation titles like *Tribune* to disseminate their case.[47] Yet the publicity imbalance in favour of the right did not necessarily afford it leverage over policy because relatively strong horizontal party structures meant the left were able to mobilise dissent through the mechanisms of the Annual Conference, NEC and trade unions meetings.[48] This puts in context CDS involvement in pressing for organisational changes as a means of achieving wider party reform. Consequently when Arthur Bax resigned as head of party publicity, activist Dick Taverne saw an opportunity to promote the Campaign's values through the appointment of a likeminded person to the vacant post:

> With our links to the Labour Party organisation we wanted to see somebody who was prepared to use advertising, there was a widespread feeling that advertising was a capitalist sort of thing- a very different attitude from certain recent elections.[49]

The CDS initially considered supporting future National Union of Teachers' leader Fred Jarvis for the job. The post eventually went to John Harris, another Campaign supporter and personal aide to Gaitskell.

Must Labour Lose? The politics of polling

The CDS's pioneering use of public relations underlined the Gaitskellites' interest in setting the media agenda and, by extension, influencing party debate following the 1959 defeat. To this end the revisionists began employing another marketing technique, public opinion research, to provide them with evidence to further their case and in doing so promoted the value of polling within a hitherto largely sceptical party. Prior to that there had been sporadic attempts to develop a programme of voter analysis for Labour. In 1947 the market research department of the Erwin Wasey advertising agency provided the party with insights into the salient topics and whether these had changed from the landslide victory two years before. One thousand respondents from 8 locations were questioned about their attitudes towards parties, unions and nationalisation. The sample identified housing, coal production and food supplies as the key issues; tax and education were deemed less important and health did not feature as one of the 14 foremost items of policy. The survey also revealed widespread support for the nationalisation of public utilities but opposition to its further encroachment on the private sector.[50] Similarly following the 1950 election Michael Young and Robert Plant of the Research Department reviewed the main poll findings from the British Institute of Public Opinion (Gallup), Research Services Limited (RSL) and the London School of Economics' pioneering psephological study of the Greenwich constituency. The report discussed the large numbers of Tory voting manual workers, including the 'irrational' self-acknowledged working-class ones. Besides class, the analysis considered age, sex, issues and non-voters. Labour was popular on health, children and food prices and less so on nationalisation, housing and tax.[51] Those supportive of polling received a boost with the appointment of former Government Social Survey executive David Ginsburg as head of Research in 1951; Ginsburg subsequently availed himself of the major psephological works on recent and forthcoming campaigns.[52] Hugh Gaitskell's election as leader in 1955 proved a significant turning point given the *Socialist Commentary* article 'Understanding the Electorate' that year in which he wrote:

> Our outlook must be in line with the ordinary elector. If we fail this, we run the risk of developing into a sterile dogmatic group, living our own illusions, growing more and more out of touch with the non-political majority, and becoming increasingly ineffective politically.[53]

Gaitskell found a willing adviser in Mark Abrams, managing director of RSL, a sub-division of the London Press Exchange agency whose executives had previously advised Herbert Morrison during the 1937 London elections. One of Abrams' first tasks was to supply data for a 1955 party study of youth, *Take it from Here*.[54] Perhaps inevitably a sustained programme of polling was stalled by a combination of poor finances and educationalist suspicion that was personified in Labour Treasurer Aneurin Bevan. Bevan and his NEC allies attacked Abrams' methods and his research, particularly one study of public attitudes towards education. Feelings ran so high that revered party adviser R.H. Tawney felt obliged to intervene to defend the pollster during one meeting where his work was likened to that of Josef Goebbels.[55] The NEC subsequently failed to award RSL a contract although Abrams continued to brief Gaitskell. Following the 1959 election the pollster again offered his services and proposed to conduct a post-mortem into the defeat but the Executive also rejected this bid. Gaitskell continued to promote the importance of understanding wider public opinion, most notably in the post-defeat address to the party conference in which he famously attacked Clause Four and Labour's commitment to nationalisation. In the speech he argued society was entering a period of increasing convenience whereby growing numbers of voters, particularly in the South and Midlands, were beginning to own televisions, fridges and washing machines and take foreign holidays. It was precisely these people Abrams was so keen to research and understand.[56]

The Labour right, like their leader Hugh Gaitskell, were keen on ensuring Abrams' study into what Denis Healey called the 'irrational electorate' took place.[57] Practical support for the pollster was forthcoming from the revisionists' monthly *Socialist Commentary* in what was a logical partnership given the journal had been promoting the electoral importance of the 'floating vote' since 1951.[58] The results of Abrams' survey of 750 voters were published in a series of articles in early 1960 and subsequently appeared later that year as a book co-authored by the pollster, political scientist Richard Rose and *Socialist Commentary* editor Rita Hinden. The volume, *Must Labour Lose?*, impressed several strategists including General Secretary Morgan Philips and Research head Peter Shore and also promoted the value of professional opinion research inside the party.[59] Leading revisionist Tony Crosland believed that polling based reports like *Must Labour Lose?* demonstrated the need for the party to develop a better 'rapport' with the electorate through a sustained programme of opinion research. Privately he counselled his leader to counsell his leader to pursue the matter with vigour given 'the Labour Party uses polls and surveys less than any other major party in the world'.[60]

Must Labour Lose? suggested there had been an 'embourgeoisement' of society whereby growing numbers of working-class were leading more affluent consumer lifestyles. This thesis linked political change to a growing individualism and erosion of strong communal ties which some activists believed would foster an 'atomised society' hostile to the collectivist ethos of Labour, the unions and organisations like the Workers' Education Association. Hinden argued the many newly 'affluent' workers' perceived the party to be 'holding them back' and even hostile to their self-advancement: 'Labour may stand 'for the working-class', but not for the increasing number who feel, rightly or wrongly, they have outgrown that label'.[61] A likeminded account quoted a working-class Conservative supporter as saying: 'it (Labour) had no time for those who work hard and want to get on. You pull yourself up a bit and then the Labour party comes along and takes everything away'. For junior MP Roy Hattersley it would be legitimate to appeal to the 'aspirations' of such voters in what was an 'increasingly classless society'. For revisionists this necessitated the reform of party organisation, policy and, to use the vogue term, image. Ultimately *Must Labour Lose?* appeared to give the Gaitskellites 'scientific' justifications for their position.[62] Unlike the Conservatives' first major polling study into *The Floating Vote*, Abrams' study had been commissioned and publicised by a journal associated with one party faction yet it still succeeded in furthering the revisionist agenda by focusing debate on how Labour was supposedly antiquated, too wedded to a declining traditional working-class vote and allegedly beholden to ill-conceived and unpalatable policies like nationalisation. General Secretary Morgan Philips effectively endorsed Hinden's analysis for *Must Labour Lose?* in *Labour in the Sixties*, a major policy statement in which he argued for an image overhaul similar to that undertaken by the Conservatives during the 1950s.[63]

The educationalist response

Many of those committed to the reform of campaigning were keen on enhancing the leadership. Inevitably they faced resistance from a formidable alliance of passive traditionalists wary of spending money on expensive professional campaigns and the more vocal opposition from radical activists distrustful of what they regarded as shallow and divisive means of political persuasion. Even Gaitskell, who stood to personally benefit from the party's adoption of mediated electioneering, was initially sceptical about using advertising because he believed 'the whole thing is somehow false':

> You see, I am a rationalist. I like to think that in a mature democracy people reach their conclusions mostly on the basis of actual evidence and argument. I do not like to think that they vote as they do because something appeals to their unconscious.[64]

The leader's educationalist style reticence in this regard may have stemmed from his background in adult tutoring. Gaitskell's donnish disposition made him appear uneasy on television, particular against his more telegenic opponent, Harold Macmillan.[65] That said, his experience of leading the Labour campaign in a general election convinced him that the party needed professional help and techniques. Gaitskell's swift conversion on this issue was, however, atypical.

'The New Necromancy'

During the run-up to the 1959 election many Labour politicians made a virtue of ridiculing the Conservatives' relationship with CPV to such an extent that attacking 'admass' politics was one of the few things that united a fractious National Executive from Eirene White on the right to left-wingers like Ian Mikardo.[66] Patrick Gordon-Walker, the party's first ever broadcasting officer and leading Gaitskellite MP, denounced the Tories' sponsorship of the 'worst sort of Americanisation' and warned about dangers posed 'by the introduction here of high pressure advertising techniques aimed at the hidden persuasion of the electors'.[67] His fellow Gaitskellite Alice Bacon, Chair of the NEC Publicity Committee, used a parliamentary debate in 1960 to outline her fear that politics would 'become a battle between two Madison Avenue advertising agencies' for the reason that 'The Conservative Party has placed itself in the hands of an advertising agency which produced the so-called image of the Tory Party by advertising methods. I believe this to be doing something alien to our British democracy'.[68] Predictably the most vociferous opposition to mediated campaigning came from the left and its most prominent leader Aneurin Bevan who, in a famous speech in which he likened the Conservatives to 'vermin', made a point of denouncing the party's 'propaganda machine'.[69] Bevan was similarly scathing about the techniques he associated with manipulation and deceit:

> (He)...despised the whole paraphernalia of psephologists' forecasts, public opinion polls, television campaigning, and the presentation of so-called party 'images'... He believed that they debased the art of politics since they were contrivances tending to increase the politicians' reliance on careful calculation and diminish his faith in political ideas and his courage in stating them.[70]

Many of the party's left and grassroots activists shared Bevan's scathing judgement and remained wedded to the educationalist belief in direct, unmediated and didactic forms of political communication. The 'new necromancy' of marketing was, according to Labour Chair Barbara Castle, antipathetic to the party's mission 'to go out and make socialists' and emancipate society.[71] Similarly Ken Garland, another party supporter and co-designer of the classic Campaign for Nuclear Disarmament logo, denounced 'Ad Men' as 'Institute of Directors fellow travellers':

> (A)ll they know about is appealing to people's greed, whereas we are trying to appeal to their ideals...we ruddy don't need (these)

tricksters... If you want a photo on let's say, Youth and Labour, you don't need a studio portrait of an impossibly smooth looking teenager wearing clothes that could only be afforded by a Mayfair call-girl. What you do need is a lively outdoor photo of the girl next door with freckles and a saucy grin, against a backdrop that could be your street or my street.[72]

The intellectual community surrounding the party shared the ideological distrust of 'admass' politics. In his first book the writer and dramatist Dennis Potter argued the Conservatives' 'selling' of themselves was debasing politics and, more fundamentally, subverting the democratic process: 'the techniques of persuasion, the ideology of the acquisitive society, have taken on new and more dangerous dimensions'. EP Thompson broadened the attack by complaining the: 'Two major parties competed like soap manufacturers to sell the "image" of their branded product'; inevitably another commentator likened the combatants to 'Daz and Omo'.[73] The widespread opposition in the Labour movement to advertising, public relations and market research had a practical policy dimension. In the 1961 party pamphlet, *First things last?*, purveyors of the 'Jack's All Right' mentality were condemned in no uncertain terms:

> Some time ago the hoardings carried a poster chosen by the advertising profession itself... 'ADVERTISING INTRODUCES YOU TO THE GOOD THINGS IN LIFE.' This means that the good things of life are only the things that are advertised. Not education or health, or adventure, or sport, or great advances in human knowledge, or explaining space...or building good homes, or fine public buildings. Not helping other countries, some of them desperately poor. Or making some great contribution to world peace. Just the rat-race. All against all- the scramble for social status, money, commercial products. Well, for the Conservatives, apparently, that's enough. Britain has never had it so good, they say. But there are many people who reject this shallow philosophy. They are to be found in all walks of life- and their number is growing. Perhaps you are one of them?.[74]

The pamphlet's sentiments were shared by other Labour inclined publications, notably the Fabian Society's report advocating *A Tax on Advertising*, as well as an influential group of MPs led by Harold Wilson, Philip Noel-Baker and Christopher Mayhew who were distrustful of the burgeoning marketing industry.[75]

'Taking the Poetry out of Politics'

Given the National Executive's failure to support Mark Abrams both before and after the 1959 election it was to be expected that the pollster's *Must Labour Lose?* findings would not be universally welcomed within the party. Pragmatists like Herbert Morrison voiced the most basic criticisms of Abrams' approach and dismissed it for encouraging the 'election as game' ethos. Nor was Morrison impressed by the method: 'I myself have never had much faith in the opinion polls, preferring an instinctive judgement produced from the indefinable atmosphere at meetings and among ordinary people on the street. It is well to know one's fellow-countrymen'. Similarly George Woodcock, a leading trade unionist and representative of Labour's principal funders, was blunt about the process and argued 'You get the answers you expect'.[76] Leading strategists like Tony Benn sought to develop a more sustained and engaging critique of polling as a technique by questioning whether it was truly able to deal with the complexities of political life:

> It is one thing to ask people which way they intend to vote and publish the results as a guide to their personal preferences and prejudices. It is quite another thing to seek snap judgements from people on a few isolated elements in intensely complicated policy questions. It would be easy to produce a public opinion poll showing that an overwhelming majority of the electorate was in favour both of lower taxation and, at the same time, greatly increased expenditure on schools, roads and cancer research.[77]

The appearance of *Must Labour Lose?* triggered an intensive debate over Labour's future and also led to a less high profile discussion of polling and its merits. *Socialist Commentary*, the journal that originally funded and published Abrams' findings, gave a right of reply to Denis McQuail and others doubtful about the research analysis whilst the agents' journal *Labour Organiser* also featured a rebuttal of the findings based on published Gallup data.[78] These critics suggested the party's defeat lay in a general distrust of Labour rather than any specific policy commitment such as the Gaitskellite bugbear of nationalisation. Others disputed *Must Labour Lose?* contributor Rita Hinden's conceptualisation of embourgeoisement not to mention its assumption that increased affluence necessarily favoured the Conservatives' electoral fortunes. Poverty had not prevented a sizeable section of the working-class from voting Tory.[79]

The more passionate Labour arguments against opinion research were not, as Mark Abrams himself acknowledged, technical or partisan in nature. Rather they were motivated by a fear that polling was 'a mortal threat to the ideological integrity of the party' or, as Bevan saw it, 'taking the poetry out of politics'.[80] One of the most forthright statements of this position was offered by leading left-winger Richard Crossman in *Labour and the Affluent Society*, his polemical rebuttal of *Must Labour Lose?*, which took issue with those intent on 'reshaping' Labour 'in the image of the American Democratic Party' so as to 'manage capitalism as competently as the Tories'. He further contended that those whose main object 'is to regain office tend to be opportunists, to hedge and to equivocate in order to appease the voter'. Nor were they genuinely Labour because 'a left-wing party which adopts such tactics destroy itself'.[81]

Several left-wing intellectuals expressed hostility towards the rapidly growing study of psephology or what E.P. Thompson termed 'ephology' only worthy of publication 'in the *American Journal of Communicational Guphology*'.[82] The most penetrating attack on polling and *Must Labour Lose?* appeared in *New Left Review*. In the piece, 'Dr Abrams and the End of Politics', socialist historian Raphael Samuel argued the business style approach to campaigning was ideologically alien as well as antipathetic to the party's traditions:

> He sees people as consumers of politics, behaving in politics much as they would – in the motivational research imagination – when confronted with mass-marketed commodities: they 'buy' political labels and allegiances as they would any brand associations it promises to afford... Dr. Abrams is not, therefore, concerned with the real nature of peoples' needs and desires – since on his view they cannot be said to have any that are truly autonomous- nor with the quality of Labour policies, since these have no validity independent of the 'identifications' they offer – but solely with 'associations', both personal ('ego-identification') and political (party 'image' and leader 'personality'), and it is with these that his survey is principally concerned.

Samuel concluded his essay by outlining his concerns about the likely consequences and impact of Abrams' work:

> If the Labour Movement were finally to abandon its traditional way of thinking about people – and that alone is truly fundamental – to

lose the faith in the power of the word to move people, and of the idea to change them, if it were to let go its conviction in the capacity of human beings rationally to choose between the alternatives which face them, and purposefully to re-shape the society in which they live, then it would be finished, and would find itself trapped in that limbo of the political imagination whose features Dr. Abrams has so meticulously outlined.[83]

Other socialists bemoaned the apparent failure of polling-obsessed parliamentarians to give a lead to the party and wider movement in the country. In the view of influential theoretician Ralph Miliband, it was symptomatic of the 'Sickness of Labourism' and further evidence of a paralysis of leadership among politicians 'haunted by a composite image of the potential Labour voter as quintessentially petit-bourgeois'.[84] In the aftermath of the 1959 general election such analysis was popular within the party and helped those strategists sceptical about incorporating marketing professionalism into electoral practices. Yet events were about to conspire to rapidly bring about the most important changes to the Labour campaign organisation since it was formed.

4
Selling the Party

The first modernisation of Labour

The 1959 election defeat led to major inquest into the state of Labour. Discussion eventually turned to campaigning and how it might be made more efficient and responsive. After a protracted debate, change was relatively swift. Pointedly the Nuffield study described this process as 'The Modernisation of Labour'. Serious reorganisation of campaigning began when key party posts fell vacant between 1960 and 1963. The sudden death of Hugh Gaitskell deprived Labour of its leader. Ill-health forced the retirement of General Secretary Morgan Philips and Arthur Bax suddenly resigned as head of publicity. In addition the death of Aneurin Bevan, Labour's arch-educationalist, removed a key impediment to the professionalisation of campaigning. Gaitkell's successor, Harold Wilson developed a keen interest in presentation. Wilson sloughed off his objections to image management and became 'a man fascinated by the media, by political techniques and organisation'. He demonstrated that non-revisionists were committed to overhauling campaigning and helped make this happen. As Chair of the Campaigns Committee set up by the National Executive Committee (NEC) in October 1961, Wilson had been central to preparations for the following election.[1] On becoming leader he proved an effective organiser, self-publicist and communicator.

Wilson carefully cultivated his public image. His Yorkshire accent, Gannex raincoat, love of HP brown sauce and pipe smoking suggested he had the common touch. Privately Wilson preferred luxuries including expensive cigars. The leader employed soundbite-type responses and popularised phrases such as 'golden handshake' in a memorable attack on exorbitant executives' severance payments in the early 1960s.

Wilson became the first major politician to really understand the media's needs and to this end used an autocue in televised broadcasts.[2] Len Williams' appointment as General Secretary helped the new leadership. His formidable predecessor Philips had outmanoeuvred elected rivals and disliked Wilson because of his 'penny-farthing' report. By contrast the more cautious Williams' promotion over proactive Research Secretary Peter Shore would help boost the profile of other headquarters' staff. In January 1962 Arthur Bax's surprise retirement, officially on grounds of ill-health but following his smearing as a communist sympathiser, created another vacancy in a key Transport House portfolio.[3] His post was re-titled Publicity Director and attracted a higher salary than did other staff on the same grade.[4] A quality shortlist resulted in the appointment of John Harris, a 34-year-old writer for the Labour supporting *Forward* newspaper. Significantly neither Harris' role as Gaitskell's press adviser nor his closeness to revisionists like Roy Jenkins undermined his position following Wilson's election as leader. On the contrary the partnership flourished and: 'Harris took on the task of moulding the Wilson image with almost academic precision'.[5] Consequently, barely three years after Alice Bacon's denunciation of the Conservatives' use of Colman Prentis Varley (CPV), Labour did a volte-face and embraced media-style electioneering. Ironically some party strategists came to regard CPV's 1959 campaign as a model of effectiveness. Labour also looked further afield for inspiration. Kennedy's 'New Frontier' struck a particular chord with Wilson, a keen student of Theodore White's study of the 1960 presidential race.[6]

Professionals and the Party

Major changes to election organisation began in 1961 with the setting-up of the traditional pre-election Campaign Committee. Chaired by Wilson, the forum encouraged contact between headquarters' officials and sympathisers working in advertising, market research and public relations. Mark Abrams was impressed with the arrangement and compared it to the Liaison Committee responsible for the Conservative campaign between 1957–59. Previously Abrams had complained of having no effective body for the discussion of his work.[7] John Harris became the key party contact for supporters in the marketing industry. In February 1962 Harris, together with Alice Bacon, senior politician George Brown and Len Williams, held a meeting with professionals at the House of Commons. In spite of a 'fruitless' discussion, some of those present agreed to run a campaign on behalf of a wealthy Constituency Labour Party (CLP) in Norfolk. Later, at an informal gathering in The Paviour's Arms public house near Transport House, Harris and his deputy Percy Clark began the first of a series of consultations with a team of designers, copywriters and advertising executives. The informality of proceedings led to subsequent meetings at Mark Abrams' own flat or the Reform Club. Harris reported back to the Campaign Committee and became something of a diplomat: 'Great care was taken not to place before the NEC or any of its sub-committees material which could spark off ideological controversy'.[8]

Granted a generous initial budget of £100,000, Harris organised the professional volunteers into three groups: strategy, press and PR, and broadcasting. Some commentators believed the new arrangements effectively dispossessed the Campaign Committee of its key functions. The nucleus of the operation lay in the strategy team led by Harris and Abrams together with the professionals Peter Davis, Benton Bowles agency director David Kingsley, Brian Murphy of Erwin Wasey and Michael Barnes of the firm Crawford's.[9] In turn they sought advice from a wider circle of contacts including the Institute of Practitioners in Advertising's ex-president Alan Eden-Green and even, covertly, an executive with the Conservatives' agency CPV. Unlike previous elections, Deputy Director of Publicity Percy Clark could now boast that Labour was using 'top people in advertising'.[10] Some executives did, however, prefer to remain nameless because, as Kingsley admitted, 'It wasn't terribly popular within the advertising industry to be seen to be working for the Labour Party'. Like the Shadow Communications Agency twenty years later, the volunteers belonged to a 'ghost' grouping which provided anonymity and flexible working relationships.[11]

The strategy group took responsibility for election planning, a major part of which involved polling analysis. A motion to the 1960 Annual Conference had called for this and the NEC eventually responded by appointing Mark Abrams as the party's official researcher in 1962. Abrams' work became crucial and, for the first time in a national Labour campaign, 'major advertising and publicity decisions were largely based on lessons drawn from surveys'.[12] With £5000 he undertook the first in a series of pre-election opinion surveys. In autumn 1962 Abrams reported his initial findings to the NEC in a briefing on 'general implications'. The research, influenced by the work of the Simulmatics Corporation for John F. Kennedy surveyed 1250 voters. The findings focused strategists' minds on the estimated uncommitted 35% of voters. Of these 'waverers' Abrams identified those living in key marginal seats as the 'target' groups Labour needed to convince. Broadly representative of the electorate as a whole, these voters were understood to view politics in a largely non-ideological way and were more interested in television programmes like 'Z Cars'. Evidence of this kind was used to challenge the widespread assumption that public opinion was evenly arranged on a linear left-right spectrum.[13] In contrast to past experience, Abrams' research was well received by the NEC. Gaitskell was an enthusiast and, shortly before his death, announced a plan to raise £400,000 for market research. Abrams even saw his influence under Wilson increase to the extent that: 'the vocabulary and thought of several National Executive members seemed permeated with the surveys' conclusions'. As an official later admitted, the polling research was 'prodigiously influential'.[14] It also provided a culture shock for some:

> A party member of fifty years' standing (thirty of them in the House of Commons) watched as a succession of young men in gingham shirts leapt to a flip-chart to explain their part of the campaign. 'I have never', he said as he left the meeting, 'seen anything quite like that before'.[15]

Labour's first sustained programme: '...concentrated on the political environment, on the electorate in terms of their background, on the communication between party and electorate, and on those who make up the "party" within the electorate'.[16] Polling helped challenge the view, ironically promoted by Wilson's 1955 penny-farthing report, that the working-class would support Labour provided the party mobilised their votes. By contrast Abrams believed workers were more heterogeneous and needed appealing to as parents of young children, women or lower middle-class people. These voters were less concerned about Labour's 'modernisation' rhetoric or the Tory's 'wasted years' in government. Though influential, research was primarily about refining the message so that those charged with conducting and interpreting findings advised 'what to concentrate on, which aspects of agreed policy should be emphasised, (but) did not attempt to re-create the product being sold'.[17]

'Let's Go with Labour': campaigning in the Sixties

Mark Abrams did research for all three of Labour's advisory groups. He helped the publicity and PR team consisting of volunteers Ros Allen, James Boswell and assorted *Daily Herald* staff. They co-ordinated the party's most ambitious pre-election campaign in a generation.

Launched in May 1963, this consisted of newspaper and poster advertising. Copy appeared in popular titles like the *Mirror* and *Express* as well as the loyal *Herald* and Co-operative *Sunday Citizen*.[18] Anticipating an autumn election, the party found itself having to sustain the promotional momentum well into the following year. Abrams' research guided the copywriters and designers preparing the advertising. Survey findings helped to identify useful themes and issues, copy-test slogans and ideas, and monitor attitudes towards politicians. The team used quantitative and less traditional, qualitative forms of feedback. The latter involved depth interviews testing voter reactions to copy. Research helped modify the team's prior assumptions. One poster had a particularly swift demise:

> It showed a delectable girl with tongue peeping saucily from between her lips, and the men on the advertising group were captivated. But Mark Abrams had 'researched' for reactions, and it was found that most women thought the girl in the ad looked like a 'tart', 'husband stealer' or 'loose woman'. So much for the Labour Party's one timorous venture into eroticism.[19]

During the run-up to the election the party built its campaign around the slogan 'Let's go with Labour and we'll get things done'. The phrase, devised by David Kingsley and Peter Davis, appeared in various guises. Taking inspiration from a gesture associated with Norman Vaughan, compere of television's *Sunday Night at the London Palladium*, designers used a disembodied hand pointing upwardly to promote the 'Let's Go' message.[20] Research helped copywriters appeal to voters with more specific messages including 'What Labour will do about overcrowded schools', 'How Labour will end the housing heartbreak', and 'I've had enough of the Tories'. The team suggested targeting women by advertising in the *Sunday Mirror*. The proposed copy depicted a mother bathing her baby alongside the caption 'Like Mother's Love... there are some things a man cannot understand'. Wilson vetoed the material, considering it both patronising and emotive. Another advert, featuring the leader with members of the public, was dropped because it made him look 'too ordinary'.[21]

In addition to occupying an important strategic position, Wilson played a major presentational role. Abrams believed the personalisation of Labour would help generate success and that was a more effective media performer than the patrician Prime Minister Alec Douglas-Home. Labour's leader developed a presidential aura by drawing parallels between his 'New Britain' rhetoric and the American Democrats' 'New Frontier' and, in doing so, became a 'Kennedy-type figure'.[22] His visionary 'white heat of technology' reinforced the difference between his party of 'modernisation' and the Conservatives.[23] Wilson did not restrict himself to a few selected themes as the pre-election advertising had done. He proved particularly adept at synchronising his speeches to coincide with evening news broadcasts. This ensured more coverage: as soon as the camera lights went on the leader would stop his speech and recite prepared text with skill and spontaneity.[24] The augmentation of Labour's Press and Publicity Department built on earlier innovations, notably the press conferences introduced by Morgan Philips during the 1959 campaign. Headquarters' staff including Gerald Corr, Philip Parry, Jonathan Boswell and ex-London Press Exchange executive Michael Pentreath were assigned to offer public relations' advice to candidates, agents and organisers in the Midlands and southern England. T. Dan Smith Associates, a firm run by the legendary Newcastle council leader, was retained to provide a similar service for those campaigning in the North and Scotland. Smith attended Publicity Sub-committee meetings in 1962 prior to the NEC's confirmation of his contract later that year.[25] The party's first significant public relations' offensive was launched in spring 1963 to coincide with its national advertising campaign.

Unlike the other groups, the broadcasting team worked for party official Clive Bradley and not the Publicity Department. A former BBC overseas service operative appointed chief broadcasting officer in May 1962, Bradley was in turn accountable to the Senior and Junior Broadcasting Committees chaired by Chief Whip Herbert Bowden and Tony Benn respectively. This bureaucracy developed because television was felt to be exceptionally influential. It did not however unduly hinder Bradley who worked closely with John Harris.[26] Some politicians like Benn were both supportive and helpful. The resulting broadcasts departed from the stylised formula introduced in 1959. Wilson and deputy George Brown felt the earlier Party Election Broadcasts (PEBs) had been too slick. Although a company, Mithras Films, shot footage of the 1963 Conference and other events, little of their material went into a final series of Broadcasts that relied heavily on Wilson's screen presence. Abrams researched public reactions to the PEBs. His findings suggested that whereas Labour supporters liked to see attacks on the Conservatives, target voters remained relatively unmoved by the same appeals.[27] Most of the PEBs were routine and consisted of the standard politician to camera format. An exception was a film featuring 'ordinary' party members at the home of a North London councillor. The event's host turned out to be publicity adviser Brian Murphy and the choice of venue was not to everybody's taste as the Nuffield study noted: 'The Murphys' well-stocked bookshelves slightly troubled the image-makers'.[28]

'You Know Labour Government Works': winning a second term

Labour won the 1964 election by a narrow margin. Two years later Wilson would go to the country in pursuit of a healthier electoral mandate. In the intervening period there was comparatively little debate over campaigning, although Wilson made the most of his premiership as an adept self-publicist willing to appeal to popular culture by awarding honours to The Beatles and being photographed with celebrities. In the wider party there were limited attempts to provoke a strategic rethink. The *Socialist Commentary* journal did, for instance, produce 'Our Penny Farthing Machine', to mark the tenth anniversary of Wilson's report on party organisation. Contributors to it wanted more professionalism and less complacency: 'Up and down the country cosy squalor and amateurism are our main hallmarks'. Largely unheeded at the time, the document's proposals were very similar to the reforms introduced by the Kinnock leadership twenty years later.[29] They included: paying advertising advisers, recruiting and training public relations staff, loosening politicians' control over PEBs; and intensifying polling efforts. In 1966 the party did not undertake the laborious schedule of preparations that preceded the 1964 election. There was also controversy over the perceived demotion of the NEC in favour of a special Officers' (or liaison) Committee involving selected party and parliamentary representatives. Similarly there was a row over an ad hoc publicity committee consisting of headquarters' officials, a representative from the Whips' Office and minister George Wigg. The controversy was partly resolved following the replacement of Wigg with NEC member Richard Crossman. The dispute underlined the organisational vacuum caused by the departure of many headquarters staff to government jobs following the 1964 victory.[30]

Less opinion research was commissioned in 1966 because 'the party felt it had learned all it needed to know before 1964'. Nonetheless, Wilson retained the services of strategists David Kingsley, Denis Lyons and Peter Davis. During a difficult period in 1965, the advisers had warned the prime minister not to use publicity to try and resolve a problem. It was in sharp contrast to 1959 when offers of professional help had been rejected. Now the leadership welcomed professional guidance to the extent that, in the words of one consultant, it became 'a sort of cargo cult' amongst the Labour hierarchy.[31] Approaching the campaign Kingsley and his colleagues reorganised into a core Planning team alongside Brian Murphy, Ros Allen, Abrams and newly promoted Publicity Director Percy Clark. Clark emulated Harris and provided a discreet point of contact for the party's advisers.[32] Denis Lyons and Peter Davis were provided with accommodation in No. 10 Downing Street, sub-groups formed to co-ordinate work on PR, political education, publications and women and the services of T. Dan Smith were again retained. Rosemary Oxley devised the core campaign message 'You Know Labour Government Works'.[33] Given their response, the voters appeared to agree. Wilson and Clark managed the campaign through discreet lines of communication. The leader was praised for being 'completely professional'. But Wilson's style also fuelled a backlash from critics of the prime minister's hands on approach and reliance on a 'kitchen cabinet' of unelected advisers.[34] As in 1964, the 1966 election in effect saw a downgrading of headquarters' role. Victories at both polls eased any resentment but it soon became apparent that the party machine was in need of attention. After a couple of poor by-election results in 1967, Crossman noted:

> In Transport House there wasn't a single person capable of considering the strategy of our propaganda, the effects of the by-elections and drawing conclusions from them. This kind of work simply isn't going on either in Transport House or Whitehall.[35]

Crossman's concerns were shared by William Simpson's committee of inquiry into party organisation set up that year. Participants discussed the 1965 *Socialist Commentary* pamphlet and took submissions from various people including trade unionist Frank Cousins and Labour MP Robert Maxwell. For his part Wilson and his advisers maintained an interest in American campaign techniques, particularly the television commercials made for Richard Nixon's successful 1968 presidential campaign. Private screenings of this 'fascinating' material were shown at 10 Downing Street.[36]

Fractiousness and factionalism: the Seventies and beyond

If the 1960s had seen dramatic changes in the party, the following decade witnessed an even greater transformation. Wilson's ability to manage the party would be put to the severest test. Earnest debate over the direction of the party followed general election defeats in 1970 and, more explosively, 1979. Inevitably this had consequences for campaigning.

'Yesterday's Men': the 1970 defeat

Harold Wilson became the focus of criticism after Labour lost office in 1970. MP Leo Abse accused Wilson of running an aloof campaign without a care for the party organisation. Key aides included the leader's political secretary Marcia Williams, press secretary Will Camp, researcher John Allen and former *Daily Herald* staff journalist Alfred Richman.[37] Filmmaker and actor Stanley Baker advised Wilson and narrated a PEB whilst the star of popular comedy series Steptoe and Son Harry H. Corbett appeared in another. The traditional Campaign Committee was aided by a smaller sub-committee consisting of the leader and his aides together with representatives from the Parliamentary Labour Party (PLP) and NEC.[38] Following recommendations by the Simpson Committee, press officers were appointed throughout the English regions to provide training in public relations and opinion research techniques. In the North and Scotland the work was undertaken by T. Dan Smith's consultancy and by Gywnoro Jones' firm in Wales.[39]

The leader's relationship with the party's advertising consultants eventually highlighted the tension between strategists in Downing Street and at the party's Transport House headquarters. Wilson took soundings from a Publicity Advisory Committee led by the 'three wise men'. These were the now familiar figures of David Kingsley, co-founder and owner of the agency Kingsley Manton Palmer (KMP), Peter Davis of Central Press Exchange and Infoscan's Denis Lyons. They continued to work with Director of Publicity Percy Clark.[40] Once largely private figures, the advisers began gaining public recognition. In a *Sunday Times* interview Kingsley revealed how commercial experience informed his political outlook: 'Ideas are coming back. They're the now thing. This is an interesting thought that has only just occurred to me- we could really sell the Labour Party on ideals in the present climate of opinion.'[41] Kingsley and his team devised pre-campaign slogans like 'Labour's got Life and Soul' and 'When it comes down to it aren't Labour's ideals yours as well?'. These were followed by another piece of copy, 'Now Britain's Strong Let's Make It Great to Live In'. More controversially the party launched its 'Yesterday's Men' advertising. This used waxwork miniatures of leading Conservatives to ridicule them as out of touch. Media critics objected to the negativity of the material whilst Labour educationalists attacked its personalised and trivial tone.[42] Kingsley was a casualty of the fallout and never worked for the party again.

Labour's programme of opinion research also proved controversial. American motivational researcher Conrad Jamieson, a potential replacement for retiring pollster Mark Abrams, was commissioned by the party to research the views of 1000 members. Officials became upset when the depressing findings of this study, *Resolutionaries not Revolutionaries*, appeared in *The Sunday Times* during January 1968. Regardless of who leaked the information, the exercise did little to build trust between the party and its consultants. This led to tension between, among others, Clark and Kingsley. Shortly after a by now an ex-adviser Jamieson lamented Labour's 'schoolboy casualness' to organisational matters.[43] The problems over polling left the party with little time to find a replacement for Abrams. Having been approached in December 1969, London based Market Opinion & Research International (MORI) began working for Labour in March 1970. Previously owned by market research firms National Opinion Polls (NOP) and Opinion Research Centre (ORC), MORI established itself as an independent company under American chief executive Robert Worcester. Wilson's decision to go to the country in June meant Worcester had to make swift preparations and only a couple of brief studies were completed during the campaign. By contrast the Conservatives' team of marketing strategists had time to incorporate sophisticated polling techniques and help leader Edward Heath to an unexpected victory.[44]

Following the 1970 defeat, the balance of power in Labour's NEC began moving to the left. Soon the debate over polling resurfaced with critics boosted by the Jamieson and Yesterday's Men controversies. The NEC banned questions on policies and personalities though Wilson continued to take discreet advice from MORI on the standing of public figures including himself.[45] The fine balance between the left and right was illustrated in 1972 when the General Secretaryship fell vacant following the retirement of Harry Nicholas. The fate of Roy Jenkins' candidate Gwyn Morgan and his left rival Ron Hayward lay with the NEC. After a dramatic tie, Executive chair Tony Benn made the casting vote in favour of Hayward. Benn personified the ideological shift underway. The new General Secretary believed staff ought to be the servants of the party and answerable to the National Executive not the parliamentary leadership. Hayward's approach brought him into conflict with Wilson.[46] The radicalisation of the party took various forms. Press and Publicity, for instance, was briefly re-designated the Information Department and marked a resurgence in left sponsored educationalism within the NEC. Public relations became, according to one critic, an afterthought and 'Achilles Heel' although it did not stop an official from bragging about how several professional agencies 'would be only too glad to have us'.[47]

Wilson's last stand

The 1974 elections saw little in the way of innovation partly because they were both called at short notice. NEC Campaign Committees were convened alongside a smaller steering group, the General Election Committee, consisting of Wilson, chief whip Bob Mellish, the NEC chair and vice-chair, the General Secretary, and three heads of department including the Director of Publicity. In practice much strategic decision-making fell to Wilson and close aides like Marcia Williams, polling analyst Bernard Donoughue, correspondence secretary Albert Murray, broadcasting expert Terry Boston and press officer Joe Haines. Additional expertise was offered by designer Mike Oxley, writer John Mortimer and, once again, the actor director Stanley Baker. Trusted advisers Denis Lyons and Peter Davis continued to play their part, working directly to Wilson; together, with pollster Worcester, they earned the nickname 'chocolate soldiers' in recognition of the Rowntree trust money used to fund some of their activities.[48] Market researcher Andrew McIntosh was also consulted. Chris Powell, an executive with the Boase Massimi Pollitt agency and adviser to the Trades Union Congress (TUC), began what turned out to be his long if punctuated relationship with the party.[49] In an attempt to placate his critics as well as the NEC's vocal left caucus, the leader liased with headquarters in a way that had not happened in 1970.

In the second election of 1974, Labour was in office and better prepared for the coming campaign. Strategists developed the slogans 'Britain Will Win' and 'Labour Keeps Its Promises'. The idea of the 'team' was also used. The party had originally planned to use this theme in the 1970 election. According to Joe Haines the campaign organisation was more effective than it had been then and was aided by Lyons and Davis' presence in a Downing Street office in anticipation of the October election. The increasing fascination with those working for and around the party leaders produced a telling comment from the Nuffield authors: 'Campaign management has become a much more elaborate and self-conscious process than in the days when Mr and Mrs Attlee drove around the country in the family car'.[50]

A great deal of preparation went in to Wilson's tour of Britain. Most effort and resources were targeted on fifty marginal seats. Designer Jack Stoddart together with Hammer films make-up artist George Blackler helped on the visual presentation whilst party youth officer Neil Vann together with David Wickes, producer of television series 'The Sweeney' took care of the practicalities.[51] If the leader's aides had comparative freedom in organising how he would be reported on news reports, they had less control over PEB production. Nevertheless some of this broadcast material did reflect the strategist's concern with communicating to key electoral groups; in one film from the February campaign Shirley Williams made a clear bid to win women by using a basket of shopping to discuss prices.[52]

The 1974 elections consolidated the relationship between Labour and MORI. From 1972 the firm experimented with so-called 'psychographic' research techniques, a method that helped to categorise voters according to their underlying value structures be they 'authoritarian', 'apathetic', 'old style' or 'new style' Labour. According to Robert Worcester, qualitative and quantitative research informed party decisions 'in matters of tactics and presentation of policy'.[53] Wilson praised survey findings, later claiming they were a valuable aid that helped him to cut through 'the fog'. Though a significant undertaking, the NEC was less than unanimous in its support for the polling operation. The opposition to opinion research continued and intensified following Labour's return to government. Tony Benn objected to research material on personalities or sensitive policies like nationalisation. Nor did the reporting of Labour's private poll findings in the *Sunday Times* endear the practice to sceptics such as General Secretary Hayward.[54]

The sudden retirement of Harold Wilson as prime minister and leader in 1976 came as a shock and created a major vacuum within the government and party. Wilson's resignation also deprived Labour's professional advisers of a committed client. The party lost a skilled conciliator able to mediate between the various officials, advisers and aides responsible for campaign development. As his political secretary put it: 'Harold was an outsider- except where it counted most: the Transport House Publicity Department'.[55] Wilson's role in developing the party's media campaigning was his organisational legacy as he personified Labour's shift from educationalism to persuasionalism. According to Rose: 'Harold Wilson's career as party leader has shown there is no necessary antithesis between leading the Labour party and being continuously sensitive to public relations'.[56] James Callaghan,

Wilson's successor, had comparatively little time for strategic matters. Callaghan's precarious government majority afforded him little opportunity to develop relationships with public relations and advertising executives. The new leader was also less media conscious and, in the run-up to the 1979 election, attacked the Conservatives' professional campaign: 'The truth is in this election the Tories are being sold as though they were Daz of Omo'. Callaghan made a virtue of his own approach: 'I don't intend to be packaged like cornflakes. I shall continue to be myself'. He did nonetheless play a key organisational role within the campaign and was no doubt encouraged by personal opinion ratings that consistently bettered those of Mrs Thatcher throughout the election.[57]

The party acquired the services of PR specialist Edward Booth-Clibborn of FD & D, advertising executive Tim Delaney of agency BBDO and Trevor Eke, the managing director of Playtex. Delaney found the experience demoralising. The group had few resources, little support from headquarters and lacked access to private polling reports. Neither did the: '... speeches objecting to soap-powder advertising techniques... help the morale of the people trying to work for the Labour party'.[58] Party chair Frank Allaun presided over a Campaign Committee consisting of up to 22 members drawn from the Cabinet, NEC and headquarters' staff. Informed observers thought the body too large to be effective. Callaghan held separate strategy meetings with press secretary Tom McCaffrey, campaign manager Derek Gladwin, personal aide David Lipsey, economics adviser Gavyn Davies, Booth-Clibborn, *Sun* journalist Roger Carroll and former Wilson adviser Bernard Donoughue. Others involved included *Daily Mirror* journalist Mike Molloy and Essex University psephologist Ivor Crewe who chaired an advisory team called the 'white room group'.[59]

Labour's NEC renewed MORI's contract in February 1978 but only after a fraught debate had ended in a 11 to 7 vote in favour. The main opposition to polling came from left-wingers who now formed a cohesive majority on the Executive. Fittingly Norman Atkinson, occupying the Treasurer's post once held by Aneurin Bevan, was the leading bane of the pollster. Speaking at an Executive meeting in 1979, Atkinson made his feelings clear: 'Twenty members of my general management committee and I can do a better job (than the polls) of assessing public opinion'. The then junior NEC member Neil Kinnock added 'Norman, why do you need the other twenty?'[60] The hostility towards marketing professionalism within the Executive could also be found in Labour headquarters. Officials like General Secretary Ron Hayward had little time for the party's advertising and polling advisers. As Edward Booth-Clibborn later admitted: 'they didn't 'understand nor even want to understand people like me'.[61] Tensions arose between the leader's office and the professionals on the one side and the NEC and headquarters on the other. Labour's increasingly fraught relationship with its external advisers frustrated Dick Leonard, an MP who lost his seat in the election. He was especially critical of the 'wilful ignorance and elitist contempt' of those responsible for managing party campaigns:

> Labour's use of survey research material has been spasmodic and, often, ill directed, the benefits derived from the money actually spent have been a great deal less than they might have been, and there has been a singular failure to draw long term valid conclusions from the mass of relevant data available in published polls and voting studies in the private polls published by the party.[62]

The party's lack of strategic unanimity was reflected in disagreements over campaign preparations. Challenging advertising copy was rejected by officials whilst other material, perceived to be of poorer quality, formed part of the actual campaign. A memorable advertisement devised by Delaney and his colleagues used a burning candle to remind voters of the power cuts under Heath's government. The image, captioned 'Remember the last time the Tories said they had all the answers', was never used because its publication had not been approved by the Campaign Committee. The promotional initiatives that did appear fared little better. One PEB was, for instance, attacked as 'stupefyingly incompetent'.[63] The production of this and the other films was undoubtedly hampered by ongoing disputes between Callaghan aides, the Broadcasting Committee and other officials. Advertising expert Winston Fletcher questioned the wisdom behind the pre-election theme 'Keep Britain Labour and It Will Keep Getting Better'. The slogan was undermined when, within weeks of its launch, the massive 'Winter of Discontent' public sector strike began. Labour eventually succumbed to an ignominious defeat. The loss was blamed on a number of factors including the public mood, economic climate, deteriorating industrial relations and growing affluence among skilled working-class families. Labour, one MP argued, was too identified with 'slums, decaying shipyards, immigrants, cloth caps and caring only for minorities and underdogs'.[64]

From bad to worse: the 1983 debacle

The years following the 1979 election were amongst the most difficult in the party's history and saw an acrimonious dispute that ended in the defection of several MPs to the newly formed Social Democratic Party. The loss of these rightwingers did not resolve the bitter debate and the party became 'very internalised'.[65] The balance of power within Labour's NEC remained finely balanced. Tony Benn and others on the left attempted to maintain their control over the Executive in face of a sustained challenge from a resurgent right led by John Golding. In the circumstances, it was hardly surprising Labour found itself poorly equipped to fight the 1983 election. A lack of coherent decision-making structures, coupled with an organisation effectively working as a collection of individuals, hindered the development of party strategy.[66] Only Research Secretary Geoff Bish remained of the senior staff that had fought the 1979 election. Jim Mortimer, appointed General Secretary in June 1982, had come from the ACAS industrial relations service. Max Madden's selection as a parliamentary candidate meant a new Director of Publicity had to be found. After some disagreement Nick Grant, press officer with the health service union COHSE was appointed in January 1983. The Publicity Department suffered a further blow the following month with the retirement of veteran Chief Broadcasting Officer Doreen Stainforth.[67]

Curiously the 1983 election saw one major innovation in Labour campaigning involving the official employment of an advertising agency. Originally hired in May 1982 and again in February 1983 for the local elections, the firm's contract was extended for the national campaign. Johnny Wright and Partners, the agency appointed, had previously offered their services before the 1979 election. During the 1983 campaign the firm had little contact with the Publicity Department and was not responsible for the new Labour logo featuring a red flag. That emblem had been created a couple of years before by Jack Stoddart, the party's long serving in-house designer. Wright, creative partner Garnet Edwards and agency colleagues were not allowed ready access to Labour's polling research and this perhaps gives some indication as to their strategic input. They did, however, have access to focus group work undertaken for the party.[68] Wright also used what he believed were Labour's strongest positions: defence of the welfare state and the unemployment crisis. After considerable discussion, the agency provided the main slogan: 'Think Positive, Act Positive, Vote Labour' and 'Are You Going to Vote Yourself Out of Job?'. The firm also produced over 100 minutes of PEBs in a relatively short space period. The Publicity Director later admitted that, given the time pressures, some of the chosen themes were 'misjudged'.[69]

MORI again faced difficulties getting their contract renewed prior to the election. Confirmation of the arrangement came in February after lobbying from union leader Clive Jenkins. MORI undertook qualitative focus group work as well as the traditional quantitative forms of research. Publicity Director Nick Grant clarified the benefits of polling:

> ... it is a tool – no more, no less – to assist in deciding how best to communicate to voters the policy of the party, and to understand in some depth what the views of the public are, so that we know better how to talk to the voters.[70]

Unfortunately for Grant, the party's advertising agents were never comprehensively briefed on the private polling material whilst the bureaucracy appeared agnostic, hostile or ill-prepared when it came to using the data. Nor did Johnny Wright attend the Campaign Committee. Given it had 40 members, the body almost certainly contained less important strategists. At the suggestion of Neil Kinnock, the agency eventually began liasing with a smaller contact group. After the defeat various people, notably Geoff Bish, party chair Sam McCluskie and sympathetic journalist Martin Linton complained that the size and scope of the Campaign Committee had hindered strategic developments. On one occasion even Michael Foot's special branch bodyguard was inadvertently admitted to what member John Golding denounced as an 'anarchist' forum.[71] This problem, compounded by the lack of inter-departmental and agency communication, was in turn exacerbated by a physical split in headquarters' functions between the ad hoc media operation in the TGWU union Smith Square offices and the party's new South London premises in Walworth Road.

Labour's campaigning problems were personified in leader Michael Foot. Unlike the archetype persuasionalist Harold Wilson, Foot was a stalwart educationalist and believed in the power of ideas not soundbites. There was however a more fundamental problem arising from the informal but nevertheless thorough restructuring of campaigning by Wilson. This soon became apparent as a more inclusive leadership sought to democratise decision-making in the Campaign Committee but failed to follow Research Secretary Geoff Bish's advice about the need to establish an effective chain of command so as to enable a small team of officials to implement plans. The Office Campaigns Committee, the group that most resembled such a body, did not function during the campaign preparations and this proved costly. Consequently there was, according to one official, the 'air of improvisation', a lack of experience and too many late decisions.[72] This resulted in poor co-ordination: halfway through the election, for instance, the party's platform colour of red changed to a more television friendly pink.

For his part Michael Foot preferred working with individual colleagues like Stan Orme and Neil Kinnock. Press secretary Tom McCaffrey, an ex-Callaghan staffer, and former *Tribune* editor Richard Clements accompanied the leader on the election trail. During the campaign, Foot spoke at several meetings where his passionate oratory on youth unemployment and other topics was enthusiastically received. Such skills sat uneasily with his role as a leader in a largely media constructed electoral race. By contrast to his speechmaking, which television largely ignored, Foot's television interviews reached an audience of millions. These were not a success if judged by the polls as his ratings duly slumped and consistently trailed those of Thatcher.[73] Unlike his main opponent, the Labour leader avoided glib answers and soundbites when under cross-examination. General Secretary Jim Mortimer was particularly scornful of the Conservatives' slick style:

> I can assure you that the Labour party will never follow such a line of presentation of politics. The welfare of human beings, the care of people and the fact that we want to overcome employment – these are the tasks before us, not presenting people as if they were breakfast food or baked beans.[74]

After the devastating defeat, a surviving MP compared the Labour campaign to the launch of the Ford Edsel, the most notorious marketing failure and one Shadow Cabinet minister dismissed his own manifesto as the 'longest suicide note in history'.[75] The trauma of the election and the loss of hitherto safe seats would provide the backdrop to the most ambitious reform of the party's organisation and policy in its history.

5
Designer Labour

Marketing politics, Left and Right

The 1979 and 1983 elections traumatised the Labour Party. The latter defeat, then the heaviest suffered by either major party since 1945, underlined Labour's organisational deficiencies. A shattered party turned to a youthful politician for leadership. Despite his left credentials, Neil Kinnock was destined to oversee a wide-ranging reform programme designed to court, in his words, 'floating voters'. Addressing his first Conference as leader, Kinnock made clear his feelings on the recent election: 'Just remember how you felt then, and think to yourselves 'June the Ninth, 1983', never again will we experience that.'[1] Given the Conservatives inflicted the defeat, it was understandable when Labour began to study their approach to electioneering. Party strategists were further encouraged by the experience of the left led Greater London Council's (GLC) campaign against its abolition. Marketing professionalism was, however, no guarantor of success as the supposedly media aware Social Democratic Party demonstrated. Expertise was of limited use if an organisation was uncertain of its core identity and message.[2]

Margaret Thatcher's leadership of the Conservatives proved to be a watershed in the development of political marketing in Britain. Central to this was the partnership between Thatcher, Central Office director of publicity Gordon Reece and Tim Bell, an executive with the party's advertising agency Saatchi and Saatchi. Their understanding led to a series of well-timed campaign initiatives including the famous 'Labour Isn't Working' poster. Scammell contends a major strategic re-orientation was underway:

> Most importantly there is evidence that the marketing concept shaped the manifesto and electoral strategy in all three elections

81

under Lady Thatcher's leadership. This is not to say that market research dictated the details of policy but it did suggest the tone and tenor and indicate that certain policy options were electorally out of bounds.[3]

Because the Conservative Chairman, the head of organisation, is a leadership appointee, the bureaucracy operates on a hierarchical basis. On taking charge Thatcher immediately installed new personnel at headquarters.

Keen polling analyst Thatcher was well placed to use market research to inform policy developments. This sits awkwardly with the popular perception of Thatcher as an ideologue driven by conviction because, as Kavanagh notes: 'The irony is that the high point in the use of public relations in British elections in the 1980s was exploited by the country's most ideological Prime Minister'.[4] That said the marketing approach understood the importance of analysing the electoral environment as well as voter attitudes. Consequently in 1979, the Conservatives exploited concerns over crime and immigration and tied these with populist policies including right to buy for council tenants. Thatcher herself came to personify the 'brand' but also demonstrated her interest in challenging the public consensus.[5] In 1981 Central Office employed Christopher Lawson to head a new marketing department. A former executive with Mars confectioners, Lawson distilled the Conservatives' message into a few appeals. Research proved invaluable to this process. Particularly important was the polling evidence suggesting that whilst voters were concerned about rising unemployment, they did not blame government.[6] In 1983 the Conservatives secured re-election by an increased margin whilst Saatchi and Saatchi briefly became the largest advertising agency in the world.

In 1983 the re-elected Thatcher government planned to abolish the Labour dominated Metropolitan County Councils. The most electorally marginal of these, the GLC, was also the subject of greatest controversy following the succession of Ken Livingstone to its leadership in 1981. Initially derided as an extremist, Livingstone proved an adept communicator determined to defend his position. Initial research suggested there was little support for saving the Council. The subsequent £14 million campaign between October 1983 and March 1985 would change Londoners' perceptions of the issue. Crucially a heavy spend on paid media generated sympathetic coverage.[7] The GLC used the innovative advertising agency Boase Massimi Pollitt and Denis Robb, the BMP executive responsible for the account used focus groups to test copy. Mock adverts were shown to groups of Londoners. Initially the copy failed to garner any sympathy for the Council. One theme did, however, provoke a strong reaction. Participants were incensed by the government's intention to cancel the 1985 GLC elections with a so-called 'paving' bill prior to pursuing outright abolition.[8] Focus group results influenced the subsequent 'Say No to No Say' campaign. Advertising was intensive and posters even appeared on Romanian football stadium hoardings during England's appearance there. The campaign heightened public awareness of and sympathy for the GLC. Though it ultimately failed, the strategy delayed the authority's abolition and rehabilitated Livingstone as a 'Robin Hood' figure.[9] Expert Winston Fletcher described it as 'the finest political campaign of the decade, perhaps ever' before concluding '(P)olitical ads have changed the face of British society. If that's not great advertising, what is?'[10]

The GLC experience challenged attitudes within the Labour movement. As recently as 1983 Kinnock had invoked R.H. Tawney's words to call for an 'offensive of education' in order to attack an economic system he believed 'lives by advertising and mobilising envy'.[11] His views soon changed and, according to BMP executive Peter Herd, the 'Say No To No Say' initiative was crucial in this respect: 'It is hard to overestimate the importance of the GLC campaign; it made advertising politically acceptable to the left'.[12] For rising frontbencher Gordon Brown the campaign: 'showed that it was possible to employ glossy public relations without diluting the basic socialist message and it is encouraging'.[13] It also helped that Livingstone was a sceptical left-winger who became an influential advocate of marketing communication. As a Labour Co-ordinating Committee pamphlet on party organisation put it: 'Who dares accuse the GLC of socialist betrayal?'[14] Educationalist sentiment, so long an influence on party communications' strategy, finally appeared to be on the wane. Ironically it was the same organisation, a Labour-led London Council, which had been responsible for showcasing the merits of professional campaigning half a century before.

The 'new professionalism'

On becoming leader Kinnock enthusiastically supported the proposal of General Municipal and Boilermakers' Union (GMB) union leader David Basnett for a Campaign Strategy Committee (CSC). Basnett advocated a 'new professionalism' and won useful backing from the Labour

Co-ordinating Committee, an internal grouping that included Patricia Hewitt, Kinnock's newly appointed press secretary. A sympathetic motion was welcomed by the 1983 Conference.[15] This in effect reversed an earlier National Executive Committee (NEC) decision to veto a similar plan to Basnett's proposal. Led by Audrey Wise, left-wingers on the Executive had sought to challenge the way in which the Campaign Committee had, without prior consultation, retained the services of Johnny Wright's agency during the election.[16] The NEC eventually ratified the Basnett plan and created a 23 member CSC that was in effect a more permanent version of the ad hoc body traditionally convened before each election. Chaired by the leader, the Committee was not restricted to NEC members and included frontbenchers and other representatives. Specific responsibilities were devolved to sub-groups such as those on polling and broadcasting or ad hoc bodies such as the one overseeing a planned reorganisation of party headquarters in 1985.[17] The existence of a polling sub-committee formally legitimatised interest in market research though there were controversies over who should and should not have access to the research. The group's first meeting considered a paper on the need for a clearer focus, image enhancement and understanding of how voters differentiated Labour from its opponents. Pollster Bob Worcester reinforced this message, suggesting the party appeal 'to the needs and concerns of people'.[18]

The new CSC was not universally welcomed. The *Tribune* diarist attacked the body as evidence of the leadership's 'Saatchi and Saatchi approach to politics'. Others feared the CSC compromised the ability of the NEC (and its key Home Policy Committee) to formulate party strategy. As Shaw argues:

> (T)he formation of the (Campaign Strategy) committee was motivated by political as much as campaigning considerations as Kinnock intended to use the body to short-circuit the NEC and thereby reduce the role of its still influential left-wing contingent.[19]

In 1984 the Labour leadership appointed Kinnock ally Robin Cook to oversee strategy. Enjoying Shadow Cabinet ranking, the Campaigns Co-ordinator mediated between the party at Westminster and headquarters. In duties, if not status, the post resembled that of the Conservative Chairman.[20] Cook proved keen to learn from his opponents and carefully studied BBC broadcaster Michael Cockerell's film 'The Marketing of Margaret'.[21] The Campaign Co-ordinator's prescription was blunt: 'Nor will we get our message across unless we learn to manipulate the media at least as successfully as they manipulate us... Labour cannot credibly pretend to be the party of the masses unless it can come to terms with the mass media'. Cook supported the use of marketing consultants and dismissed 'the obstacle of Left purism'. He was not, however, averse to using his own ideological rhetoric: 'The GLC campaign over abolition has shown the techniques of the marketing industry can be turned against the capitalist society that spawned them.'[22] There was growing evidence to suggest Cook's view would prevail. Shortly after the 1983 defeat, the Publicity sub-committee had considered the motion that the 'NEC should not retain an agency'. Coming before the leadership election, the vote was inconsequential but for the fact that it rejected the proposal. Participants were perhaps mindful of advice from Battersea Constituency Labour Party (CLP): '(The) party must master the techniques of mass persuasion including advertising, marketing, public relations and other media techniques and use them to win the electorate to socialist policies.'[23] Early recognition of this came in 1984 with the appointment of former Shelter and Friends of the Earth executive Steve Bilcliffe as head of Sales and Marketing. In post Bilcliffe co-ordinated a direct mail effort that brought healthy returns.[24]

Ad hoc initiatives

Labour headquarters' official Jim Parish, journalist Irene Reid and public relations consultant Ellis Kopel together with Campaign Co-ordinator Robin Cook became central to the re-establishment of an effective campaign structure in time for the European and local elections of 1984. Both contests saw modest Labour gains. Cook had not wanted to use an advertising agency and preferred to run the operation through the cultivation of certain advisers.[25] This was in line with an earlier proposal to the NEC for a Labour Marketing Group. Finally in November 1984 a Communications Advisory or so-called 'breakfast' group was established.[26] Those involved included pollster Bob Worcester, marketing consultant Tim Steel of TBWA, lobbyist Richard Faulkner, BMP executive Chris Powell, Les Butterfield and Paul Southgate of the Abbott Mead Vickers agency and Patricia Hewitt, the leader's press secretary. Market researcher Colin Fisher, another associate, observed that year's US presidential elections on the party's behalf. In February 1985 the group delivered a 'Marketing plan for the Labour Party'. Another adviser, PR consultant Francis Beckett, admitted that whilst not all the proposals were taken up this effort saved the party a considerable amount of money in consultancy fees.[27]

Though campaigning during the early period of Kinnock's leadership was characterised by its ad hoc, flexible approach, his aides managed to assume the key strategic roles. They included Leader's Office members like Hewitt, Chief of Staff Charles Clarke and policy advisers such as Cambridge economist John Eatwell. Kinnock's aides made contact with sympathisers in the marketing industry. In 1985 the party hired high profile PR consultant Lynne Franks to develop Labour's profile on women's rights, 'Green' issues and the textile industry. Young people were the focus of other initiatives involving the promotion of an exclusive Katharine Hamnett designed T-shirt range.[28] Kinnock himself featured in Tracey Ullman's pop video 'My Guy'. His willingness to appear in such a format reflected a desire, or desperation, to communicate with a group seen as crucial to the party's future success. BBC Radio One's Andy Kershaw was one of several young celebrities to meet Labour politicians in early 1985. To him the leadership appeared somewhat naive:

> We were shown into a room in the House of Commons, and there sat Kinnock, surrounded by bottles of claret and bowls of crisps, asking me what should be done about young people. It was all a bit sad and bizarre, and I felt sorry for him. None of us were ordinary young people leading normal lives.[29]

In a more promising move Labour sought advice from Peter Jenner, manager of singer-songwriter Billy Bragg, and contacted other artists prepared to campaign for the party. These meetings culminated in the formation of 'Red Wedge' in November 1985. Those involved included Bragg, Paul Weller, Sade and the actor Tim Roth. In marked contrast to future campaigns, Red Wedge was relatively free of party control. From the beginning of 1986 volunteers appeared at sell-out events designed to mobilise a traditionally anti-Conservative if disinclined youth vote.[30]

After months of planning, the CSC's first major initiative came in April 1985 with the launch of a 'Jobs and Industry Campaign'. The offensive promoted Labour fiscal policy and was informed by focus group findings that suggested the public associated the party with economic mismanagement.[31] The campaign was promoted through regional and national media. Celebrities including Hamnett and Bragg volunteered their support. Ambitious in scope, the campaign also involved grassroots members and specialist materials were produced for internal as well as public consumption. Even with its clear educational dimension some still viewed the project as ideologically suspect and claimed it studiously ignored the consequences of the momentous miners' strike.[32]

Red Rose discipline

1985 proved to be a major turning point for Neil Kinnock. Up until the Conference that year, the leader was perceived to have been following rather than directing events in his party. Kinnock took the unusual step of addressing delegates twice. Reports of his main speech were dominated by his attack on the Militant Tendency, the Trotskyite organisation operating within the party at the time. The denunciation of Militant constituted the most high profile aspect of Kinnock's efforts to enhance the authority of his position.[33] In his other speech Kinnock opposed a motion calling on an incoming Labour government to compensate striking miners penalised during their yearlong dispute. Kinnock articulated an electoralist philosophy that would dominate his leadership:

> As you vote be sure that you can convincingly justify the way you vote, not just here in the tight circles, the comfortable warm circles of a Labour Party conference, but in the street, to your neighbours, at work, wherever you go, in interviews, justify it there, justify it there![34]

Streamlining headquarters

In its first editorial of 1985, *Tribune* had identified a groundswell of support for 'realignment on the left' behind Kinnock.[35] The same month saw Larry Whitty appointed General Secretary. A GMB research officer, Whitty had been favourite to replace Jim Mortimer over former MP John Garrett and future Trades Union Congress (TUC) chief Norman Willis. Kinnock's decision to back Whitty was one of the last times he voted with the NEC's left.[36] The new General Secretary's first major task involved the implementing of an NEC report on party organisation. The plan amounted to the most wide-ranging programme of headquarters' reform since 1918. Whitty supported the reforms, believing 'there is no contradiction between socialism and professionalism' before conceding there would be 'no Reaganite packaging of our campaigns'. Similarly Kinnock's allies in the Labour Co-ordinating Committee argued that the party should make use of the media and polling, launch a national membership scheme and streamline headquarters.[37] The reorganisation meant ten Departments became four Directorates. Sections including Press and Publicity were abolished in a bid, the reformers hoped, to make the headquarters more goal oriented.[38] Existing staff assumed three of the new Directorships. When head of publicity Nick Grant resigned, the vacancy for the Campaigns and Communications portfolio was opened to others. The shortlist included former National Union of Journalists' President Denis MacShane, *The Scotsman* journalist David Gow, GLC press officer Nita Clarke and television producer Peter Mandelson. In the first ballot 11 NEC members supported Mandelson against 10 for Clarke and a handful for the others. Kinnock's support made Mandelson the leadership's choice and he secured appointment with three more votes in the second round.[39] The new Director would continue to polarise opinion throughout his career.

The grandson of Herbert Morrison, 31 year-old Peter Mandelson became a key figure in his five years as head of Campaigns and Communications. A friend of Kinnock's influential Chief of Staff Charles Clarke, Mandelson had previously worked with the British Youth Council, TUC Economics Department, frontbench MP Albert Booth and served on Lambeth Council before taking a job with London Weekend Television as a producer on the current affairs programme 'Weekend World'. The position gave him an insight into the media, opinion research and the opportunity to meet influential politicians.[40] On becoming Director of Campaigns and Communications, Mandelson was soon cultivating publicity. In his first major interview he described himself as 'an extremely talented, bright highflyer'. His interrogator Kathy Myers concluded her subject was motivated by a desire 'to effect... a shift in internal party ideology, as well as the hearts and minds of the public'. Labour's more centralised 'Central Office' structure would greatly aid the reformist leadership.[41] The Campaigns and Communications Directorate (CCD) was particularly important because it became a 'clearing-house for all contacts between the party and the media' and eventually 'came to supplant the much older Organisation and Policy Directorates as the most powerful body at Head Office.'[42] Its budget rose from £35,000 to £300,000 per annum within a few years. Deriving 'his sole authority from Kinnock', Mandelson became a formidable organisational politician and gatekeeper guarding media access to key party people and meetings.[43] According to Shaw this meant that: 'Although Mandelson was in theory accountable to the NEC, in practice he acted on behalf of the leader working closely with his aides, particularly (Charles) Clarke'.[44]

His burgeoning power created difficulties including a protracted dispute with his deputy John Booth after the latter's exclusion from the Director's unofficial advisory Shadow Journalist Group. Mandelson's authority was further underlined when, following disagreements with Lynne Franks, the PR consultant left the party's service.[45]

The Shadow Communications Agency

While the CCD was a formal part of headquarters, the Campaign Management Team (CMT) and Shadow Communications Agency (SCA) were more ad hoc bodies. The CMT, set up in October 1985, to help implement CSC directives comprised senior headquarters' officials, Leader's Office aides and Robin Cook.[46] The Team reported to Kinnock until the traditional pre-campaign consultative body was convened in 1986. Though now re-designated the Leader's Committee, it still drew in membership from the NEC, parliamentary frontbench and affiliated trades unions. In March 1986 the CMT helped set-up another key group, the SCA, for sympathisers working in marketing.[47] The immediate background to the Agency lay in calls from members, notably in the LCC, for the party to embrace professional techniques. A sympathetic Conference motion was passed that year and Cook and his 'breakfast group' were keen on the opportunity provided by the formation of 'shadow agency'.[48] Retiring Publicity Director Nick Grant recognised a major rethink was underway:

> Labour has, at last, come to terms with the need for a clear concise marketing approach- not in order 'to sell politics like soap-powder', but in order to understand the need to develop political marketing as part of the science of communication in the multi-media society in the Britain of the 1980s and 1990s.[49]

The blueprint for the SCA dated back to a report commissioned by Grant's successor Peter Mandelson shortly after his arrival at headquarters. For this purpose Mandelson hired advertising executive Philip Gould, a former executive with the agency Doyle Dane Bernbach turned freelance consultant for progressive organisations like the Anti-Apartheid Movement and trade unions including USDAW.[50] Gould conducted his 64 page 'communications audit' in late 1985. The report recommended major changes and urged the party to improve its mediated campaigning, overhaul the 'stagnation' within its own structures and questioned the efficacy of grassroots electioneering. On the electorate it was suggested that Thatcherite values 'still hold sway to an extent' and that the 'main medium for key target groups appears to be tabloid newspapers, dominated by the Conservatives'. Gould alleged other deficiencies, including Labour's association with minority interests, its 'cloth cap' image, ability to score 'own goals', activist centred nature, reactive strategy and unco-ordinated use of advertising and broadcasting. The leadership was doing well in 'distancing itself from unacceptable, beyond the pale elements'. Citing the example of the Conservatives in 1979, Gould advocated the use of a more coherent public relations approach designed to engage voters rather than convert them with a better targeted, more simple and well-orchestrated message.[51] Gould concluded that Labour needed an advisory team of sympathisers working in marketing. Some suggest the U.S. Republicans' Tuesday Group was the role model.[52] However, given the earlier use of such expertise by Herbert Morrison and Harold Wilson, the SCA can be seen as more of an evolutionary than revolutionary development. Morrison's own grandson Peter Mandelson acknowledged the work of those professionals who had worked for the party during the 1960s and 1970s shortly after becoming Communications Director.[53] Likewise Campaigns Co-ordinator Robin Cook had played a key role in creating a sympathetic environment for the SCA having promoted the importance of advisory bodies through his 'breakfast group'.[54]

Where the SCA differed with previous advisory bodies was in its influence over party strategy. From the outset Philip Gould envisaged the Agency would be 'an organisational mechanism that can act both as a catalyst and a continuing force for change'.[55] Gould convened the SCA with business partner Deborah Mattinson, a market researcher formerly with Ayer Barker. The Agency derived its name from Labour's designation as the parliamentary opposition. 'Shadow' was apt description for an organisation whose members offered their services anonymously in order to protect their contracts with Conservative supporting businesspeople. Apart from a retainer paid to Gould Mattinson Associates, SCA professionals were not remunerated. Gould calculated this arrangement saved Labour hundreds of thousands of pounds in preparing for the 1987 election.[56] Barry Delaney, one of the most prominent volunteers involved, described the Agency as:

> ... a loose knit and ever changing group of volunteers from advertising and marketing and public relations who gave their services free to the Labour Party and consequently the Labour Party get very

high quality people, better people arguably than they could get by hiring a single agency, the quality of whose work might vary greatly. They pick and choose, the Labour Party. It's worked well for them.[57]

The secretiveness of the SCA enabled Kinnock and his allies to further control campaigning and, by extension, other aspects of party strategy and organisation. The Agency arrangement necessitated close liaison between a small group of aides, officials and advisers. Mandelson was at the centre of this network. He established his authority over the SCA operation by cultivating Robin Cook's contacts in advertising having simultaneously 'purged those from journalism and PR'.[58] The Agency's steering committee was co-chaired by BMP DDB Needham executives Chris Powell and Peter Herd, both veterans of the GLC campaign. Twelve working groups were convened to co-ordinate approximately 150 volunteers. The teams covered management and planning, creative, broadcasting, design and other tasks. BMP executives were heavily involved and the agency became a hub of expertise in the way London Press Exchange had for Morrison fifty years earlier. The company became, in effect, the party's agency.[59] Besides BMP's Ross Barr, Paul Leeves and Alan Tilly, other SCA personnel included Leslie Butterfield of Abbott Mead Vickers, Geoff Howard-Spink of Lowe Howard-Spink, Andrew Cracknell of Wight Colins Rutherford Scott, ex-Ted Bates' executive Kay Scorah, former McCormick Publicis director Gerry Moira and Richard Faulkner, the managing director of Westminster Communications.[60]

During the mid-1980s Labour made its first enduring links with foreign political consultants. Those consulted included the eminent American campaign specialist Joe Napolitan and his colleague Sally Hunter. Philip Gould and Patricia Hewitt had met Napolitan during an International Association of Political Consultants conference at which Hewitt had shown Tracey Ullman's pop video featuring Kinnock.[61] Early on the American counselled his client on the need for research 'that will allow Labour to design and modify a campaign in progress'.[62] Focus groups would be one obvious source of such data. Leslie Butterfield and Paul Southgate of advertisers Abbott Mead Vickers together with Roddy Glen of the Strategic Research Group consultancy had used the method and presented their findings at a November 1985 meeting of those associated with Robin Cook's breakfast group held at the offices of Tim Steel's TBWA agency. The newly recruited Philip Gould was particularly impressed by the way the data and analysis highlighted the apparent disparity between popular attitudes and a party associated with high tax, unilateralism and nationalisation. It was further contended that voters liked choice and were 'completely divorced' from the 'minority agenda of the emerging metropolitan left, of militant rights in welfare, race and gender'. This analysis accepted the distorted ideological misrepresentations of the so-called loony left that were so prevalent in the Tory press at the time.[63] Younger women were worried about society breaking down and appeared introspective and primarily concerned about their families. The researchers concluded 'everybody wants to be middle-class these days', an observation that underlined the potency of Eric Hobsbawm's influential thesis that the shrinking manual workforce threatened to undermine Labour's electoral base.[64] Subsequently the SCA's secretary Colin Fisher and Roddy Glen developed an extensive programme of qualitative research. Approximately 200 group sessions were held prior to polling day. Their work was particularly important during the run-up to the 1986 Labour Conference, the last before the general election. Fisher belonged to the Strategic Research Unit, a consultancy with strong party links and which boasted prominent executives including Dennis Stevenson and Peter Wallis, the cultural commentator better known as Peter York.[65]

Value free campaigning? The repackaging of Labour

The SCA and their 'client' representative Peter Mandelson provided the impetus behind the re-launch of Labour in 1986. In contrast to previous initiatives, the campaigns that followed were highly disciplined exercises. As Mandelson admitted: 'Communications means throwing your net much wider than publicity. It means deciding what we say, how we say it, and which spokesmen and women we choose to say it'.[66] The name of each campaign betrayed the party's marketing conscious approach: 'Freedom and Fairness', 'Investing in People' and 'Modern Britain in a Modern World'. All three were highly media-centred operations. Input from the party faithful was limited to purchasing mugs and other merchandise from the revamped Sales and Marketing department. Launched in the run up to the 1986 local elections, the Freedom and Fairness campaign became a journalistic story for its manner as much as its theme.[67] Devised by a team including advertising executive Trevor Beattie, it featured a nine-year old reaching skywards. The campaign was praised in *Tribune*, *The Observer* and *The Guardian*, the latter of which called it 'light years ahead' of previous efforts though not all the coverage was favourable: 'One day the twee nuclear family living in a semi in a suburb will have vanished from our TV screens altogether – except, of course, in the Never Never Land of commercials for Milton Keynes and Labour Party Political Broadcasts'.[68] Some in the party were, however, dissatisfied and claimed the decision to use grey rather than traditional red epitomised the initiative's 'anodyne and meaningless' symbolism. There was also growing concern at headquarters over the burgeoning role of Mandelson.[69]

The idea for Freedom and Fairness had emerged from CSC discussions of reports from pollsters Market Opinion and Research International (MORI) and the qualitative research programme. This feedback pointed out apparent shortcomings in the Jobs and Industry campaign. It also identified significant voter antipathy towards so-called 'scroungers' and, by implication, Labour policies devoted to helping these 'undeserving poor'. The promotion of such language was a marked feature of New Right Strategy had been popularised through the Tory press during the late 1970s.[70] Lamentably it now began to inform opposition thinking. In his first major qualitative-based study for the party, Philip Gould argued the party's 'minority agenda' was a major electoral handicap.[71] Consequently Freedom and Fairness was tailored to appeal to what marketers, and particularly those associated with BMP DDB Needham, termed the burgeoning 'aspirational' electorate. This strategy was outlined to CSC members at a SCA presentation on the topic of 'Society and Self'. The Agency's message was not universally welcomed. Tony Benn was particularly alarmed by the meeting: 'Labour was associated with the poor, the unemployed, the old, the sick, the disabled, pacifists, immigrants, minorities and the unions, and this was deeply worrying'. Benn was further troubled by what he saw as the proposed remedy of Thatcher-style leadership. Some like *Tribune* columnist Hugh MacPherson were more sympathetic because 'presidential style public relations are highly relevant in politics'. Benn, however, was unequivocal following the Society and Self briefing: 'I came out feeling physically sick; I'm not kidding I felt unwell, because if this is what the Labour Party is about I've got nothing whatever in common with it'. He was not alone in opposing those advocating a more presidential approach. Pollster Bob Worcester cautioned against such a move in an internal memo of August 1986.[72] It made little difference as Shaw notes: 'Because it became the Agency's task not only to accumulate the information but also to draw out its inner meaning and significance, it was increasingly able to shape the parameters of strategic debate.' Consequently alternative understandings or contradictory findings from the research data were invariably 'filtered' out of discussions.[73]

Labour launched its 'Investing in People' campaign later on in 1986. The initiative was accompanied by music from Brahms and Vivaldi and superficial praise from the press. There was again some dissent within the party. Questioning the benefits of 'value free' campaigning, NEC member David Blunkett argued: 'If we fall into the trap of merely presenting isolated and uncommitted policies, we will fail fundamentally to challenge the ideology of the right which permeates much of the Western world at the moment.' He continued: 'We may win an improvement in percentage points temporarily in the opinion polls, at the expense of failing to win people over to what we believe in'.[74] Similarly *Tribune* editor Phil Kelly attacked the campaign for appealing to voters' individualism rather than collective group identities. Another critic suggested the campaign accepted and endorsed the Conservatives' 'privatisation of people'. Kelly also raised concerns about the strategic implications: 'Given the plethora of overlapping policies, the image-makers can pick and choose. Some policies fit better than others' and argued 'modern marketing techniques' were being used to further the 'moderniser' position at the expense of more 'traditionalist' opinion inside the party.[75]

The defence policy campaign 'Modern Britain in a Modern World' had the potential to be more explosive than either 'Freedom and Fairness' or 'Investing in People' yet received less coverage than it might have expected. Initiated by a 1985 Conference motion, promotional efforts only began late the following year. Controversially the campaign linked Labour's unilateralist nuclear policy with a commitment to increase conventional defence spending. Whereas 'Investing in People' had promoted options favoured by the leadership, the 'Modern Britain in a Modern World' proposals amounted to a de facto change of policy.[76] Unlike Kinnock, Mandelson had little sympathy for the Campaign for Nuclear Disarmament and reportedly said 'the less said about defence the better' prior to the 1987 election. Similarly Labour's American consultant Joe Napolitan regarded unilateralism as a vote loser and likened it to US Democratic candidate Walter Mondale's commitment to raise taxes in the 1984 presidential race.[77] This lack of empathy helps explains why 'Modern Britain in a Modern World' was not a high profile campaign. By contrast Labour's most well publicised launch of 1986 came with the introduction of a new logo just before the Conference that autumn. The rose emblem replaced the short-lived red flag insignia developed in 1981.[78] The new design had been chosen from hundreds of alternatives produced by the Wolff Olins consultancy team of Michael Wolff, Philip Sutton and Clare Hamilton. The final choice was, as Kinnock acknowledged, informed by other European social democratic parties' use of the rose. General Secretary Larry Whitty believed the symbol embodied Labour's new 'corporate image'.[79] The cultivation of celebrities formed another dimension to this strategy. Like Wilson before him, Kinnock appeared in public with famous supporters at Arts for Labour events. Prominent sympathisers included dramatist Alan Bleasdale and actors like Julie Walters and Julie Christie.[80]

The perceived success of the SCA consolidated Mandelson's influence within the party. By contrast, the politician other than Kinnock most involved with the Agency suffered through his involvement. Thus Campaigns Co-ordinator Robin Cook's portfolio gave him a lower parliamentary profile and it greatly contributed to the loss of his Shadow Cabinet place in the annual ballot of MPs in 1986. It was something of an irony that the same post enabled Cook's successor Bryan Gould to become a popular figure within the party.

The 'Victory' of 1987

The 1987 election is widely perceived to have been a major stage in the evolution of Labour as a marketing organisation. The party developed increasingly sophisticated machinery for the twin tasks of news management and firming up electoral support. According to two protagonists, their achievement was to devise 'one of the most effective pieces of disciplined communication of modern British politics'.[81] The campaign was, however, more an object lesson in stylish advertising than strategic marketing.[82] Arguably more important changes followed an election that, though it ended in defeat, succeeded in promoting the benefits of professional campaign communication.

Labour entered the official four weeks of the election well behind the Conservatives and with only a narrow lead over the SDP-Liberal Alliance. Pre-campaign initiatives had gone poorly. A goodwill visit by Kinnock to Ronald Reagan only underlined the President's opposition to Labour defence policy. Domestically the party fared little better. An inaccurate press campaign against the so-called 'loony left' councils damaged Labour's image. The offensive, led by Conservative supporting tabloids, attacked supposed extremism in local government, particularly within London. The issue dominated the Greenwich by-election in early 1987. Labour lost the seat to the Alliance. Soon after a memorandum from Patricia Hewitt was published by *The Sun*. In it Kinnock's press secretary argued the loony left tag was damaging the party's credibility. Rather than countering media misrepresentation, strategists appeared to be attempting to insulate the party from the Labour led councils involved.[83] By contrast the party's official campaign went well and promoted the core 'brand' value of caring.[84] *Guardian* columnist Hugo Young reported on its impact:

> Labour, the last party to be captured by marketing men, needs them more than any other, and yesterday received their climatic ministrations. The manifesto was launched in a new-tech conference hall, amid vulgar fanfares and shameless glitz... the scene persuaded those taking part that they were, after all, the acme of modernity.[85]

Campaign materials emphasised the party's policies on health, education and employment. Expertly choreographed by CMT members Mandelson, Hewitt and Andrew Fox, the strategy had taken shape during the summer of 1986. CMT officials together with the Shadow Agency co-ordinators took responsibility for implementing decisions agreed by the Leader's Committee. The SCA significantly enhanced the profile of consultants within the party.[86] In addition a number of specialists such as acclaimed photographer John Clarridge contributed their services. Clarridge supplied images for a hard-hitting series of adverts, one of which featured a queue of unemployed people reminiscent of the infamous 'Labour Isn't Working' poster designed by Saatchi and Saatchi for the Conservatives.[87]

In a dramatic departure from tradition Labour strategists devoted an Election Broadcast to the leader's personality and vision. Hubert Humphrey had earlier demonstrated the power of the 'biopic' in his 1968 US presidential bid and there were similarities between his 'What Manner of Man' and a Party Election Broadcast that became known as 'Kinnock The Movie'. This was perhaps not so surprising given Joe Napolitan advised both parties. Advance publicity had encouraged viewers to watch and 'See a side of Hubert Humphrey you've never seen before'. This was also the aim of the Kinnock portrait made by Oscar winning director Hugh Hudson and the Broadcast ended with the red rose adorning the leader's rather than the party's name.[88] Some hailed it 'the most effective piece of political communication in recent political history' and claimed it had increased Kinnock's ratings by 16%. In reality this figure reflected the shift of opinion amongst existing Labour voters. The presidential tone was replicated in other publicity and Kinnock featured in advertising proclaiming 'The Country's Crying Out for Labour'.[89] Having not authorised this copy he, like the public, first saw it on poster hoardings.

Despite suffering a third defeat, those involved promoted the merits of Labour's election strategy. Even dissenters like Tony Benn called it the 'best campaign since 1959'.[90] Others argued the poor results spoke for themselves. A Conservative strategist went further and argued considerable 'nonsense' was talked about Labour's performance.[91] Much was made of the effect the party's approach had on opponents. Labour's professionalism unsettled the Conservatives and, following a rogue poll on so-called 'Wobbly Thursday', Central Office was the scene of infighting between rival strategists with differing interpretations of conflicting opinion research reports from agency Saatchi and Saatchi and their unofficial rivals Young and Rubicon. The row usefully demonstrated the contested and deeply political nature of electoral marketing choices.[92] Furthermore the uncertainty compelled Thatcher to revisit a charge once made against her party by attacking Labour for 'packaging politics like some washing powder'. She felt sufficiently aggrieved to return to this subject in a post-election interview:

> First they tried to hide their socialism. What floated to the surface was Labour's Iceberg Manifesto. Then they tried to repackage socialism. They wrapped it in cellophane and roses, sweet smelling for a day, but oh, so transparent.[93]

Labour strategists believed their campaign thwarted a potentially serious Alliance challenge for second place. They also judged Kinnock's performance a success. The strategy, heavily based around his image, promoted the leader to an internal audience who might otherwise have become restless in defeat. For Richard Rose, the promotion of Kinnock was such that it threatened to make his party redundant.[94] *Tribune* journalist Hugh MacPherson summed up the importance of the campaign:

> He has now established himself, beyond any shadow of doubt, as the Labour leader for the next election- and almost beyond that as well... As it is his performances and the organisation of the campaign has been little short of brilliant in its use of television and radio.[95]

This reflected the thinking of key strategists who contended that the leader together with their energetic professionalism had saved Labour from a worse result. Some influential party figures disagreed but they failed to mount any sustained challenge to the leadership at this potentially vulnerable time. Indeed the setback would be used to argue for the further embrace of marketing as a guiding rationale for Labour.

Part III
The Marketing Age

6
Market Research Socialism

Labour's turning point

Paradoxically the 1987 defeat strengthened Neil Kinnock's position and enabled him to pursue major policy changes. He was far from alone in advocating reform. Shadow Cabinet colleagues like Gerald Kaufman argued the party's own manifesto had undermined the campaign effort and that Peter Mandelson had merely provided Labour with 'a whole new style and façade... but, of course it was a facade. You can't sell something that people don't want however well you package it'. The Campaigns Director agreed, concluding 'the product kept seeping through'.[1] According to a more detached account Labour did not 'market' itself in 1987 but sought to build a campaign around the 'peculiar narratives of deprivation and poverty and the moral worth of British socialism'.[2] Far from undermining the Kinnock leadership, the defeat served to reinforced the party hierarchy's determination to pursue further reforms. In overseeing the resulting Policy Review, the chosen vehicle for change, Mandelson would become one of the most influential non-elected politicians in Labour history.

The electoral imperative

Following the election, Kinnock launched the Policy Review. The idea had originated from party Director of Research Geoff Bish but it was leadership ally Tom Sawyer who advanced the project as chair of the National Executive Committee (NEC) Home Policy sub-committee. He commissioned a report from Adam Sharples, a researcher with his union NUPE. They concluded that to be successful, a review needed to consider every policy's electoral relevance to the 'needs and concerns of groups of voters'.[3] Opinion research would be essential to this process. The report also suggested greater attention be given to targeting voters, future social trends, the 'communications' imperative' and the experiences of social democratic parties abroad. The paper gained a sympathetic hearing from an NEC already sympathetic towards plans to 'woo the affluent worker'.[4] Some were concerned by the proposals and a candid admission by Campaigns Co-ordinator Bryan Gould in which he said: 'What we ought to be doing is looking at where policies ought to come from, what the demand is, what interests we ought to be serving. In that way we can make sure that the policy includes its popular appeal from the market'. Deputy leader Roy Hattersley castigated such 'electoralism' as the 'SDP approach' to politics:

> What we do, we send out a lot of marketing men into the country, just as the Democrats in America did 20 years ago, and say, 'what are the policies people want and then when we find out what they'll vote for, we'll write it into our manifesto' – that is not the sort of politics I want to be involved in.[5]

The NEC placated Hattersley by allowing him to draft a new statement of Labour's 'Aims and Values'. But, by comparison with what critics dismissed as his 'visionary utterance', polling commissioned for the Review had considerably more influence.[6] From the outset considerable resources were invested in conducting public opinion research. The initial results, contained in a briefing entitled 'Labour and Britain in the 1990s', were presented at a joint meeting of Shadow Cabinet and National Executive members held in the T&GWU's Transport House headquarters on November 20th 1987. Kinnock's intention was for the gathering to focus on the declining level of public support for Labour and its policies. In marked contrast with the early 1980s, feedback from voters in the form of research would now become integral to the party decision-making process. Gould, who was centrally involved in the proceedings, commented that this was a 'defining moment in Labour's history'.[7]

Peter Mandelson co-ordinated the 'Labour and Britain in the 1990s' programme with the help of academics, market researchers and Shadow Communications Agency (SCA) co-ordinators Gould and Deborah Mattinson and several of those involved spoke at the special November meeting. Psephologist Roger Jowell suggested that though the public had not embraced Thatcherite values, many voters were, to use the increasingly commonplace term, aspirational people particularly keen to buy their own homes. Political scientists John Curtice and Andrew Shaw from Liverpool University reinforced Jowell's message. They outlined several factors hampering a Labour recovery including its declining working-class support; public hostility towards certain policies, particularly on defence; a reputation for poor economic management; and the perception of the party as an outdated, male dominated organisation against people realising their aspirations.[8] Economist Paul Ormerod reinforced the point about the increasing importance of such voters and cited socio-economic trends likely to further reduce Labour's appeal including: rising home ownership; a growing service sector; the flight to suburbia; and increasing personal wealth among key voter groupings. Presentations by IFF Research and the party's Political Intelligence Officer reinforced the impression of an overwhelmingly negative public perception of Labour.

The November meeting was something of a leadership success if judged by reports in the opinion forming newspapers. *Tribune* focused on how the polling had highlighted 'the party's extremist image' and the widespread public belief that 'Labour is no longer for us'. *The Guardian* reported the research as revealing that, in contrast to the Conservatives, more people supported Labour out of habit. Other journalists mentioned the 'loony left' image and leadership problems, both collective and individual. According to the key contemporary account of Hughes and Wintour, the Transport House meeting proved 'explosive' as well as 'crucial' to subsequent party debates.[9] Yet many of the findings replicated previous material included in Philip Gould's 1985 communications' audit, the SCA's 1986 'Society and Self' presentation and the writings of politicians such as Austin Mitchell.[10] In its content and methods 'Labour and Britain in the 1990s' resembled the 1960 study *Must Labour Lose?*. It too had followed a third consecutive election defeat. The critical difference between the two reports lay in their status as publications. Unlike *Must Labour Lose?* 'Labour and Britain in the 1990s' received fulsome support in spite of ongoing cuts to the headquarters' budget. Thus the latter report enjoyed a formal role denied its predecessor and influenced subsequent discussions to the extent that 'in the 'new model party', political demands would be inseparable from the communications' imperative'.[11]

Managing the review

The Review provided what appeared to be an early concession to the party's educationalists by holding a series of public consultations entitled 'Labour Listens'. Some believe the meetings were 'a critical part of the whole exercise' because they conveyed an image of a 'listening' organisation. Yet these partial, unfocused exercises were of minimal importance as journalist Colin Hughes observed: '(T)he true value of "Labour Listens" was as a campaigning tool: to convey a message to voters that Labour was willing to bend to their wishes, and to tell Labour's own cohorts that they were part of the process. Having served that softening-up purpose, the campaign was consigned to oblivion.'[12] The perceived failure of the exercise favoured those who wanted more 'passive' sources of feedback.[13] This took the form of commissioning an ambitious programme of quantitative and qualitative opinion research. It helped that Peter Mandelson had an understanding and interest in focus grouping arising from his time with Weekend World in the early 1980s. Speaking in December 1987 Mandelson used qualitative research material to argue Labour was out of touch and associated with 'strange things', 'Marxists' and 'gays'.[14]

The Policy Review consisted of seven groups, each jointly convened by a Shadow Cabinet and NEC member. The Campaign Management Team (CMT) helped to co-ordinate the process. Every group was assigned a theme covering a policy area. Journalists Paul Anderson and Phil Kelly were not impressed: 'The policy review groups had titles with vague, advertising-agency invented names which correspond neither to existing government departments (where the policies will have to be implemented) nor to the way ordinary people think about their world'.[15] Opinion research feedback was made available to all of the groups throughout the Review process. Frontbencher Harriet Harman believed the decision to widely circulate the material was a welcome departure from past practice. Certain findings were particularly influential, notably the feedback suggesting large numbers of potential supporters discriminated between a 'deserving' and 'undeserving' poor. Labour's continued association with the latter implied traditional social democratic thinking or 'Croslandism' was now outmoded.[16] More ominously the party appeared unwilling to challenge the 'scrounger' mythology orchestrated by New Right theorists and propagated in tabloid newspaper from the late 1970s onwards.[17] The research also questioned specific policies, notably on nuclear disarmament. MP Austin Mitchell described the party's unilateralist stance as 'Labour's Edsel', recycling a phrase he first used to condemn the entire 1983 manifesto. The eventual abandonment of the policy meant 'defence was the paramount symbol of the review'.[18] Research also fostered the view that the party-union link was an 'electoral handicap' that could be countered through Labour's acceptance of Conservatives' controversial industrial relations policies.[19] More widely the leadership accepted the primacy of market forces and sought an accommodation with big business and the City. This was pursued through initiatives such as the so-called 'prawn cocktail offensive' led by John Smith and Mo Mowlam. There were other minor but symbolic changes in policy. Given marketing now played a central role within the organisation, it was perhaps fitting that Labour should also begin to publicly espouse the economic benefits of the process.[20]

Kinnock later admitted that he ensured the research commissioned during the Policy Review was repeatedly used to emphasise the negatives: 'I saw to it that meetings were conducted in such a way as to make people remember the weaknesses for longer than they remembered the strengths'.[21] The state of public opinion had been a significant factor in changing the leader's views and would now play a key role in challenging party attitudes. According to ally Tom Sawyer: 'It was Neil's Review and everything that happened in that Review, he was, at the end of the day, the master of it. He knew what he wanted in the Policy Review and he got more or less what he wanted in the Policy Review as well.'[22] Kinnock became focused on winning over the aspirational electorate or, at the very least, with reassuring those undecided middle and skilled working-class voters identified by the private polling. In his first conference address after the 1987 defeat the Labour leader revisited popular understandings of class citing union leader Ron Todd's observation that, even a docker could now earn £400 a week and holiday in Marbella.

Having closely observed Kinnock's journey from left-wing orator to publicity conscious leader, his former deputy Hattersley remarked: 'It's very strange that Neil Kinnock, who is I should think the great evangelist politician of this half century presided over a Labour party which was less interested in evangelism than it was in the graphs, diagrams and figures.'[23] Early on Peter Mandelson recognised and was sensitive to the charge that the Policy Review was polling driven and, in the early stages of the process, commented: 'What we are doing is selling socialism, selling our party as a party that's fit to govern. What we are not engaged in is marketing' having caricatured the latter as 'finding out what people want and, no matter what that may be, designing your product accordingly in order simply to make a profit or, in our case, to win votes'. Similarly the highly partial 'insider' account of the Policy Review strongly contested the 'absurd' notion that the exercise was polling led and unconvincingly claimed it was designed 'to shift and lead opinion'. Mandelson was however more candid towards the end of the process and unequivocally answered 'no' when asked 'is there any policy of Labour's that you would not be prepared to abandon if you thought it would gain votes?'. As the architect of Review Tom Sawyer put it, the 'moderate programme' that emerged was 'pitched where the electorate is' and was a logical consequence of the preference accommodating approach that had steered it.[24]

Though Policy Review proposals were ratified at successive Conferences, the process encountered opposition. In 1988 leading left-winger Tony Benn formally stood for the Labour leadership having criticised Neil Kinnock's 'authoritarian and intolerant manner' and the way 'pollsters and public relations people have now effectively replaced policy-making and political campaigning as the basis of the party's work'.[25] Benn feared a 'US style politics' was engulfing the party and disparagingly contrasted the professionals' work with the struggles of labour movement heroes the Tolpuddle martyrs.[26] Though widely derided at the time, the challenge came at the defining moment in modern Labour history. The subsequent margin of the leadership's victory over the left strengthened their position but did not silence the critics. Kinnock's poor public and media profile continued to depress his poll ratings and the party's American consultant Joe Napolitan even suggested the leader should resign in early 1988 and again in 1991 following the removal of Thatcher. Within the hierarchy this was a rarely voiced viewpoint but it was a logical one given the highly personal, even presidential nature of British politics at the time and given, as Rose saw it, the Labour leader had effectively begun to displace his own party structure. Yet serious internal discussion of Kinnock's standing with the electorate was suppressed and actively ignored by key strategists like Philip Gould.[27] This was somewhat ironic given the leader's own predilection for using opinion feedback to structure discussions so that they dwelt on apparent party weaknesses rather than strengths. Significantly the research had a discernible impact on policy although some did not share the leadership's enthusiasm for the Review and accused its documents of being bland, platitudinous and devoid of inspiration. In a celebrated speech Ron Todd, leader of Labour's largest affiliate the T&GWU, criticised the 'opinion polls, advertising and all the rest if the flim-flam' and the 'modernisers' driving the policy process courtesy of their 'sharpsuits and cordless telephones, clipboards and scientific samples'.[28] Others used marketing terminologies to highlight perceived shortcomings in the Policy Review. At a 1988 conference entitled 'Hard Labour' critics and leadership supporters vied to position themselves as the authentic 'modernisers'.[29]

'New Model' Labour

Towards the end of the Policy Review strategist Philip Gould began privately writing about the emergence of 'new' Labour. Though this specific phrase did not become common currency there was a widespread belief that the party policy and organisation had changed in very real and meaningful ways. A highly sympathetic 1990 account of the period reflected this in its title, *Labour Rebuilt: the New Model Party*, and dealt with the Review's machinations and outcomes.[30] This well informed if somewhat partisan book demonstrated the important role played by the SCA, Campaigns and Communications Directorate (CCD) and Leader's Office within the process. Significantly these groups would now be at the forefront of publicising an electoral offering they had helped create.

The primacy of the Shadow Communications Agency

Labour's 1987 election promoted the benefits of image management and public relations to the media as well as an internal party audience. The campaign also enabled the party to draw upon the expertise of a range of specialists not available to it in the 1983 defeat. The Review process ensured this nexus of professional strategists, aides and advisers became a permanent feature within the party organisation. The leadership ensured this burgeoning network was funded with so-called 'Short' money paid by the state to opposition parties for research and other expenses. By 1992 this not inconsiderable sum had risen to over £1.4 million.[31] The SCA arrangement helped conserve this money. It also heralded a strategic transformation similar to that which took place in American politics two decades before. Then the relationship between presidential candidates, their parties and hired election strategists changed because: 'advertising agencies have simply been muscled out of the business by the new corps of political media consultants'.[32] The rise of professional specialists diminished the importance of the national bureaucracy and the formal relationships between party organisers and agency executives were replaced by more fluid partnerships between a new cadre of consultants and aides representing those aspiring to be president. This change was motivated by a belief that an ad hoc team provided for more responsive, flexible and decisive campaigning. That it helped undermine the accountability of candidates to national party officials and committees was an added benefit.

The SCA emerged as an integral part of what Shaw terms Labour's 'strategic community'.[33] Without the formalised party-agency partnership that existed in 1983, a consultancy based arrangement made it easier for Kinnock's aides to liase with marketing advisers. Effective National Executive supervision of the party's opinion research programme, broadcasting and other campaign initiatives was curtailed: 'Although the NEC and its Campaign Strategy Committee (CSC) were formally charged with overseeing all aspects of campaigning and communications, in practice both were shunted into the background, their functions transferred to new institutions and the informal networks they spawned.'[34] The diminution of Executive control over campaigning reduced the trade unions' influence over strategy. This did not perhaps matter because leaders of the main affiliates had tended to support Kinnock's organisational and policy reforms. Like the party, the unions had subjected themselves to a period of self re-reflection and were keen not to embarrass the Labour leadership. Some in the movement had talked of the need for so-called 'New Realism' as well as marketing campaigns to recruit members.[35]

During the Policy Review, the SCA had emerged as a 'potent instrument of leadership power'. The Agency, formed to encourage the participation of a wide-ranging group of professionals, 'became more institutionalised and cohesive'. Guided by co-ordinator Philip Gould, it increasingly focused around a marketing rather than academic or journalistic agenda.[36] Whereas the party-Agency partnership intensified, Labour's longstanding relationship with pollsters Market Opinion and Research International (MORI) ended after the 1987 campaign. The firm's chief executive Bob Worcester believed this happened because Peter Mandelson was determined to control the way research findings were disseminated in the party. Mandelson told Worcester 'I want no information that will cause interference with what I know is the right thing to do'.[37] Later Labour hired ex-Conservative pollsters National Opinion Polls (NOP), a firm recently acquired by party sympathiser Clive Hollick. NOP did not perform the same functions as MORI and this enabled the SCA to emerge as the 'key source of strategic recommendations'.[38]

Labour strategists sought advice from professional consultants based overseas. These liaisons went beyond discussions with officials from sister parties and followed the contacts made prior to the 1987 election. In preparing for that campaign Kinnock had used the

Washington based Fenton Communications consultancy to help with media relations during his trip to meet President Reagan. Philip Gould's involvement with the International Association of Political Consultants led to further contacts and overseas work, most notably in Nicaragua where he advised President Daniel Ortega prior to his and the Sandinistas' defeat in the 1990 elections.[39] Labour forged links with the polling firm of Mark Mellman and Ed Lazarus. They advised the party to use 'people metering', a system used to monitor public reactions to televised adverts and speeches. NOP adopted the technique and organised groups of around 60 floating voters to test various materials. Potentially more controversial were the links party strategists made with 'hard bitten' negative campaign specialists David Doak and Robert Shrum.[40] Like Mellman and Lazarus, their consultancy was associated with the Democrats. They gained prominence in 1988 by helping congressman Richard Gephardt to mount a serious challenge for the party's presidential nomination. Two years later Doak and Shrum were responsible for a hard-hitting campaign against Texas Governor Ann Richards. Despite being accused of drug abuse, Richards fought off their candidate's challenge for the Democratic nomination. Prior to the 1992 election the consultants met members of the Campaigns Directorate, SCA co-ordinator Philip Gould and leading Agency volunteer Barry Delaney. Questioned about alleged links with these and other American consultants, Jack Cunningham denied the party had any before conceding his advisers 'are likely to consult with (such) people'.[41] The Campaigns Co-ordinator was aware that public acknowledgement of these consultants' existence would more than likely provoke resentment within the party.

The changing party culture

Having played key roles from the outset, members of the Leader's Office, SCA and CCD continued to help manage the Policy Review. They became a formidable network working directly to the leader and took responsibility for a series of initiatives to promote each phase of the Review. These campaigns took the form of a series of 'pre-manifestos' that starting with 'Social Justice and Economic Efficiency' in 1988. May 1989 saw 'Meet the Challenge, Make the Change' complete with theme. Reports of qualitative research findings suggesting Labour 'lacks a positive identity' encouraged the party to invest more resources in its campaigning.[42] In a bid to maintain the momentum provided by the Review other events followed including 'Looking to the Future' (1990), 'Opportunity Britain' (1991) and 'Made in Britain'

(1992). The last two featured a concerted attempt to use patriotism and the Union flag in what one commentator described as Labour's 'glitzkrieg'. Each launch was co-ordinated for media consumption by Campaign Directorate staff such as Jim Parish. SCA members were available to offer advice and the shadow health team took particular advantage of their help in combating a £2 million advertising promotion of government policy.[43]

During the Policy Review Party Political Broadcasts were often made by Sid Roberson and Barry Delaney. Many of their films were 'real people' documentaries designed, as Roberson put it, to 'hook' viewers with 'a style laced with analogy and imagery... intended as a cameo of life or experience for one or other group of target voters.'[44] In preparing for the election those working on Broadcasts were joined by ex-SDP supporter David Puttnam and 1987 campaign veteran Hugh Hudson. Barbara Follett provided Labour spokespeople with presentational advice. Her work as an image consultant to Robin Cook, Harriet Harman and others provoked considerable media interest and it was perhaps inevitable that commentators would begin writing about the 'marketing' of Labour.[45] Supporters like Follett and Puttnam were also involved in new fundraising initiatives. These included high profile £500 a head fundraising dinners organised by PR Consultant Julia Hobsbawm. Though their main purpose was financial, the gatherings also helped associate Labour with fame and success. The number of actors involved led media critics to deride the events as 'Luvvies for Labour'. Left-wing MP Eric Heffer protested that these opulent dinners compromised the party's solidarity with the less fortunate.[46] Less controversially the party used direct mail firm WWAV and telemarketers Pell and Bates for its more routine fundraising. Direct response marketing was also incorporated into the party's canvassing and targeting work.[47]

The media intensive Review launches intensified the links between those promoting the party and a select number of opinion forming journalists including Alastair Campbell, Andrew Grice, Nicholas Wapshott, Donald MacIntyre and Patrick Wintour. According to a critic, *Guardian* correspondent Wintour became 'Mandelson's amanuensis'.[48] By contrast other journalists resented their lack of access and the contrived nature of party campaigns. Nowhere was this more acute than at the Annual Conference. During the 1988 gathering party managers staged debates that 'might harm the image of the 'new' Labour Party' during the breaks for children's programming that punctuated the live televised proceedings.[49] Carefully designed platform sets reinforced the image of a party engaged in impression management. Genuine debate appeared to no longer occur at a Conference that had descended into what *Today* political editor Paul Wilenius called a cross between 'the Nuremburg rally and EastEnders'. Similarly, giving the journalists' vote of thanks at the event, Roy Jones of the *Morning Star* paper commented: 'I thought I would say something about politics in this speech, but why bring the subject up so late in the week.'[50]

The lack of engaging discussion within the party during and following the Policy Review unsettled those on the left such as MP Jeremy Corbyn. He attacked Labour's 'new agenda': 'It's soft-soap populism. We do our opinion polls, find out what people want, and say 'OK, you can have it', without asking what kind of society we have now, and what kind of society we want to replace it'.[51] For fellow dissenter Ken Livingstone, the party was losing its faith: 'We're talking about what humanity is about. You can't understand that by marketing. It's what you have to believe, it is about moral choices, about right and wrong, it is not about percentages, about how much you can get people to buy this, that or the other product'. Less predictable was a telling point made by former SCA member and market research specialist Kay Scorah in which she questioned the direction of the Review:

> There is a tendency now for them to overuse the research and that's beginning to concern me. They are allowing the electorate to dictate policy rather than using the research to help them communicate their policy. I don't think we elect people to tell us what we already think. I think we elect people to lead and if you don't get leaders anymore you just get the same old shit.[52]

Former Kinnock supporters such as *Tribune* columnist Hugh Macpherson also began to express their disillusionment: 'The Labour Party is now a public relations led organisation, whether it be reassuring American capitalists of the European Commission or trailing around the boardrooms of Britain telling them that they have nothing to fear from Labour.'[53] More surprising were comments in a paper from the largely pro-leadership Labour Co-ordinating Committee (LCC):

> Too much sanitisation and voters lose any real sense of what we stand for. The politics are in danger of becoming the servant of public relations, instead of the other way round... Labour seems to lack passion and confidence in its alternative. This is simply not a problem of presentation. It is a problem of political strategy.[54]

The LCC document reflected unease throughout the party that went right up to the highest levels. The more sceptical 'soft left' Shadow Cabinet members were subjected to attacks in unattributable press briefings. Those targeted included Bryan Gould, John Prescott, Michael Meacher, David Blunkett, Denzil Davies, Norman Buchan and union leader Ron Todd. It was widely assumed that Peter Mandelson was responsible for these stories. One of the frontbenchers criticised in the reports complained: 'It smacks too much of the way Mrs. Thatcher runs things.'[55] Though Mandelson denied any part in these briefings he did later explain his own organisational role: 'My job was as much as a political manager exercising political judgement and driving things forward politically as it was making sure the set look good, the edit was fine, the hair was in the right place. I left all that to other people.'[56] For a headquarters' official Mandelson attracted enormous attention. According to one profile, he became 'the main point of contact between Labour and the press, because he decided on day one that it was newspapers which set the agenda for TV and radio, and TV and radio which turn people's votes'.[57] By contrast Kinnock failed to develop a rapport with certain media. *Mail on Sunday* editor Stewart Steven argued this problem had been exacerbated by Mandelson who, soon after his appointment, had given the impression that he believed newspapers 'were no longer very important' compared to television and had consequently blocked print journalists' access to the leader.[58]

Given his now pivotal role as a gatekeeper, Mandelson increasingly provoked hostility from within the party. Tony Benn had been critical since the attempt by the Campaigns Director to prevent him from appearing on BBC television's 'Question Time' in 1986.[59] Benn wrote in his diaries: 'I find Mandelson a threatening figure for the future of the Party... he and Kinnock work closely together. Whitty is just a figurehead, and Geoff Bish has been pushed into the background.'[60] When his tenure at headquarters ended in 1990, Mandelson had acquired a reputation unmatched by any official since Morgan Philips' time in the 1950s. He had also made vital alliances with those whom he had enthusiastically promoted as part of his job. Fortunately for him one of the politicians he courted was Tony Blair. Ultimately Mandelson had been dependent on the patronage of Neil Kinnock, the person he acknowledged was most responsible for Labour's marketing transformation and a Review 'driven by him, and if not achieved single handedly, certainly won by dint of his Herculean efforts' rather than by 'backroom boys and marketing consultants'.[61] The Director's eventual departure from his headquarters' job was marred by controversy.

After an acrimonious contest he secured the parliamentary nomination for the Hartlepool seat. Some on the National Executive doubted whether a candidate could remain in charge of campaigns. Gordon Colling, the chair of the NEC Communications sub-committee mobilised this dissent and, in a rare show of Executive independence, helped force the issue. Following his resignation the former Director commented: 'I may be changing my role, but the Mandelson machine lives on.'[62]

There were a number of candidates who vied to succeed Mandelson. Despite competition from Roy Hattersley's aide David Hill, General Municipal and Boilermakers' Union (GMB) official Phil Woolas and chief press officer Colin Byrne, John Underwood was appointed following a secret ballot of NEC members. Television journalist Underwood's credits included working as a news correspondent and producer with innovative Channel Four series 'After Dark'. The editor of *Tribune* welcomed Underwood's arrival: 'It's the best decision the NEC could have made. It's a vote for professionalism ahead of factionalism.'[63] The new Director contemplated making changes and considered using a single agency rather than the SCA during the forthcoming general election campaign.[64] But Underwood was frustrated in post and resigned following protracted disagreements with his deputy Colin Byrne. His departure attracted considerable media attention. The leader's failure to support Underwood ended an uneasy relationship that had earlier deteriorated following Kinnock's decision to let Mandelson oversee the crucial Monmouth by-election campaign in 1991. According to journalist John Pienaar, Underwood's departure demonstrated the extent to which 'Kinnock holds party in vice-like grip'.[65] For Charles Clarke, the leader's chief of staff, this 'unquestioned control' was essential for strategic development.[66] The vacant Campaigns Directorship went to David Hill. His background as press spokesperson for Roy Hattersley did not prevent him getting involved with every aspect of the campaign and he renamed the SCA the Communications Agency in an attempt to make it sound less secretive. The Agency nevertheless retained its considerable influence over the development of strategy.[67]

It's not time for Labour

The ultimate test for Neil Kinnock's 'new model' party came in the 1992 general election. The campaign, fought over the first three and a half months of the year, would be as arduous as it was bitter. Labour also faced a new opponent, Prime Minister John Major, who set about abandoning Margaret Thatcher's 'flagship' poll tax and promoting a more consensual image. The Conservatives' re-branding made it difficult for Labour to reposition itself after such an exhaustive policy review. Kinnock's position subsequently came under renewed pressure following his party's slump in the polls after Thatcher's resignation.[68]

Labour reconvened its CMT for the coming election in mid-1988. The CMT drew together the strategic expertise of Campaigns Co-ordinator Jack Cunningham, headquarters officials and aides from the Leader's Office. Alternatively known as the General Election Planning Committee, the Team was strengthened by the later addition of Kinnock's aide Patricia Hewitt and SCA co-ordinator Philip Gould. Cunningham also chaired the Campaign Advisory Group of senior party and SCA strategists. Their weekly meetings discussed the latest polling and advertising plans. The CMT and CAG were in theory accountable to the party's CSC and the pre-election Leader's Committee. In practice things worked differently in that NEC or CSC control over the campaign as well as the then largest 'war chest' ever assembled amounted to 'little more than a facade'.[69]

Labour entered the campaign hoping to capitalise on public anxiety over economic recession by launching a Shadow Budget statement including modest tax proposals. This continued the party's repositioning of itself on economic matters. The Conservatives and their vocal press allies mercilessly attacked their opponent's past performance and future plans with the advertising slogans 'Labour's Tax Bombshell' and 'You Can't Trust Labour'. The party replied with 'It's time for a change, It's Time for Labour'.[70] Unfortunately for them the new Tory premier had already transformed the image of the government and was far more personally popular than Kinnock. Labour strategists responded to this problem by deploying a team of spokespeople including the Shadow Chancellor John Smith, a politician markedly more effective than his incumbent opponent. Others beneficiaries of the approach included Margaret Beckett, Tony Blair and Gordon Brown. Labour had difficulty in setting the agenda of what quickly became a stale campaign. This changed followed a Labour Party Election Broadcast (PEB) entitled 'Mandy'. Its depiction of a child's health problems provoked outrage in the Tory press. The film, created by Boase Massimi Pollitt (BMP) executive John Webster and 'Four Weddings and a Funeral' director Mike Newell, was accused of exploiting Jennifer Bennett, the child on whose case the PEB was supposedly based.[71] Health Secretary William Waldegrave likened the party's approach to Nazi propaganda.

Once the so-called 'war of Jennifer's ear' subsided, the issue became Labour's fitness to govern.

During the campaign Major emphasised his common touch. Conservative MP Edwina Currie compared his efforts unfavourably with those of Kinnock and credited the Labour leader for his statesmanlike tour of the country in a limousine. This was integral to justifying his status as 'Britain's Next Prime Minister'. His sober, establishment image sat uneasily with Kinnock's naturally ebullient personality.[72] This was demonstrated in the week before polling day at the Sheffield Rally. Coverage of the event ignored Kinnock's imaginative oration and concentrated on his 'We're all right, we're all right' greeting of the audience. According to deputy leader Roy Hattersley the medium became the message:

> Neil Kinnock made the finest speech I think I've ever heard him make and that's pretty high praise. It was full of ideas. It was full of passion. It was positive. It was about a key subject, education. And instead of being reported we had the photographs of the big screen, of helicopters landing, we had photographs of fireworks. Next time less fireworks, more ideas in speeches.[73]

The party's campaign experienced other largely self-inflicted problems. Labour raised constitutional issues but Kinnock failed to clarify his stance on electoral reform and made the rival leaders appear more resolute. He also seemed somewhat weakened by his political longevity and was pilloried in the Tory press for now abandoned commitments to nuclear disarmament, public ownership and union rights.[74]

The denouement

The post-mortem into Labour's fourth defeat was curtailed by the need to find a new leader following Kinnock's resignation. There was however a candid if brief exchange of opinions over the modernisation strategy and the marketing approach underpinning it which revealed dissenting views at every level of the organisation. Deputy leader Roy Hattersley believed his 'enormously respectable' party failed because it did not 'inspire' and 'excite' voters. Shadow Cabinet colleague John Prescott focused his criticisms on the SCA and its methods, claiming the group favoured 'beautiful people' and had been 'out of control for far too long'.[75] The perception that unaccountable advisers had wielded too much influence was reinforced when CCD official Jim Parish contended that major decisions ought to have been taken by 'politicians advised by professional staff with politics in their blood-stream'.[76] Such a contention drew support from the wider party. At the 1992 Conference delegate Teresa Pearce was warmly applauded for articulating grassroots' feelings:

> We have allowed ourselves to be marketed by paid image-makers, but in whose image are we being made? It is not an image I recognise. It is not an image I want to recognise. We should be aware of the paid image-makers. These are people, mainly middle-class graduates, who have learned their socialism from market research and opinion polls.[77]

Co-ordinator Jack Cunningham and strategist Patricia Hewitt were understandably indignant about the criticisms of the campaign. Likewise Neil Kinnock was contemptuous of those who questioned the modernisation strategy and its cautious approach.[78] Peter Mandelson was similarly unrepentant 'the party's credibility problems were to do with the policies... (which) required a political solution. Labour itself had to be rebuilt- modernised in terms of policies and appeals'.[79] Given the role of market research in Policy Review it was almost inevitable that the party's polling would became the subject of some controversy.

Leys believed 'market research socialism' and its abandonment of policy commitments was symptomatic of the leadership's crisis of confidence.[80] Another argued 'rigorous social analysis' as opposed to the party's reliance on commercial methods might have inspired more genuinely radical thinking.[81] Similarly in a televised debate on the future of the left the leading Fabian Ben Pimlott spoke of the 'consumerist' strategies of 'morally desperate' politicians. Pimlott's colleague and author of *The Culture of Contentment* John Kenneth Galbraith argued that for the sake of democracy 'it is much better that there is a voice rather than a victory'. By contrast fellow guest Tony Blair demonstrated his instinctive bias for 'preference accommodating' rather than 'shaping' electoral positioning when he argued 'of the one thing I am absolutely sure is that Labour did not lose the election because it was too moderate'.[82] Such thinking pervaded the party hierarchy as dramatist David Hare found during the extensive research and interviews he undertook with leading party figures and strategists whilst writing the play *The Absence of War*. Hare concluded the decision to 're-model itself as a paragon of sobriety has not only left the electorate wondering why they should vote for the imitation when they might as well vote for the original; it has left a Labour party terrified of controversy, terrified of internal argument'. The resulting 'play safe strategy' attempted to respond to rather than reshape the public agenda and in doing so revealed a timidity that did little to challenge the prevailing orthodoxy that the Conservatives were the best party for the economy.[83] Events were about to have a decisive impact on this perception. In turn the electoral prospects of Labour were about to be dramatically changed.

7
The New Right Ascendancy

The legacy of the Policy Review

Campaigning played a significant role in changing and redistributing power within the Labour Party during the 1980s so that, by the end of the decade, the organisation was unrecognisable from the one defeated in 1979. Far from being about peripheral presentational exercises, the adoption of a marketing driven approach became integral to the leadership's reassertion of control. Furthermore this activity extended to influencing popular opinion and was concerned with convincing the party of the need for reform. The Policy Review programme began as a process of 'internal' marketing that culminated in the launch of 'new' Labour. The function of 'agenda-setting' is central to understanding how the Review and subsequent leadership exercises were able to restructure the party. Cohen identified the core feature of this concept when he wrote: 'the press may not be successful much of the time in telling people what to think, but it is stunningly successful in telling its readers what to think about'. Having been popularised in a celebrated study of election campaigning, Lukes used the term to describe one of three 'faces' of power that determine organisational outcomes.[1] Others adopted the concept in studying Labour decision-making procedures during the 1970s and early 1980s, a period characterised by 'crisis management' and a determined attempt by grassroots' activists to diminish the power of the parliamentary leadership in order to reassert the right of the party Conference to make key decisions.[2] The body, labelled the 'parliament of the movement' by Attlee, provided a delegatory form of self-governance embodying a commitment to internal democracy.[3] This quality, largely absent from the other main parties, state institutions and most media organisations, helped explain Labour's historic distrust of the latter in particular. Significantly the modern party's embrace of marketing afforded the media considerable influence over its internal affairs with important consequences for what remained of the organisation's federal, participatory structures.

To better understand the changed nature of party organisation it is vital to consider the increasingly central role played by three actors in shaping and determining decision-making outcomes. Firstly, and most importantly, there has been the growth in size and importance of what Panebianco calls the 'electoral professionals' responsible for implementing and, increasingly, devising strategy. With the emergence of this elite there has been a parallel growth in the party's reliance on the media allies Ostrogorski termed 'auxiliaries'.[4] In return for privileged access, these sympathetic journalistic outlets have been responsible for the conduit of leadership viewpoints to general as well as internal publics. This is not a new phenomenon given it was Michels who made the telling observation: 'The press constitutes a potent instrument for the conquest, the preservation and the consolidation of power on the part of the leaders'. Finally, in terms of the input side to the debate, there has been an increasing preoccupation on the part of the electoral professionals with floating voters. The attitudes of this so-called 'opinion electorate', as represented by polling research, have been used by the leadership and its strategists to inform and influence successive party debates and reforms.[5]

Empowering the electoral professionals

During the Policy Review the media helped the leadership dominate the party agenda. By doing so Labour was reconstituted as a more hierarchical, professional organisation. Phil Kelly, the editor of *Tribune*, speculated on such an outcome at the beginning of the Review:

> If it becomes a mass party which takes it membership seriously, and involves them in policy-making and implementation, then it will need a system of internal management based on consensus. If it descends into a media-orientated marketing organisation for top politicians, then it will need internal discipline which will make the Fifties seem liberal by comparison.[6]

Prior to the late 1980s party agenda setting was understood to mean an ability to influence policy and organisational decisions through the mobilisation of internal opinion. The increased importance of marketing complicated the process by intensifying politicians' reliance on the mass media as a vehicle for persuasion. This in turn eroded the power of previously influential horizontal decision-making structures such as the Annual Conference. Given its already privileged position, a leader with coherent strategies now became virtually unassailable not least because:

> His office now housed an unprecedented proliferation of aides, assistants and advisers, with an overview of, and involvement in, all aspects of party activity and all dimensions of the links with the unions. In effect there was now an Executive Office of the Leader... (providing) the basis of a centralised power structure unique in Labour Party history.[7]

Neil Kinnock's burgeoning 'executive' was funded by the parliamentary subsidy of Short Money paid to opposition parties for research.[8] The beneficiaries of this resource were leadership aides, marketing consultants and Campaigns Director who formed the core of the 'strategic community'. Increasingly it was these advisers, rather than the increasingly titular National Executive Committee (NEC), who directed party affairs. An obvious manifestation of this was the growing prominence and perceived importance of so-called 'spin' and 'spin doctors'.[9]

The influence of media auxiliaries

The marketing-conscious Review process involved targeting non-electoral groups including party members, donors and affiliates with an interest in policy and organisational developments.[10] The leadership was uniquely placed to co-ordinate a sustained public relations effort designed to influence internal audiences with the help of external media 'opinion formers'. Unlike conventional politics, intra-party debates offer particular opportunities as well as challenges:

> The mixture of intimacy and opposition is conducive to tensions, but when the interactions and relationships are distilled and exaggerated into news reports, the mixture is doubly explosive. Immediate relations are refracted through the prism of media publicity, itself often clothed in extravagant gladiatorial imagery.[11]

Before the Policy Review Labour agenda setting centred on influencing Conference and NEC decisions in tandem with a mediated debate which flourished in left journals like *Tribune*, *New Statesman* or the in-house *Labour Weekly* and *New Socialist*. The latter two publications' closure was symptomatic of the leadership's concentration on the anti-Conservative *Guardian* and the *Mirror* group of newspapers owned by former MP Robert Maxwell for the dissemination of their reformist ideas from the late 1980s onwards. During this time both papers, and contributors like *Mirror* political editor Alastair Campbell and *Guardian* correspondent Patrick Wintour in particular, were invariably supportive of Kinnock's leadership and their advocacy helped frame broadcast media coverage of internal party matters. The importance of the papers stems from their circulation figures: throughout the early 1990s these titles' readerships both outnumbered the estimated Labour membership of 300–350,000. Their organisational significance became obvious given an estimated 35% of those belonging to the party read the *Guardian*, 27% the *Mirror/Record*, 7% the *Independent*, 15% others and only 13% no daily.[12] The two most popular papers were thus able to each reach a larger audience than the combined strength of the main Labour supporting publications *Tribune*, *New Statesman*, *Labour Briefing*, *Chartist* and *Socialist/Red Pepper*. The latter group's tendency to be more critical of the leadership than their mass-market rivals once mattered because of their opinion-forming, activist readerships yet their potential agenda-setting influence waned as the party abandoned its horizontal democratic structures in favour of more passive forms activity including membership ballots for parliamentary selections, leadership elections and constitutional or policy referenda.[13]

Researching the opinion electorate

Private polling, that is opinion research commissioned by parties, is not new to British politics. Nevertheless the importance attached to this form of data as a source of feedback was borne out by the increase in the amount as well as types of study being commissioned during the 1980s. Parties that previously relied on quantitative opinion research methods such as the large-scale questionnaire now began funding ongoing qualitative studies of voter attitudes, typically in the form of a focus groups consisting of 6 to 10 people sharing a weak partisanship and/or similar socio-economic background. In such sessions a trained moderator would facilitate a recorded discussion aimed at exploring participants' deeper value and attitudinal structures. Qualitative findings increasingly complemented quantitative electoral analysis because, as Neil Kinnock put it, they 'get behind the figures'.[14] Parties have long used such research in their electioneering work. The inter-war Conservatives held cottage coffee mornings to target women voters whilst Labour did the same with impromptu back street meetings. Though primarily propagandist in intent, both offered potentially valuable feedback. In the 1960s so-called depth interviewing of individual voters became a feature of campaigns. Interest in qualitative techniques intensified with the use of these methods by Conservative strategists and also the Save the GLC initiative in the 1980s.

The 1988 US presidential race offered the most disturbing insight into focus groups' potency. During the campaign a pro-Republican organisation tested voter reactions to Democrat candidate and Governor of Massachusetts Michael Dukakis' policy of rehabilitating criminals. The consultants discovered the unrepresentative case of a re-offending parolee, Willie Horton, and he subsequently featured in a highly negative anti-Dukakis advert. The Democrats' failure to counter the spot proved a turning point in the campaign. For E.J. Dionne Jr, the use of 'Pavlovian' focus groups threatened to undermine the credibility of the entire political system as well as a particular candidate.[15] In Britain the Labour leadership took a different view and began using the method to monitor changing trends in opinion from the mid-1980s onwards. The subsequent Policy Review ensured selected material from focus groups of floating voters became integral to debate because, according to Kinnock, the process had to be 'reinforced periodically by using the Shadow Communications Agency (SCA) to give presentations which...assisted in the efforts to sustain the movement of the Review in the desired direction'.[16] The practice of using research findings in this way would outlive the Kinnock leadership.

The 'modernising' agenda

The fourth consecutive defeat in 1992 triggered a further period of introspection within the Labour movement. The supporters of Kinnock launched a determined defence of his reform strategy during the immediate post-mortem period and beyond. In doing so they used public relations and selective opinion research findings to influence the debate over the party's future. Brivati identified the two issues that defined their position:

> The British Labour Party has a long memory and a conservative nature. There are two key elements in its conservatism which have been the subject of controversy over the last thirty years and which the current leadership would like, in an ideal world, to reform. The first is the link with the trade unions, particularly the block vote

system. The second is Clause IV of the Party's constitution. Both are retained because of their historical importance rather than their contemporary relevance, and the modernisers in the party feel they are an obstacle to winning power.[17]

The so-called 'modernisers' scored a notable coup by appropriating a name that had been fought over since the early stages of the Policy Review. That they were able to do so was largely a result of the intensely mediated nature of modern internal party debates. Like them, the modernisers' journalistic sympathisers characterised their opponents as 'traditionalists', a negative term most in the party associated with conservatism. Unsurprisingly many of those designated as such did not like or use the name and claimed it was they who were the authentic radicals with a modernising agenda.[18] Nevertheless the print and broadcast media discourse couched the debate in terms of modernisers versus traditionalists, thereby giving the former added credibility. Yet the labels were misleading if not meaningless as few Labour partisans were not prepared to countenance policy and organisational changes.[19] To use more conventional terminology, the debate was largely constructed through a media prism according to terms governed by a publicity conscious grouping on what can be termed the party's 'new right'.[20] Significantly this faction of former 'soft left' sympathisers differed from their Gaitskellite forebears and successors on the conventional right in that their political identity was not founded upon trade union backing nor preoccupied with mainstream social democratic concerns such as class and poverty. Rather the grouping wanted to consolidate mentor Neil Kinnock's legacy by building an electoral alliance based on relatively affluent supporters, an accommodation with free market capitalism and the espousal of an authoritarian rhetoric more commonly associated with the Conservatives. As Marquand later put it: 'on the central question now facing the political economies of western Europe, new Labour and the new right are one'.[21] This provides useful context to the Labour's new right response to the 1992 defeat which amounted to calling for a more consumer-centred politics as a means of challenging vested 'producer' interests be they business or, more pointedly, union.[22] By adopting the title of modernisers they effectively neutralised their internal Labour rivals' ability to claim the mantle of the 'left' against their own less attractive but more accurate 'right' label. This proved an asset in a succession of debates, be these constitutional and concerned with the union link and Clause Four or more specific and related to events like the

American Democrats' 1992 electoral victory or the unexpected leadership contest of 1994.

End of the unions?

The 1992 election ended Neil Kinnock's leadership but not what he had come to regard as 'the project'.[23] In discussing the defeat most of his party rivals avoided attacking Kinnock personally and preferred to focus on the role played by the SCA, a key agent of his reform strategy. The SCA was, however, spared some criticism when this muted post-mortem was diverted by the 'extraordinary fixation' with the union link 'on the part of an influential minority who had important prompters and allies in the media'.[24] Behind this sustained attack was a straightforward calculation:

> Labour's social democrats used to argue that the block vote was a democratic measure representative of trade union opinion. But once the union block vote swung against them, they complained that it was undemocratic and unrepresentative. Perspectives change according to whether a practice helps a group win a struggle with challenges or not.[25]

Consequently, within days of the defeat, former Campaigns Directorate official Colin Byrne alleged 'behind the scenes fixing' involving unnamed trade unionists who had long sought to undermine Kinnock.[26] This coincided with stories that several general secretaries were supporting John Smith for the leadership. Media attention turned to these affiliates' role and the resulting coverage was almost entirely hostile and reminiscent of the kind of biased coverage analysed by the Glasgow Media Group in the 1970s.[27] An *Independent* editorial denounced the party-union link as 'constitutionally wrong' whilst a *Sunday Times* feature by Andrew Grice warned of 'The Red Barons Return'. The unions were also accused of being 'rooted in the past', 'undemocratic', a source of 'extremism' and having 'cloth cap' images.[28] The myth of the monolithic 'barons' was a persistent feature of journalistic reports but took no account of a more complex reality in which the affiliated unions were frequently divided over many issues.[29]

Discussion over the union link began to dominate Labour's post-mortem and thwarted a sustained reappraisal of Kinnock's reform strategy. Leaked findings from the party's own private focus groups furthered the anti-union media agenda. Reports from sympathisers like

Donald Macintyre reinforced the new right's case: 'Labour lost the election because floating voters saw it as union-dominated and outdated and because they believed voting for it was not in their financial self-interest, according to confidential post-election research circulating in the party's high command'. Similarly Patrick Wintour of the *Guardian* wrote about 'devastating' feedback which suggested the party was 'too old fashioned, too tied to the past, too linked to minorities and old images of the trades unions'; the latter were blamed for offering 'an old fashioned, bureaucratic image (to) key suburban swing voters'. Other opinion forming papers reinforced the rapidly emerging consensus that Labour was 'backward-looking' and identified with 'industrial strife', 'the winter of discontent', 'inflation and economic failure', 'heavy industry', 'the traditional working class', 'the past', 'downwardly mobile' and 'minority groups'. It was argued that the union 'interest' reinforced these negative associations.[30] Shadow Cabinet and NEC member Clare Short suspected the leaks were being used to divert attention away from the SCA's flawed campaign strategy and, somewhat bizarrely, it was left to the Conservative supporting *Daily Telegraph* to point out the benefits of the party union link. Stuart Weir detected an orchestrated attempt to scapegoat Labour's founding allies:

> During the election, the Conservatives tried to make Labour's links with the trade unions into an electoral issue and failed. None of the polls picked up any signs of the trade unions damaging Labour's rosy image, and the first post-mortems by specialist writers entirely disregarded them. But within a few weeks a highly influential group *within* the Labour Party had rewritten history. They firmly identified the trade unions as the root cause of the electorate's distrust of Labour – apparently as the first stage of a campaign to break the party/trade union connection.[31]

The immediate post-mortem failed to seriously address other possible negatives such as the so-called 'Kinnock factor'. This was a notable omission given the presidential nature of modern campaigning combined with this leader's widely recognised unpopularity with voters. This self-denial had, however, been unofficial policy as Philip Gould had consistently suppressed damning public feedback on Kinnock's performance in successive strategic presentations out of loyalty to the leader.[32] By contrast Gould showed no such reluctance to apportion blame to those identified in a memo of his that appeared in the media post-mortem on the fourth defeat. For him the 'polling was clear': Labour was still a party of the 'past'.[33] By contrast the official party report on the election, published the same month, was more cautious but came too late to influence the debate over the link. It did however indicate that barely 7% of voters had mentioned unions as a reason for not supporting Labour. The more common explanations given were general party image (30%); economic competence and tax (20%); Major and Kinnock (20%); and tax on its own (10%). All four of these concerns were comprehensively explored in *Labour's Last Chance?*, the British Election Study's lengthy analysis of the outcome. The BES team's conclusion emphasised the contribution of the more general factors like competence and image rather tax to the party's defeat. Tellingly the report limited its discussion of union influence on the result to the longer-term electoral consequences of declining membership.[34]

One more heave? The leadership of John Smith

The convincing victory of the leading traditional right-winger John Smith in the 1992 leadership election underlined how much the party had changed in a decade. Smith's consensual style contrasted with that of his more frenetic predecessor. This was a reflection of his personality but also of the enormous powers bequeathed to him by Kinnock. Smith moved quickly to disband the SCA and replace it with a more formalised client-firm partnership. In 1993 the party appointed former SCA volunteer Leslie Butterfield's BDDH as its advertisers. The agency assumed a relatively low profile in an arrangement designed to make the firm more accountable to the National Executive rather than the leadership. To this end Smith allowed his senior colleagues ready access to the party's private opinion research where Kinnock had continually restricted the circulation of this material. This did not, however, dramatically change a strategic outlook that still remained in the view of seasoned observer David McKie wedded to 'targeting middle income and Middle England'.[35]

Labour enjoyed a period of relative calm and unity during John Smith's leadership. The re-elected Conservatives were soon besieged by crises arising from the Exchange Rate Mechanism debacle and the government's controversial mine closure programme. Labour's new right became agitated by what they perceived to be the leader's 'one more heave' strategy despite having supported his candidacy against the more obviously radical Bryan Gould. Journalistic sympathisers such as Andrew Grice and Martin Kettle acted as conduits for the group's view on Smith's performance by focusing on his alleged unwillingness to give a lead in what was now a heavily centralised party.[36] Yet the leader's relaxed approach also enabled the new right to dominate the internal agenda and attract considerable media coverage for articles like the provocatively entitled 'Sleep Walking to Oblivion'.[37] In advocating of further change, the group's cause was to be further galvanised by a seismic political event overseas.

The 'Clintonisation' of Labour: the electoral post-mortem by proxy

The debate over Labour's defeat was initially side tracked into a manufactured but politically expedient row over the union link which in effect postponed the post-mortem. This changed with Bill Clinton's victory in the US presidential election of November 1992.

The 'New' Democrats

Bill Clinton's victory enabled the so-called 'New' Democrats to promote their agenda for government. Their origins lay in the right-wing Democratic Leadership Council set up following the 1984 presidential election defeat. The DLC believed their party had to shed its perceived 'tax and spend' image and detach itself from 'minority interests' in order to establish a reputation for financial rectitude. Critics, however, feared this would consolidate the economic orthodoxy being established under Reagan and questioned why the special interest groups identified were unions and others associated with the left rather than the large and politically influential corporate sector.[38] The 'new' Democrats also associated themselves with a less liberal penal agenda and developed policies to combat anti-social behaviour. In the run-up to the election Clinton underlined his own moral conservatism as Governor of Arkansas by executing a mentally incapacitated murderer.[39] His subsequent victory inspired Labour's new right in a way their party's fourth defeat had not. Links had been forged when several headquarters' staff visited the United States to support the Democrats' campaign. Former SCA co-ordinator Philip Gould also experienced the election and identified what he believed were the campaign's key lessons for Labour. Media reports interpreted them as the proposed 'Clintonisation' of the party.[40] Gould lauded the Democrats' rebuttal of the Republicans claims about their tax policies and argued Labour's inability to do likewise was a key failing of the 1992 campaign despite having earlier advocated the need for a 'rapid reactions unit' in his first report for the party.[41] Gould was fulsome in his praise of Clinton's key strategist James Carville and a flexible 'war room' which ensured his team were able to quickly respond to opposition claims. The Democrats' strategic clarity was conveyed by Carville's phrase 'It's the Economy, Stupid'.

The Labour new right's agenda was furthered by a conference on 'Clinton Economics' held at the beginning of 1993. The event featured Clinton strategists, American trade unionists and other analysts. Pollster Stanley Greenberg explained the campaign had aimed to broaden the Democrats' class appeal, emphasise the economy and sustain a critique of the government. Strategist Paul Begala spoke of how: 'Clinton's genius was to understand that the Democratic Party did not operate on a Left/Right basis and he changed the nature of the dialogue to that of between the old and the new, between elitism and populism'.[42] Several British commentators argued the Americans offered Labour a blueprint for abandoning its image as 'a party of the poor and the past' by embracing the 'working middle-classes'.[43] Philip Gould and Patricia Hewitt launched the party new right's own journal *Renewal* with a widely reported article entitled 'Lessons from America'. It suggested Labour needed to follow the Democrats' lead by divesting itself of its 'tax and spend' image and developing a reputation for economic trustworthiness in order to win more middle-class voters. The analysis, presented as something original, was in reality little different to that offered in the aftermath of the 1987 defeat. More novel, but less commented upon, were the observations from some of the party officials who had worked on the Democrats' campaign.[44] Following Clinton's victory the leading Labour new right-wingers Gordon Brown and Tony Blair began visiting Washington to meet Democratic colleagues and Shadow Cabinet members began discussing fashionable American books like 'Reinventing Government' and its promotion of the 'enabling state'.[45] Shadow Home Secretary Blair cited the communitarian ideas of Amitai Etzioni and others associated with Clinton in formulating a 'new' political agenda. He argued debates about major themes such as state versus market provision tended to overshadow the need for individuals to recognise they had responsibilities as well as rights. This stance informed Blair's more socially authoritarian 'tough on crime, tough on the causes of crime' rhetoric.[46]

The politics of focus grouping

Qualitative research methods became a more prominent feature of electoral analysis following the opinion polls' failure to predict the outcome of the 1992 general election.[47] Both politicians and journalists became increasingly interested in focus group data as an apparently scientific type source of some authority. Labour MP Giles Radice, a long time supporter of Kinnock's reform strategy, used the results of focus groups to explore public attitudes towards his party. His autumn 1992 pamphlet *Southern Discomfort* drew on findings based upon discussions involving voters from five Tory held marginal 'new town' seats in south eastern England.[48] The undisclosed number of participants aged between 25–50 had all intended to support Labour in the recent election but ultimately opted for the Conservatives. These people were seen as particularly important because, in effect, they counted twice: the impact of losing one of their votes would be doubled if they supported the opposition. The *Southern Discomfort* focus group evidence suggested these predominantly routine non-manual (C1) and skilled (C2) voters perceived the party to be out of touch, extremist, overly concerned with minorities, supportive of high taxation and antagonistic to their aspirations. It usefully reinforced the impression created by the research findings leaked in the aftermath of the defeat which is hardly surprising given the firm of Philip Gould and his colleague Deborah Mattinson were responsible for conducting both pieces of research on which the analysis was based.[49] Radice departed from the findings to argue for the repeal of Clause Four of the party constitution, which embodied a commitment to public ownership, as a means of demonstrating the 'new Labour party' was serious about change. This call, not to mention selected contents of the pamphlet, gained widespread coverage in the media.[50]

The findings of *Southern Discomfort* were broadly endorsed in a confidential briefing from party Campaigns Director David Hill. The contents of Hill's leaked memo received considerable press attention when it appeared at the height of the Clintonisation debate. His focus group based analysis offered further support to the new right case; this was understandable given the alleged source of the leak was Peter Mandelson. Philip Gould also later admitted to having also passed material to the *Sunday Times* during this time following encouragement from Tony Blair. For his part Mandelson had apparently obtained his documentation from NEC members Blair and Gordon Brown and passed it to his longstanding contact Patrick Wintour of *The Guardian*.[51] The subsequent front page scoop, headlined 'Losers' verdict divides Labour' and 'Leaked memo warns of voters' distrust', went on to suggest voters felt the party was too beholden to the poor, minorities and other vulnerable groups.[52] Wintour and likeminded journalists were keen to dwell on the party's credibility 'problem' at a time when it was enjoying a near record 20% lead in the polls and it was unquestionably the Conservatives whose popular standing was in freefall.[53] It was ironic that the 'modernisers' should accuse their 'traditionalist' opponents of being backward looking whilst simultaneously arguing that divisive events a decade ago were in part to blame for Labour's current predicament.

The partial results of leaked focus groups produced skewed analysis around a narrow range of issues because, as critic John Prescott saw it: 'a political agenda can be pursued through the kind of answers you get in a poll which are reflecting the way a question is put'.[54] Others noted the absence of any significant commentary on Neil Kinnock's role given his perceived unpopularity and past 'inconsistency over positions'.[55] No sustained discussion of the leader's performance featured in Gould Mattinson Associates' research for the *Southern Discomfort* study despite several participants having voluntarily mentioned Kinnock in response to a query about their attitudes towards the party.[56] By contrast there was extended commentary on other aspects of the qualitative findings notably on the unions and this, together with almost uniform interpretations of the leaked research, hindered alternative understandings of voter opinion. Most commentators failed to note that each successive instalment of focus group findings had in fact added comparatively little and that the only novelty was provided by the sensationalism and degree of 'spin' in the reporting of evidence.[57] As Labour spin doctor Charlie Whelan later admitted the nature of this kind of research enabled Alistair Campbell and himself to invent findings in an attempt to further undermine John Major's premiership.[58]

Aside from the skewed representation in the coverage of what were already selective 'leaked' findings, the inherent limitations of the methods and results were not acknowledged in much of Labour's focus group based debate. This did not stop discussions becoming saturated and distorted by choice quotes originating from qualitative studies with little or no reference to quantitative based research material. This contributed to the simplification of findings for media consumption which, combined with journalistic licence, helped to obscure more complex social and political realities.[59] Such reports also neglected the generalisability of the findings as well as the psychological dynamics inherent within the artifice of a focus group consisting of strangers brought together because of their similar background. Both *Southern Discomfort* and the leaked party research involved a narrow sample of Labour inclined but ultimately Conservative voters living in marginal seats who shared a need to justify and post-rationalise their decision to change allegiance during the 1992 election.[60] This reflected a tendency of market research methods to privilege the worries and aspirations of the individual as consumer. By contrast other contemporaneous qualitative research pointed to the continuing importance of collective identities including race.[61] Cumulatively Labour's qualitative based studies reinforced support for the contentious psephological thesis that the party's primary deficiency was its failure to convince 'aspirational' southern English skilled and routine white-collar workers rather than a wider cross-section of the public. Furthermore, although the *Southern Discomfort* study acknowledged the popularity of the *Sun* among its subjects, it failed to recognise that of the five constituencies featured two represented the paper's third and seventh highest readerships out of more than 650 seats nationwide.[62] It is interesting to speculate whether this subconscious absorption of tabloid influenced research may have had some consequences for Labour's subsequent political trajectory; certainly it did little to discourage it.

Perhaps most critically of all the commentary reported from the various focus group studies associated with Labour followed a pattern established before and during the Policy Review in that it was overwhelmingly negative about the party. This animosity was interpreted as being exclusively aimed at Labour rather than, as other researchers found, at a wider (and widely mistrusted) political elite that included a soon to be discredited Conservative government.[63] Yet the undermining of the party's own public image was endorsed by those responsible for commissioning, conducting and analysing the focus groups studies. The existence of such a strong moderator bias can be seen as a manifestation of the leadership's own loss of self-confidence whilst their deployment of 'scientific' methods in pursuit of change neglected adequate consideration of the representativeness, generalisability and validity of such qualitative based research findings.[64]

Marginalising the 'Traditionalists'

Partial reports of focus group research findings continued to influence the parameters of the debate over the party's future re-ignited by the Democrats' victory. Though they avoided using the term, those supportive of so-called 'Clintonisation' had a clear objective: 'The outbreak of public skirmishing over the relevance to Labour of Mr. Bill Clinton's US election victory is really coded debate about the extent to which the party must address the values and prejudices of the middle classes'. For John Prescott this was part of an ongoing 'battle for the soul of the Labour Party' underway against those 'obsessed with image rather than ideological conviction'.[65] The most thorough statement of the left position was contained in Peter Hain's pamphlet *What's Left* which contended the trade union movement was a defensible 'vested interest' and criticised the Labour new right's devotion to mass mediation at the expense of a Gramscian style political education programme designed to combat alienation. Hain further argued the consequence of such activities would result in the party's further detachment from its core working-class constituency and, by extension, the relationship these people and the democratic system. And to this end the Clinton victory was crucial in that, according to Clare Short, it was being used 'to get rid of our old values, be embarrassed about the unions, and don't talk about the poor'.[66]

The trade unions' potentially influential role in opposing Labour's new right had inspired the mediated attacks on them following the fourth defeat. Their legitimacy came under renewed scrutiny in the reporting of a special NEC Review Group convened to discuss the party union link over the summer. The committee's initially cautious suggestions were opposed by the new right and subsequently dismissed by *The Guardian* editorial as a 'shabby compromise' in favour of minority interests.[67] Debate intensified throughout 1993 and culminated in John Smith's proposed 'One Member, One Vote' (OMOV) for parliamentary candidate selections and leadership elections. OMOV would remove the collective right of union branches to participate in these contests. Smith together with unexpected support from the previously sceptical John Prescott forced change in what amounted to 'a symbolic assertion of the will of the party modernisers, directed at the electorate. Conducted in the rhetoric of democracy and modernisation, the debate maximised the apparent independence of the party from the unions.'[68] The narrow margin of victory was helped by the increased voting strength of individual Conference delegates not to mention the continuously anti-union agenda setting in those newspapers favoured by Labour members. The growing influence of the media over the party's internal affairs would be further demonstrated in an unexpected leadership contest.

The Blair succession

Following John Smith's death Tony Blair emerged as the frontrunner to be his successor. Blair's rise to prominence had begun under Neil Kinnock and was greatly helped by Communications Director

Peter Mandelson's deployment of him as a television spokesperson.[69] The importance of this work was noted in a sympathetic profile that acknowledged how unnamed Blair's critics portrayed him as 'a light-weight, just a creation of the Labour's marketing team'.[70] Yet such media recognition proved invaluable in establishing his leadership credentials. With mourning Labour politicians refusing to comment on the succession, Sarah Baxter of the *Evening Standard* filled the vacuum by becoming the first of many Westminster based journalists to make the case for 'the Labour politician the Tories fear most'.[71] BBC reporter Steve Richards detected signs of a heavy 'spin' in, as well as on, this and similar features: 'The reports of Blair heading for an easy win were obviously based on little more at that early stage than a desire by most newspaper editors and political correspondents for such an outcome'. Opinion polling evidence reinforced the perception that he was the prospective leader most likely to ensure a Labour victory at the next election.[72] The press amplified this message:

> The media made a massive contribution to giving Blair a headstart over his rivals... The official moratorium in declarations of candidatures left the field entirely free for the media, in which Blair immediately emerged as a clear favourite. The advantage Blair obtained from this early endorsement cannot be overstated; his cause had a virtually unstoppable momentum before nominations even opened. The apparent certainty of his victory attracted contributions from donors who regarded his leadership campaign as part of a wider campaign for a Labour general election victory.[73]

When the official race began, Blair, the new right candidate, could boast over half the parliamentary party as supporters and campaign contributions amounting to £88,000. His centre-left rivals Margaret Beckett and John Prescott received fewer endorsements and only collected £17,000 and £13,000 respectively.[74] The electoral college involving approximately 400 MPs and MEPs, a few hundred thousand party members and four million union and socialist society affiliates meant most participants would receive their information through the media rather than at party hustings. This further advantaged the early frontrunner and weakened potential rival Robin Cook who was dismissed as lacking telegenic, voter friendly qualities. Blair's 482 appearances in national newspaper reports during the crucial weeks prior to the official race also dwarfed the 182 of nearest rival Gordon Brown and discouraged the latter from standing.[75] The Blair campaign was organised by Jack Straw, Mo Mowlam and Peter Kilfoyle with discreet help from Peter Mandelson. Mandelson took the codename 'Bobby' to conceal his presence and deter the kind of speculation that might have damaged the candidate's image. Blair betrayed his psychological reliance on Bobby during the leadership campaign when he was filmed running away from a reporter's questions on an industrial dispute. Having taking advice from Mandelson on a mobile phone, Blair gave the journalist a diplomatically worded reply in order to ensure the potentially damaging footage was not aired.[76]

The leadership race was a model of restraint and good humour by previous standards which, given the tragic circumstances, was understandable. Consequently the press played a crucial role providing informed speculation and occasional controversy. In the ballot Blair gained approximately 57% of the vote, winning a majority in each of the three parts to the electoral college. Prescott became his deputy, unseating Beckett in a reversal of the result two years before. The individual member and affiliated trade unionist majorities for the winner demonstrated the extent to which the transformation of Labour under Kinnock was more than surface deep and was a further tangible legacy of the marketing driven Policy Review.[77] Blair's leadership was, however, founded upon a denial of this interpretation.

Relaunching the party (again): the Clause Four debate

Tony Blair's first major act as leader was to launch a debate over Clause Four. Previously he had avoided the issue and during the leadership campaign had argued:

> I don't think anyone actually wants the abolition of Clause Four to be the priority of the Labour Party at the moment. I don't think that anyone is saying now, in the run up to an election, that this is what we should focus on. The vast majority of the British people don't sit out there and debate the intricacies of the Labour Party constitution.[78]

Within three months of his election Blair changed his mind by claiming the Clause's promotion of a more equitable society through public ownership was irrelevant and anachronistic. In his first Conference address as leader, he declared 'Let us say what we mean and mean what we say' yet relied on press officers to brief journalists present that this meant he intended to re-write Clause Four.[79] If Blair's exhortation excited some media commentators it failed to move delegates two days later when a motion reaffirming Clause Four was passed by a narrow margin. *The Guardian* headlined with 'Vote for past defies leader' and reported how the leadership had 'airily dismissed' the defeat.[80] The next time the subject was debated at a national Labour event the agenda would be considerably more favourable to the leadership.

Many MPs including Tribune Group chair Janet Anderson backed the proposed change because there was a need to revise the organisational mission statement so as to 'market the Labour Party... with a clear message of what we stand for'.[81] Blair hoped a successful re-write would enhance his own status both within the party and without. In this he was helped by a considerable organisational effort, sympathetic media coverage, an unfocused opposition not to mention a clearly defined objective. Early Market Opinion and Research International (MORI) poll results in late January 1995 appeared to vindicate Blair's position and suggested floating voters might be more inclined to support Labour if Clause Four was re-written. This was, however, challenged by Gallup evidence two weeks later indicating 72% of voters surveyed had failed to recognise the Clause when shown it; interestingly 37% of the same sample endorsed the existing wording with 33% opposed and 28% undecided.[82] The result, whilst inconclusive, suggested public ownership could even offer Labour a profitable campaign theme as columnist Keith Waterhouse argued:

> What privatisation now means, in the public mind, is a license to print money to pay the bonanza and other jackpot benefits of chief executives. Privatisation is now private in the sense of hands off, keep out. And Tony Blair chooses this moment to tour the country persuading the brothers and sisters to ditch Clause Four. Some sense of timing.[83]

Most of the opinion research cited during the debate favoured the leadership's position. Giles Radice, aided by Stephen Pollard, had embarked on further focus group based analysis of key voter groups for the pamphlets *More Southern Discomfort?* and *Any Southern Comfort?* Both advocated the dropping of Clause Four.[84] Research commissioned by certain trade unions also reinforced the case for change by suggesting most members supported the proposed change.[85] Taken with the conflicting Gallup data from the *Daily Telegraph*, the figures suggest the survey question used was the determining factor.

Tony Blair, and his deputy John Prescott redrafted and presented the new Clause Four during March in anticipation of a specially called conference vote six weeks later. Their text made no mention of public ownership but included the phrase 'the enterprise of the market and rigour of competition'. By then 91 Constituency Labour Parties (CLPs) had declared their support for the existing Clause Four. The leadership responded by encouraging constituencies to ballots members and abandon the previously binding CLP Committee system of voting. Almost all of those who did this supported Blair.[86] The only union to hold a plebiscite was the Communications' Workers Union and it affirmed the change though, like the constituencies that balloted, did not formally choose between the new and old versions. Both *The Guardian* and *Daily Mirror* gave prominent coverage to the result. Other union executives conducted their consultation exercises through the usual constitutional devices of meetings and workplace liaisons. When Unison and the T&GWU, the two largest union affiliates, restated their commitment to the original wording, a *Daily Mirror* editorial denounced them as 'undemocratic'.[87] Similarly those Labour MEPs who declared their allegiance to Clause Four with a front-page advert in *The Guardian* on the day Blair came to address them in Strasbourg were labelled 'Stalinist' in an editorial the following day. Much was made of the leader's denunciation of those behind the advert as 'infantile incompetents'.[88] By contrast most Westminster MPs were overwhelmingly supportive of the re-write, if only because some feared what would happen should Blair fail.[89] The press contrived to help strengthen the leadership's case. Thus the Scottish party conference decision to support Blair made *The Guardian* front page and merited an editorial whereas the Greater London region's vote against change two weeks later received minimal coverage.[90] The final decision lay with a special party meeting in April 1995 that voted in favour of the new version by 66% to 34%. The leadership's management of the debate combined with a sympathetic agenda setting press had been central to an outcome that greatly benefited and reinforced Blair's position. This highly controlled approach to political communication would come to dominate the leadership's approach to campaigning and, eventually, government.

8
Brand 'New' Labour?

Renewing the 'Project'

Tony Blair's rebranding of his party began with his proposed rewriting of Clause Four and the launch of 'new' Labour at the 1994 Annual Conference. Thus was a diverse, complex past simultaneously and erroneously dismissed as 'old'. Blair's casual ahistoricism did not prevent the revised name gaining wide currency. Yet the concept, like the scale of change, was not that novel.[1] In 1989 MP Giles Radice had written about the 'new Labour party' in defending the Kinnock reform strategy whilst Shadow Communications Agency (SCA) co-ordinator Philip Gould had used the term in a private memo. Dennis Kavanagh usefully summarised the thrust of this analysis:

> Perhaps the key distinction is less between left and right than between the 'old' and 'new' Labour Party. 'Old' Labour is associated – negatively for much of the public – with manufacturing industry, union power, inner cities, council housing and in general with the declining forces in Britain. It is on the new issues, such as the environment, training, citizenship and women's rights – as well as public services – which centre left parties elsewhere have scored.[2]

Blair revelled in claiming that, under his leadership, Labour was 'literally a new party' and took this message to one of the party's fiercest critics, Rupert Murdoch, at a 1995 conference hosted by the media owner.[3] Like the Murdoch newspapers' subsequent support for Labour, the use of 'new' might be better understood as a cosmetic exercise in re-branding in that rhetorical flourishes overshadowed the significant continuities of personnel, substance and approach between Kinnock and his successor.[4] Blair's highly image-conscious strategy led critics like Roy Hattersley to question whether Labour was now 'less of a moral crusade and more a marketing exercise'. Leadership supporters were sensitive to the charge and felt obliged to challenge this increasingly widespread perception. One MP argued 'New Labour is not a neat marketing ploy but an accurate description of a party reborn'.[5] Yet arguably the reverse was the case in that Blair's re-branding 'ploy' was based upon the substantial changes already brought about by the market research driven Policy Review process.

If any party had significantly changed since 1992 it was the Conservatives who, in the aftermath of the Black Wednesday debacle, had suffered major internal recriminations and a significant loss of public support. Consequently Blair inherited the leadership with Labour in an almost unprecedented position of strength. To retain this advantage and maintain momentum, the hierarchy followed up the revision of Clause Four with a series of announcements designed to show how Labour had, in the words of the new mission statement, embraced 'the rigour of the market'. Blair's aim was to divest the party of its supposed 'tax and spend' image, downplay the importance of ideology and castigate the failings of both 'old left' and 'new right'.[6] The Mais speech keynote in 1995 and Singapore the following year underlined the leader's enthusiasm for the free market and private sector. Labour also promoted a 'new' politics encompassing themes such as 'stakeholding', 'partnership with the people', 'young country', 'rights and responsibilities' and the once liberal Conservative concept of the 'one nation society'.[7] The claim for novelty obscured a more familiar motivating factor as Freeden noted: 'ideologies are recurrent action-oriented patterns of political argument, and it can be empirically demonstrated that New Labour is definitely endowed with these'.[8]

Labour's re-branding exercise invoked the works of 'gurus' such as philosopher John MacMurray, social theorist Amitai Etzioni and sociologist Anthony Giddens.[9] Etzioni's communitarianism had inspired Blair's populist soundbite, 'tough on crime and tough on the causes of crime', and Shadow Home Secretary Jack Straw's declaration that the party would favour 'zero tolerance' policing to combat anti-social behaviour. These and comments on two parent 'family values' brought unprecedented praise from right-wing opinion formers such as the *Daily Mail*. Similarly a row over Blair's eldest child's grant maintained schooling saw him promoted as a dedicated father and advocate of the type of parental choice opposed by his overwhelmingly pro-comprehensive party. This and other controversies reinforced a growing perception that Labour had an 'obsession' with 'Middle England and marketing'.[10] Blair did little to discourage this view by praising Giles Radice's *Southern Discomfort* work for 'turning the attention of the party towards lost voters in the South' and by speaking about how meeting a 'bloke' washing a car during the 1992 campaign convinced him that the election was lost. Labour's failure to convince this 'Sierra Man' was, he argued, symptomatic of its image problem. MP Judith Church took this message somewhat literally and argued the party should target the owners of BMWs with long driveways.[11] The irony of Labour increasingly courting the middle-class whilst the Conservatives simultaneously attempted to cultivate manual workers was not lost on some.[12] For critics the consequences of such activities were far reaching: 'Labour's days as the political wing of a broad based social movement, seeking to educate public opinion and to lead a popular drive for social transformation, were clearly over'.[13] The result was not so much a 'new' but, as was noted in the previous chapter, a 'new right' Labour shrouded in an attendant discourse of modernity and renewal but espousing authoritarian populism and an accommodation with neo-liberalism.[14]

Tony Blair's election as leader led to the reformation of the strategic community that had served Neil Kinnock. Peter Mandelson resumed his position of influence having been a marginal figure under John Smith: his designation as civil service spokesperson did not stop critics calling him the party's real deputy leader.[15] Former colleague Bryan Gould identified Mandelson as the leading conspirator in 'the project', a term used by Kinnock and subsequently adopted by his successors.[16] Another of those intimately involved in this process was Philip Gould, now reappointed to supervise the party's opinion research. He quickly re-established himself as a key adviser and underlined his perceived importance when one of his leaked memos overshadowed the 1995 Trades Union Congress (TUC) conference proceedings.[17] In the document, 'The Unfinished Revolution', he argued for a more transparent command structure because the party was 'unfit to govern' and lacked 'a political project that matches the Thatcher agenda of 1979'. Gould even adopted a Conservative slogan from that campaign in writing of 'Labour's Right Approach'. Most commentators failed to acknowledge that the proposed solution of giving the leader untrammelled powers had already been delivered through the Kinnock leadership's undermining of National Executive independence.

Press Secretary Alastair Campbell was one of Blair's most prominent appointments. The former *Mirror* and *Today* political correspondent worked to establish relations with a largely hostile 'Tory press' by exploiting their disillusionment with the government. Campbell assiduously courted Rupert Murdoch's best selling *Sun* and *News of the World* with exclusive articles by Blair and others. Party spin-doctors also attended to the broadcast media. Famously, when the live culmination of OJ Simpson's trial threatened to overshadow Blair's 1996 conference address, Campbell urged Independent Television News (ITN) and BBC news to lead with the speech.[18] The Corporation's 6pm bulletin did as their rivals simultaneously broadcast Simpson's dramatic acquittal. Blair's other key recruit was new chief of staff Jonathan Powell, a Washington based diplomat whose main link to Labour was his brother and former SCA chair Chris.[19] Elsewhere David Miliband was appointed to oversee policy development whilst Blair's long serving secretary Anji Hunter continued to run his private office. Former head of Labour campaigns Sally Morgan joined the leader's staff to take charge of party liaison. Blair's allies and those prepared to acquiesce to him dominated the parliamentary frontbench. Shadow Chancellor Gordon Brown's entourage included adviser Ed Balls and spin-doctor Charlie Whelan. The previously outspoken John Prescott became more guarded on becoming Blair's deputy and many of those who served under Kinnock and Smith retained their places if not their portfolios.

Blair's control over Labour enabled him to concentrate on building dialogues with those outside the party. He made clear his sympathy for the defectors who had joined the Social Democrats during the 1980s and sought advice from ex-Social Democratic Party (SDP) leader Roy Jenkins and theoretician David Marquand. Marquand and assorted former Social Democrats joined or rejoined Labour. Three of these recruits, Andrew Adonis, Derek Scott and Roger Liddle, became Blair advisers in the leader's office and the latter co-authored a guide to 'new' Labour thinking with his friend Peter Mandelson.[20] In 1995 Conservative MP and former Thatcherite minister Alan Howarth became the most surprising convert and further underlined the government's unpopularity not to mention the Labour leadership's desire to reach out to disillusioned Tories. Blair also cultivated the private sector by consulting with pro-Labour businesspeople like Chris Haskins and Swarj Paul and newer corporate allies like Body Shop owner Anita Roddick, Barclays Bank chief executive Martin Taylor and David Sainsbury of the supermarket chain. Labour set up a unit to raise money from wealthy supporters and this helped bring in £2 million by 1996. Some contributions were held in so-called 'blind' trusts whereby secret donors could support Blair's burgeoning office costs in the belief that anonymity would protect Labour from accusations of sleaze. Others including £1 million benefactor Matthew Harding made public gifts or attended one of the many £500 a head fundraising dinners.[21] The growing links between Labour and the corporate sector led to Shadow ministers and party officials taking classes on administration and organisational change at Oxford University's Templeton College and Cranfield School of Management. Tom Sawyer, the veteran National Executive Committee (NEC) member who took over as General Secretary from Larry Whitty in 1995, was a keen advocate of such training.[22] Sawyer led an experienced permanent staff that included Election Co-ordinator Margaret McDonagh and Chief Party Spokesperson David Hill. In 1995 BBC correspondent Joy Johnson was appointed Director of Communications but, like John Underwood four years before, found her position undermined and subsequently resigned. Campbell and Mandelson took over Johnson's functions and extended their already considerable influence.[23]

The 'Millbank Tendency'

During the mid-1990s the leadership physically relocated the party to Westminster having first downgraded and then abandoned the former headquarters in Walworth Road. In 1980 James Callaghan had welcomed the then new South London location because it placed Labour directly among its 'own' people. The next premises could not have been more different and occupied two floors of Millbank Tower, an office block close to Parliament. The party had originally rented space there for campaigning purposes following recommendations in a management consultants' report.[24] Prior to the general election £2 million was spent on refurbishment and the creation of a new purpose built media centre. The resulting corporate style headquarters soon became a symbol of change and controversy with critics lamenting the emergence of a so-called 'Millbank Tendency' of powerful, unaccountable advisers based around Blair.[25] The premises formed the hub of a permanent campaign from where Peter Mandelson chaired the General Election Planning Group and played a role similar to that of the Conservative Chairman. Mandelson reportedly talked of 'my Millbank' and, together with Blair and Gordon Brown, oversaw a team of several hundred officials organised in interlocking teams.[26] Alastair Campbell's news management team were greatly aided by a massive so-called Excalibur database of searchable information which helped them quickly rebut opponents' claims. Margaret McDonagh managed the 'key seats' strategy that focused efforts on the 90 marginal constituencies the party needed to take office.[27] When some of these fell vacant in by-elections it gave the leadership an opportunity to campaign as 'new' Labour. 1994 saw the party comfortably win the highly marginal Dudley West. The following year Labour fought a more controversial campaign in the Littleborough and Saddleworth by-election. Peter Mandelson's strategy demonstrated the party's authoritarian rhetoric on crime by accusing the Liberal Democrats candidate of being 'soft' on drugs. The campaign proved a defining moment for Blair as some began to seriously question Labour's direction. Centre-left MP Richard Burden crystallised this unease by attacking the party's populist stance. Blair dismissed this and other dissent by claiming his critics were either 'in need of therapy' or prejudiced by an anti-leadership 'betrayal thesis'.[28]

The Labour leadership recognised the party's union affiliates formed a more serious threat to their project than an alliance of discontented MPs and members. In 1995 the combined votes of Unison and the Transport and General Workers' Union (T&GWU) had prevented a landslide majority for the new Clause Four. A subsequent press report featuring unnamed party spokespeople accused T&G General Secretary Bill Morris of being 'confused, muddled and pusillanimous'. Unsurprisingly the Labour hierarchy supported ally Jack Dromey's failed challenge for Morris' job.[29] More widely the leadership were willing to take affiliates' money whilst denying them influence, a stance positively endorsed by Clinton pollster turned Labour consultant Stan Greenberg who advised of the need 'to reassure... voters again and again by visibly restraining the influence of the unions'.[30] The party routinely disassociated itself from industrial action and favoured new working partnerships between workers and employers. Tension mounted during the 1996 TUC conference following trade spokesperson Stephen Byers' suggestion that Blair intended to sever the union link through a membership referendum. In the event a vote did not take place and affiliate representatives continued to sit on the National Executive. However as this body's importance waned so did the unions' influence.[31] Their diminished status was symbolically reflected during the controversial selection of Swindon North's candidate. Despite widespread allegations of malpractice the NEC refused to overturn the victory of a London based television producer over a local branch convenor.[32] By contrast the Executive willingly intervened, on ideological grounds, to remove left-winger Liz Davies as Leeds North East's candidate in 1995. Her treatment contravened the long honoured Mikardo Doctrine which held that selections could only be challenged for procedural reasons.[33] Davies was evidently not Peter Mandelson's 'ideal' prospective MP:

> This model candidate is sort of youngish, about 40 years old, more women than ever before, very articulate, passionate about education, very strong in commitment to family life and values, and very tough indeed on law and order. In other words our model candidates fighting for new Labour in this election are exactly the same as those target voters whom our message is directed at.[34]

The leadership's efforts to control entry to the Parliamentary Labour Party (PLP) were matched by a desire to exert greater influence over its existing membership. Significantly Blair gained the right to select the Chief Whip and appointed Donald Dewar who introduced a more rigid disciplinary code for MPs.[35]

The increasing role of external media in party affairs meant several policy entrepreneurs were able to exert greater influence. This was especially true of the two major Labour think tanks, the Fabian Society and Institute of Public Policy Research (IPPR). These were joined by newer groupings like Demos, the publicity conscious organisation that helped popularise communitarianism. Reflecting on these entrepreneurs' role, Gerald Holtham, the IPPR's outgoing Director, argued many of those now working for think tanks were 'concerned less with concrete policy' and preferred 'social description and brand creation'.[36] Among the other media aware organisations linked to the party that flourished during the 1990s were Emily's List, a forum launched by Labour image consultant Barbara Follett to support prospective women candidates, and the Labour Finance and Industry Group set up to facilitate contact between business and political elites. Factions also became increasingly image conscious and determined to communicate their case through the media, the most high profile being Progress and the Labour Co-ordinating Committee on the right and the centre-left Labour Reform.

The entrepreneurial groups and factions' activities mimicked, of course, the central party's approach. Millbank continued to demonstrate its belief in highly orchestrated media events with the Road to the Manifesto campaign of 1996. This process, designed to allow members a say on Labour's draft manifesto, followed a party decision to sanction the kind of policy related referenda used during the Clause Four debate. The fact that the Road to the Manifesto document could only be accepted or rejected but not amended curtailed meaningful deliberation over a programme primarily designed to appeal to floating voters. On a 61% turnout, 95% supported the draft in an affirmative vote that was promoted as a demonstration of party unity. Leadership supporters applauded the new 'democratic and inclusive' procedures in condemning the previous 'Soviet' style representative system.[37] Yet the hollow populism and illusory accountability of the process provided further demonstration of the leadership entourage's power as well as their preparedness to draw inspiration from unlikely role models such as US Republican Newt Gingrich's 1994 'Contract with America'. Shadow Cabinet minister Clare Short made this point in a rare and candid interview: 'I think the obsession with the media and the focus groups is making us look as if we want power at any price and that we don't stand for anything'. Short blamed this on unnamed leadership aides whom she memorably characterised 'the people who live in the dark'. Yet the party's commitment to such methods was substantial, ongoing and came directly from the top as Blair himself admitted when he willingly endorsed Bill Clinton's observation: 'There is no one more powerful today than a member of a focus group. If you really want to change things and you want to get listened to, that's the place to be'.[38]

The 'War Room' and 'War Book': the 1997 general election

The 1997 election was fought in a climate that greatly favoured Labour. The Conservatives had lost their reputation for economic competence and their discipline following divisions over European integration and sleaze. In 1995 Cabinet minister John Redwood challenged Major for the leadership running on the slogan 'No Change, No Chance'. Many voters and journalists appeared to agree and, shortly after the election was called, the *Sun* announced 'We Back Blair'.[39] Labour's cultivation of Rupert Murdoch had evidently worked. Millbank maximised the government's discomfort, its spin-doctors' growing confidence reflected in the way they questioned the judgement of respected reporters like BBC correspondent Nick Jones and his brother George of the *Daily Telegraph*. Behaviour of this kind intensified journalistic interest in what had previously been a largely private activity to the extent that Labour's medium became part of its message.[40] The party's professionalism was further underlined by the Millbank organisation and its £15 million campaign budget. Gordon Brown and Peter Mandelson continue to supervise a large staff of press,

IT and policy specialists. The entire team worked in a central 'war room' comprising an open plan office designed to facilitate interpersonal communication.[41] Agreed strategic themes were included in a grid covering the weeks before and during the formal campaign. Boase Massimi Pollitt (BMP) DDB became the first agency to officially advise the party in a general election since 1983. BMP's publicised role reflected the changed party culture not to mention the cache now attached to the contract. That said the firm's team had only 'subordinate status' at headquarters despite being headed by SCA veteran Chris Powell.[42] Strategy was informed by National Opinion Polls (NOP) polling data and some 300 focus groups conducted by Philip Gould before the campaign. According to former Mandelson aide Derek Draper, Blair would 'pore over' this material in order to help him determine what Labour should do. Following the announcement of the election 70 more focus groups were conducted. Bill Clinton's consultant Stan Greenberg supported Gould's work although strict security at Millbank meant most journalists were unaware of his presence there.[43]

Opinion feedback underpinned the campaign plan contained in the party's so-called 'war book'. Identified 'swing voters' included 'mortgage holders, younger, higher incomes' and reflected the guiding strategic assumption that the party should focus its greatest efforts on appealing to the middle-class and those aspiring to join it.[44] The report selected other target groups such as women, people nervous about change or less likely to vote. The plan suggested campaign themes and issues designed to contrast Labour with the Conservatives including leadership, attractive policies and 'something for all people'. Five manifesto commitments, chosen to project the party's message, appeared on a pledge card devised by aide Peter Hyman and widely distributed throughout the election.[45] The specific promises involved punishing young offenders, guaranteeing to not raise direct taxes, and reducing class sizes, youth unemployment and NHS waiting lists. Labour spokespeople stayed 'on message' by reciting the pledges with formulaic regularity. This behaviour bored journalists but strategists reasoned that repetition was the best means of communicating to a heterogeneous electorate.

Party advertising reflected the war book's concern with promoting Labour as changed, trustworthy, economically responsible, future oriented, 'for the many not the few' and a vote for 'enough is enough'. Other copy highlighted Tory weaknesses, counter attacked or reiterated the pledges. Popular slogans included 'Britain Deserves Better' and 'Same Old Lies'. A memorable final Party Election Broadcast (PEB) featured actor Pete Postlethwaite as an angel lamenting the Conservatives' record.[46] The adoption of D:Ream's 'Things Can Only Get Better' as the campaign theme helped build the momentum. The song, a special video aimed at first time voters and 'Now Wash Your Hands of the Tories' club and pub toilet stickers attempted to connect with the young. Similarly so-called '*Daily Mail*' or 'Worcester' women were targeted with copy in publications such as *Chat*, *Take A Break* and *Woman* and Asian voters with broadcast adverts on the Zee TV station.[47] Predictably Gould's war book highlighted Tony Blair's 'young', 'strong' and 'dynamic' character and he featured in campaign publicity and an innovative PEB made by Molly Dineen. Dineen, famous for profiles of subjects like singer Geri Halliwell, produced the 10-minute film from hours of 'fly on the wall' footage and portrayed her subject as a dynamic leader, concerned parent and 'bloke'. Prior to the election the Conservatives had attracted considerable attention by depicting Labour's leader with sinister 'demon eyes' but most commentators believed Blair was an electoral asset. Some eulogised him and journalist friend Martin Kettle made the dubious assertion that Labour might not have won under John Smith.[48] American observer Joe Klein briefly challenged the prevailing consensus by comparing Blair's synthetic qualities to those of Bill Clinton and noting the similarity between both politicians' vacuous rhetoric celebrating 'the weary trinity of opportunity, responsibility and community'.[49]

Philip Gould further isolated the economy and patriotism as particular Conservative strengths and both subsequently featured in Central Office copy produced by the Saatchi brothers. They were, however, unable to capitalise on the first and found it awkward to exploit the latter because of their own divisions over Europe. Blair counter attacked by promising to defend the national interest in Europe and Mandelson promoted Labour's patriotism by using the ultimate symbol of Britishness, a bulldog called 'Fitz', in a PEB. Another PEB promoted Labour's economic competence and featured corporate supporters lauding Gordon Brown's financial acumen. Brown even indicated support for further privatisations and thus underlined the leadership's pro-market credentials. Most significantly Blair's photograph and signature appeared in a final week poster promising not to increase direct taxes. The leadership's rhetorical emphasis on 'new' Labour helped offset other alleged weaknesses identified in Philip Gould's report including public distrust of the 'hidden left', 'unions' and 'inexperience'. Blair attempted to counter these perceptions and the Conservative's 'New Labour, New Danger' slogan by pledging in the *Daily Mail* to keep the 'most restrictive' labour laws in the western world. 'Everything' was carefully 'market-tested for conformity with the prejudices of swing voters in target marginals'.[50]

The 1997 general election rewrote the record books in terms of the vote swing and seats gained. Labour won many constituencies where it had been in third place during the 1980s and assorted media pundits attributed this victory to the party's cultivation of Middle England. Understandably party strategists claimed their efforts had made the difference because, in Peter Mandelson's view, they formed 'the finest, most professional campaigning machine that Labour has ever created'.[51] Academic commentators were more circumspect about the Millbank 'myth' and noted how the relatively poor turnout and electoral system had contributed to the landslide. Compelling evidence indicated the outcome had ultimately been determined by the ERM crisis in 1992 from which the Conservatives never fully recovered their reputation or unity.[52]

'On message' in office

Tony Blair's first public statement as Prime Minister underlined his determination to continue with the marketing driven strategy that had helped him to office: 'we were elected as New Labour and we will govern as New Labour'. His government's preoccupation with image had already been demonstrated that morning by the carefully choreographed welcome from party workers in T-shirts emblazoned with the slogan 'Britain Just Got Better' that had greeted Blair on his arrival in Downing Street.[53] This controlled piece of public relations underlined the Labour leadership's continuing desire to influence the media agenda and stay 'on message'. This had of course been a priority since the Policy Review and it was no coincidence that those holding the key positions of responsibility were nearly all graduates of the 'strategic community' that had sustained the process. They included Blair and Gordon Brown, both of whom had joined the Shadow Cabinet during the Review, and others who had come to prominence in the course of it including Jack Straw, Mo Mowlam and Harriet Harman. Many of Neil Kinnock's main advisers from that era also enjoyed influence, most obviously Peter Mandelson whose non-Cabinet Minister without Portfolio title belied his more powerful role. The two other key Kinnock aides, newly elected MPs Charles Clarke and Patricia Hewitt, both enjoyed meteoric rises in government before joining the Cabinet. Similarly other Review veterans took major strategic roles within the

Blair leadership: Philip Gould continued his work as polling consultant as did Tom Sawyer as party General Secretary. Alastair Campbell took over the Downing Street communications' operation from where he consolidated the basis of the 'public relations state'.[54]

The public relations state

Alastair Campbell initiated a review of operations on becoming the Prime Minister's Press Secretary that culminated in the Mountfield report and an enhanced role for those responsible for promoting and protecting the government in a competitive 24-hour news media environment. Symbolic of the changes was the Government Information Service's renaming as the more proactive sounding Government Information and Communication Service. At the apex of the Service a new Strategic Communications Unit was established by No. 10 Downing Street in 1998 to co-ordinate publicity and news management activities across Whitehall and the various Departments of State.[55] The work of the SCU was itself strengthened and complimented by the setting up of other new units like those for Media Monitoring and Research & Information. This together with a greatly enlarged number of ministerial special advisers helped Campbell promote the value of maintaining good internal and external channels of communication. Blair underlined his belief in the importance of 'joined up government' by making Peter Mandelson responsible for co-ordinating and directing the flow of information between different ministries. It was not long before the work of Mandelson, Campbell and other 'spin doctors' began to attract criticism from the same media they hoped to influence as some journalists began to complain about being misled, bullied or ignored.

The influence of the Prime Minister's Press Secretary within government was such that ministers were expected to clear key speeches and co-ordinate major announcements through his Downing Street office. Where conflicts did arise, such as in a 1998 stand off between Social Security Secretary Harriet Harman and her deputy Frank Field, Campbell reprimanded the pair for conducting their row through the media. It was early demonstration of the power that favoured appointees now wielded over elected politicians. Later a then disgruntled ex-minister Field attacked such spin-doctoring aides and their methods as a 'cancer at the heart of government'.[56] Nonetheless secretive off the record briefings and leaks to favoured journalists from unnamed sources continued to be a prominent feature in the reporting of government. The furtive media interest in these stories contrasted with the coverage of a House of Commons dominated by a largely loyal, even obsequious PLP.[57] Allied to this the government's own practice of making announcements outside of the chamber further marginalised Parliament and provoked a rebuke from Speaker Betty Boothroyd within a year of the election. The difficulty in holding this government to account was highlighted by the Select Committee on Public Administration's investigation into the GICS when, despite the opposition MPs' searching questioning, the Labour dominated body's final report was largely uncritical: the inquiry into spin had been spun.[58]

The culture of spin established itself as a recurrent feature in the reporting of the government. This was hardly surprising when, within months of the election, Cabinet member David Clark was complaining about being undermined by off the record briefings.[59] More high profile victims included Mo Mowlam, one of the most popular Labour politicians, who unnamed sources suggested was not quite up to her ministerial job. This provoked a scathing attack on spin-doctors by novelist and party supporter Ken Follett who accused Blair of condoning these 'rent boys' of politics.[60] The potentially destabilising consequences of secretive briefings was most acutely felt when another undisclosed aide accused Gordon Brown of having 'psychologically flaws'.[61] Nor was Brown's by then Cabinet rival Peter Mandelson spared from criticism, particularly when his career ran into difficulties and the many journalists previously subjected to his abrasive style of media relations keenly followed up accusations of ministerial impropriety and contributed to his two resignations from Cabinet office. The furore surrounding Mandelson's first downfall also led to the resignation of Chancellor's press secretary, Charlie Whelan, when it was suggested that he had been briefing against the Trade Secretary. Symptomatic of media obsession with spin was the way Whelan's departure received more coverage than the launch of the Euro during the same week.[62]

Predictably Tony Blair's opponents attempted to exploit the recurrent controversies surrounding its spin-doctors. In his 2000 conference speech Conservative leader William Hague likened Labour's immersion in 'spin' to the 'sleaze' that had undermined his own party's credibility.[63] Though Hague did not reap any discernible benefits from his attack, the government continued to suffer from its image as a body obsessed with controlling the media agenda. Alastair Campbell's high profile role resulted in more journalistic coverage than most Cabinet members and a biographical account that labelled him 'the real deputy prime minister'. Controversy about Campbell's supposedly manipulative activities resulted in lobby comments becoming attributable to him and his eventual re-designation as the less publicly interventionist Director of Communications and Strategy.[64] The change in Campbell's role did not stop critics from continuing to complain about the unprecedented increases in the numbers of ministerial special advisers and other partisan appointees responsible for promoting policy. Some feared these aides' robust involvement in all aspects of Whitehall business challenged the traditional impartiality and role of the civil service. The government consistently denied this but the swift departure of 25 heads of information following the 1997 election suggested otherwise and reinforced a perception that the greatly increasing numbers of special advisers cum spin-doctors were politically indispensable, able to act with impunity and in a position to bully neutral civil servants into undertaking partisan tasks.[65] These changes reflected the centralising tendency of the Blair leadership, an instinct demonstrated in opposition and now translated into the running of a 'Bonapartist' style government.[66]

The people's prime minister

The Labour government's aggressive public relations underlined its preoccupation with engineering consent for its policies although Blair took care to promote the message that his ministers would be 'servants of the people'. An obvious manifestation of this 'corporate populism' was the publication of an annual company style report.[67] Blair also made strategic appearances in less formally political programmes outside of election time including GMTV, This Morning, Des O'Connor Tonight and Jimmy Young's Radio 2 show and invited high profile celebrities to receptions at Downing Street. These formats underscored Blair's desire to communicate with a wider range of voters and demonstrated his awareness of popular culture and sentiment. For supporter and media entrepreneur Waheed Ali this kind of promotional activity was essential because 'new' Labour was a brand like Nike and, like the latter, 'we're selling a lifestyle, we're selling an image'.[68] Blair's presentational strategy both responded to and encouraged an increasingly emotionalised public discourse and, in the most memorable intervention of this kind, he paid tribute to Diana Spencer as the 'people's princess'. The use of this type of 'contrived spontaneity' and rhetorical device became a marked feature of his governing style; former Cabinet colleague Clare Short has gone as far to suggest that Blair 'thinks in soundbites'.[69] The Prime Minister's relatively youthful image was reinforced by occasional references to his three school age children and the birth of baby son Leo. Media interest in the family led to the appointment of Alastair Campbell's partner Fiona Millar to handle public relations on behalf of the Prime Minister's wife Cherie Booth.

Campbell and Labour's robust news management techniques continued on taking office. The new government's abrasive approach to broadcasters was demonstrated early on following a bruising encounter between Radio 4's John Humphrys and Harriet Harman over the controversial withdrawal of single parent benefits in December 1997. Humphry's questioning of the Social Security Secretary led to a highly public confrontation between Downing Street and the BBC over the editorial line being pursued by the Corporation's flagship news programme. This tension subsequently manifested itself in a variety of ways over the course of the parliament. In contrast to their robust treatment of public service broadcasters, government spin-doctors were more considered in their dealings with the privately owned and partisan national press. The Strategic Communications Unit cultivated several titles with articles under the Prime Minister's by-line: so numerous were these articles that Blair was named freelance of the year in 1999. Selected papers were also the beneficiaries of exclusives courtesy of privileged information from within Downing Street.[70] This formed a key dimension to the Labour leader's 'big tent' strategy of maintaining a dialogue with opinion formers on the right of the political spectrum. Those involved included high profile social commentators such as Chief Inspector of Schools Chris Woodhead, columnist Paul Johnson and others associated with the *Daily Mail* and the various publications owned by Rupert Murdoch. These relationships publicly cooled following Blair's attack on the 'forces of conservatism' in 1999 though a leaked memo written by him the following year showed a remarkable synergy between his concerns over the family, crime and asylum and those of a published editorial in the Daily Mail of the same date.[71]

The *Sun*, Murdoch's best selling daily, was particularly indulged by government yet it did not prevent the paper from making a front page denunciation of the Prime Minister as 'The Most Dangerous Man in Britain' over his pro-Euro commitments at an EU summit in 1998.[72] More humiliatingly the paper published a handwritten letter from Blair following its attack on his alleged mishandling of crime, asylum and the NHS two years later. Shortly afterwards Blair's continuing desire to reassure 'Middle England' led to further embarrassment when he was handclapped slowly by a section of the audience during his address to the Women's Institute. Ironically though only a small minority objected to this avowedly least ideological of Prime Minister's 'political' speech, the subsequent television footage and media reaction conveyed an impression of indecisive leadership. Tony Blair's largely emollient response to his right-wing detractors contrasted with the more combative rebukes given to critics in the party or writing for newspapers like *The Guardian* and *Mirror*.[73] Such behaviour was emblematic of a so-called Third Way philosophy that sought to transcend the dichotomy between old left and new right but revealed, at the very least, a rhetorical bias towards the latter and neo-liberal 'marketisation'. Symptomatic of this was the adoption of a framework to sustain public sector reform through the Private Finance Initiative and even privatisation, the implementation of which had raised the ire of the unions and given Blair 'scars on my back'. More generally the leadership's preoccupation with living down Labour's alleged 'tax and spend' image led to the promotion a 'prudent' economic strategy that made a virtue of being 'discreetly redistributive' through measures like the Working Families Tax Credit.[74]

In promoting the Third Way the Prime Minister welcomed the increased liberalisation of international trade, so-called globalisation, and associated developments including the technologically driven new economy. Yet Blair consciously avoided acknowledging the role of ideology and preferred to talk about his administration having pragmatic, managerialist motives devoted to finding out and implementing 'what works'.[75] On welfare reform this was interpreted quite literally with paid employment including 'workfare' schemes seen as the best means of providing citizens with a sense of 'opportunity, responsibility and community'. To this end the government made clear its intention to impose Tory originated benefits cuts on vulnerable social groups such as single mothers and the disabled. More widely Blair's key objectives were supported by a vocal range of policy entrepreneurs associated with the party and beneficiaries of corporate sponsorship including the Institute of Public Policy Research, Foreign Policy Centre, New Local Government Network, Demos and the Social Market Foundation. Think tanks were amongst those most supportive of Labour continuing the Conservative belief in intensifying business involvement in government through assorted public private partnerships. Critics were quick to suggest that most high profile manifestation of this policy, the Millennium Dome, was symptomatic of Blair's obsession with style rather than substance.[76]

The Dome became a huge media embarrassment for the government and, almost inevitably, it featured in the opinion research feedback presented to Blair. The Prime Minister's image as a polling obsessed politician became a journalistic truism.[77] It was more than a cliché and fostered by the existence of an intensive and largely secret programme of market research by which ministers were able to monitor public opinion through conventional polls as well as so-called citizen juries or 'people's panels'. Aside from the cost critics also complained that Labour's fixation with polling research privileged short-term tactical rather than longer-term strategic policy decisions and singled out the failure of ministers to take proactive measures to address Britain's transport problems.[78] Philip Gould continued to undertake focus group work for Blair and was, within weeks of victory, advising the prime minister that: 'Our bottom-line mandate is to govern as New Labour: responsible on the economy; strong in Europe; tough on unions. Failure with any of the above will automatically be considered betrayal'.[79] Gould was reportedly one of those who urged him to be resolute in demonstrating the government's populism by implementing the Tory inspired cuts to single parent benefits in 1997. Financially the measures were of greater symbolic than practical importance but were supported by Alastair Campbell who allegedly feared their abandonment would trigger a media backlash orchestrated by the *Sun*.[80] Gould's secretive role as an advisor was highlighted when several of his private memos to the Prime Minister were leaked to journalists with *The Times* and *Sun* and used by William Hague to attack Blair in parliament. It was somewhat ironic then that an editorial in the *Sun*, one of those media most feared by Labour strategists, should criticise Gould for a 'pessimism' derived in part from appeasing opinion-forming newspapers. In a revealing memo entitled 'Getting the Right Place in History and not the Wrong One', the adviser argued the 'new Labour brand has been badly contaminated', was out of touch with popular opinion and that there was 'no shared agreement about what is the new Labour project for government'.[81] The exposure and existence of such frank advice undermined and contradicted its counsel for strong, determined leadership. The perception of Blair as a vacillating, polling conscious politician had been reinforced by his actions (or rather inaction) and nowhere more so than in his failure to persuade a largely sceptical electorate about the merits of the Euro in advance of a referendum on British membership of it. Now it was confirmed in a stark warning from an adviser who told him his focus groups were indicating that 'He lacks conviction, he is all spin and presentation, he says things to please people, not because he believes them'.[82]

Gould's self-acknowledged populism was reflected in his preference for taking 'tough' rather than 'soft' positions and being 'pro-family' to guard against losing the support of the 'mainstream majority' and 'middle Britain' to the Conservatives because: 'People feel (the government) has put asylum seekers first, has put Europe first and has put minorities first'.[83] His analysis resembled that of Downing Street aide Peter Hyman and Dick Morris, the strategist responsible for popularising the strategic concept of 'triangulation' during his time working for Bill Clinton's re-election. Morris argued democracy was an increasingly 'continuous' rather than representative process in which candidates needed to disavow 'ideological constructs' and realign themselves with their principal (i.e. right-wing) opponents, particularly on issues where the rivals had a lead.[84] Unlike the Democratic candidate Labour was comfortably ahead in the polls but this did not diminish the leadership's preoccupation with cultivating Conservative inclined floating voters. The importance attached to this effort was reinforced by the recruitment of two disaffected Tory MPs during the parliament. By contrast Tony Blair was more complacent about sections of Labour's core support because, in his calculation, they had 'nowhere else to go'.[85] It was this sentiment that triggered minister Peter Kilfoyle's resignation in protest at government ambivalence towards the problems facing the working-class constituents in his 'heartlands' seat. Kilfoyle, a member of Blair's leadership election team, gave public vent to a concern shared by many on the centre-left. The Prime Minister's response was pithy: 'the whole country is our core constituency'.[86]

Party into powerlessness

Philip Gould's advocacy of opinion research was motivated by his distrust of 'progressive elitism' and a doubt as to whether the party's structures were able to appreciate public attitudes and values. Similarly Peter Mandelson endorsed a more responsive form of politics based on a civic dialogue through 'plebiscites, focus groups, citizens' movements, and the internet':

> It may be that that the era of pure representative democracy is coming slowly to an end. We entered the 20th century with a society of elites, with a very distinct class structure. In those days it seemed natural to delegate important decisions to members of the land-owning elite, the industrial elite or the educated elite. When Labour emerged as the party that represented the industrial working class, it developed its own elite of trade union bureaucrats, city bosses and socialist intellectuals. But the age has passed away. Today people want to be more involved. Tony Blair's government has already held

two referendums and three more are at some stage in prospect. This requires a different style of politics and we are trying to respond to these changes.[87]

Plebiscites had featured in the Clause Four and Road to the Manifesto but their subsequent absence from decision-making processes in the run up to the 2001 election merely underlined their limitation as a genuine means of consultation. Neither did the organisational reforms in the 1997 *Party into Power* document amount to 'A Framework for Partnership' as claimed. Rather the re-launched National Policy Forum worked alongside a Joint Policy Committee of Shadow Cabinet and National Executive members and primarily served to dilute the already limited role of the Annual Conference. The Forum's novel procedures and low media profile enabled the leadership to outmanoeuvre opponents and remove potentially divisive items from the agenda for discussion at the more public Conference. It also had limited input into a 2001 manifesto largely shaped by ministerial special advisers.[88] Like their PLP colleagues, dissenting Conference participants faced a formidable executive power in a series of stage-managed, convention style 'debates'. To ensure favoured outcomes the platform even took to deploying a misleadingly named 'Delegate Support Office'. This and other measures meant the leadership was only defeated once during the government's first term; and the sole lost vote on pensions policy only occurred following the extraordinary intervention of revered ex-Cabinet minister Barbara Castle.[89]

The *Party in Power* proposals rendered the National Executive a largely administrative forum although persistent questioning from the centre-left Grassroots' Alliance caucus provided the NEC with a source of debate. Nevertheless the body's loyalist majority persistently defended the government and oversaw the imposition of candidates on local and regional parties from the first parliamentary by-election in Uxbridge onwards. In so doing leadership supporters compromised their professed commitment to One Member One Vote by allowing block votes and panels to prevent the selection of popular left inclined politicians like Ken Livingstone, Rhodri Morgan, Dennis Canavan not to mention a whole swathe of the European Parliamentary Labour Party. By pursuing these ideological motivations Blair was doing something he often accused his internal opponents of doing, that is re-fighting the battles of the 1980s. Such 'control freakery' went against 'new' Labour branding and may have been forgotten but for the negative electoral repercussions and rejection of Blair's favoured candidates despite sustained leads for the party in the polls.[90] This kind of behaviour hardly endeared the leadership to the membership, a sizeable number of who began leaving the organisation.

The leadership's considerable resources, a quiescent National Executive and the ingrained bias of the revamped Forum system limited the unions' ability to mobilise dissent. Collectively these affiliates' strength lay in their power as lobbyists and donors and as such formed the only serious potential threat to the party's stifling centralism. The leadership met this challenge by reiterating their belief in offering the movement 'fairness not favours' whilst seeking alternative sources of funding from rich individuals and the corporate sector.[91] This was not without problems as Blair found when, early on in his premiership, he was forced to refund a million pound donation from Bernie Ecclestone, the Formula One owner whose business received a Downing Street sanctioned opt out from a newly enacted ban on tobacco sponsorship in sport. Government favouritism towards large corporate interests was further highlighted by Greg Palast's *Observer* investigation into the conspiratorial dealings between business lobbyists, former leadership advisers and a senior government aide.[92] This so-called 'lobbygate' scandal together with a range of subsequent measures designed to the private sector helped further alienate Blair's decreasing number of allies in the union movement. One of them, TUC leader John Monks, criticised the Prime Minister for treating his members like 'embarassing elderly relatives'. Remarks of this kind did not stop Blair from maintaining his distance from the unions and declaring he was 'absolutely proud' of millionaire donors like Christopher Ondaatje, Paul Hamlyn and David Sainsbury.[93] To this end Millbank maintained a high donor unit, organised expensive fundraising dinners and arranged various conference sponsorships including a controversial deal with Somerfield supermarkets for their name to appear on delegate passes. These relationships, not to mention the resources they generated, reinforced the perception of Labour as a brand. This impression was strongly supported by a range of promotions that included the markedly commercial style 1999 European PEBs and assorted merchandising and conference logos.

Apathetic landslide: the 2001 general election

The foot and mouth crisis ravaging the British countryside delayed a widely anticipated May election but did not noticeably affect Labour's public standing. Millbank's open plan 'war room' was again central to

Labour's campaign preparations and many of the 200 involved were veterans of the 1997 election. Chancellor Gordon Brown resumed command of the operation as Chair of Election Strategy and oversaw the compilation of another 'war book'. The twice-resigned Peter Mandelson was unable to continue in his intended campaign role and his duties were taken over by MP Douglas Alexander, a Brown ally and key strategist in the first post-devolution Scottish elections.[94] Alastair Campbell spent some of the campaign at headquarters working alongside his former Downing Street colleague turned party Director of Communications Lance Price. The party's news management operation was strengthened by the presence of Colin Byrne and David Hill, former press officers turned lobbyists. Their efforts were supported by the Rapid Rebuttal system managed by Spencer Livermore. Livermore's team was one of several taskforces with responsibility for a specific aspect of the campaign. Elsewhere in the 'war room' official Greg Cook, Philip Gould and Stan Greenberg monitored and analysed public opinion via polling and focus groups.[95]

Labour's manifesto 'Ambitions for Britain' was drawn up by aide Ed Richards and adopted the pledge device used in the 1997 election.[96] The five chosen policies highlighted the key party themes and main target audiences. A pledge to maintain sound public finances echoed the Clintonite mantra 'It's the Economy, Stupid' and promoted government prudence. This message was conveyed in a special business manifesto as part of an overall effort that evidently impressed corporate opinion formers in the media who applauded Blair for being a 'credible conservative' wedded to 'consolidating' Thatcher's legacy.[97] Three further pledges promised thousands of extra nurses, doctors, police officers and teachers were especially designed to appeal to public service dependent parents and were promoted by a women's magazine style publication *Your Family*. Somewhat controversially the manifesto linked these ambitious targets to a reform programme involving greater private sector involvement. The final promise to maintain a minimum wage and pensioners' winter fuel payments was the only pledge to explicitly address the more vulnerable. Some of the most telling criticism of this 'Middle England strategy' came from Labour sympathisers rather than the Conservatives.[98]

The Conservative campaign focused on attacking asylum seekers, taxation levels and the Euro.[99] This strategy was undermined by Labour's authoritarian rhetoric on immigration and exploitation of Tory confusion over their proposed spending cuts. By contrast Chancellor Brown resolutely confirmed there were no plans to increase direct taxes in spite of evidence suggesting voters were increasingly sympathetic to such a proposal to fund public service renewal.[100] Similarly Blair's renewed commitment to hold a referendum and 'not bounce' Britain into the Single Currency undermined Conservative leader William Hague's contention that the election offered voters their only opportunity to save the pound. Hague's tactical mistakes were compounded by his low ratings in public polls and private focus groups.[101] Unsurprisingly the more popular rival leaders featured heavily in their parties' campaign publicity. Blair also appeared on less political programmes like GMTV and talked about his son. This helped communicate his personality to an audience containing a sizeable number of target voters. To this end Blair's partner Cherie Booth played a more prominent role in this campaign and made a high profile appearance presenting the main honour on Independent Television's British Soap Awards. Her 11 million strong audience dwarfed the 2.5 million watching her husband over on BBC1's Question Time and served as an obvious reminder of Blair's family image to less involved voters.[102]

TBWA, the party's new advertisers appointed in 2000, included prominent Labour supporter and former adviser Trevor Beattie. Its pre-campaign copy stressed government achievements with the themes 'The Work Goes On' and 'Thank You', a series of images featuring beneficiaries expressing gratitude to the party's 1997 voters. Perhaps reflecting on their incumbency the symbolic practice of prefixing Labour's name with 'new' was largely abandoned for the campaign. Another advert, 'Just William', mocked the teenage Hague making his first party conference speech. The most striking image of the campaign superimposed Thatcher's hairstyle on the Conservative leader's head to suggest he was her clone. Negativity also featured in horror film style posters and PEBs. Other PEBs targeted young voters by with singer Geri Halliwell and actors from the teenage soap Hollyoaks. Halliwell's previous denunciation of Blair as a 'marketing man' informed Iain Duncan Smith's response: 'This is all spin and she's crossed over to Labour and caught their disease'.[103]

This Conservative attack chimed with a discernible unease about the nature of a campaign that began with complaints about Blair's 'nauseating' announcement of the election to an audience of children.[104] Labour, in particular, were criticised for creating artificial photo opportunities, threatening the BBC and convening male dominated news conferences. The party's preoccupation with news management heightened interest in unplanned events involving dramatic encounters between Blair, John Prescott, Jack Straw and members of the public concerned about health, country sports and police reform. Significantly Prescott's remarkable altercation with a man received more coverage in the national media than the launch of the party's manifesto earlier that day. Blair attacked this style of reporting for being preoccupied with the process and responded to it by giving more access to the less irreverent regional press and broadcast networks. This change of emphasis led to many of the national reporters accompanying Blair on his battlebus to complain about being neglected and barred access to the Labour campaign; towards the end of the election the photojournalists onboard went on strike over the issue. The apparent failure of the party, not to mention the election, to engage public opinion was a marked feature of the campaign. Labour partisans including former advertising adviser Chris Powell feared this might have a disproportionate impact on the outcome:

> The concentration by the public and the media on the packaging rather than the product can only fuel a cynicism that it is all a game. Everywhere artifice, nothing natural and true to itself. This, combined with the poll-fed impression that it is in the bag, could lead to record levels of abstention.[105]

Labour's concern about stay at home voters was reflected in the decision to designate its strategy 'Operation Turnout'. Consequently from December 1999 resources were concentrated on defending the 90 key seats won by 'Operation Victory' in 1997 as well as 66 unexpected 'far side' gains.[106] The initiative involved contacting approximately 50% of the electorate living in these battleground constituencies in an attempt to identify potential switchers and doubters. Central to operations was a new call centre in Tyneside able to contact up to 10,000 people every night. Resources were also put into targeting swing voters with direct mailings and videos featuring their MP and actor Tony Robinson.[107] New media devices such as phone text messages and an 'R U up 4 It?' website were designed for younger voters. By contrast there was little face-to-face communication although some campaigners conducted 'blitz canvasses' involving high profile visits to a specified community and 30 second meetings with potential supporters. Almost all of this activity was aimed at the less committed although focus group evidence of likely abstentions among the core vote, and working-class women under 45 in particular, prompted a change of tactics and an eve of poll visit by Blair to Labour's fourteenth safest constituency.[108]

In past elections this level of non-participation would almost certainly have disproportionately damaged the party's prospects. Now the majoritarian electoral system punished the Conservatives and enabled the government to retain almost all of its 146 'priority' seats despite a modest loss of support. Though Labour could take comfort from the result, more detached observers expressed deep concern that fewer than 60% of the electorate had bothered to participate. For the Nuffield study it was nothing less than 'a fundamental indictment of modern campaigning under the present electoral arrangements and public communication system'.[109] Though ultimately victorious, Labour's strategy was neither a success in terms of mobilising core supporters nor capturing the public imagination; in the absence of an effective opposition the party had achieved an 'apathetic landslide'.[110]

Conclusion: Everything Must Go

A defining characteristic of the so-called 'new' Labour project is its ignorance of history. This is self-evident in a strategy that has continually emphasised the importance of the present and future over the past.[1] The party's approach to political communication is offered as an example of how much Labour's image has been transformed or, to use Tony Blair's preferred phrase, 'modernised'. By contrast this study has attempted to place recent developments in historical context and is mindful of theorist Philip Kotler's observation: 'Campaigning has always had a marketing character. The new 'methodology' is not the introduction of marketing methods into politics, but an increased sophistication and acceleration in their use'. Drawing on his own experience the eminent practitioner Winston Fletcher has developed this point:

> So far from political advertisers copying baked beans and detergents, as the oft-repeated cliché has it, baked beans and detergents have been copying political advertisers, for ages. This should not be surprising. Persuasive communication is the essence of politics, and has been since the dawn of time. The marketing of branded consumer goods is a relative newcomer to the scene.[2]

The preceding chapters have traced Labour's evolution through the identified stages of propaganda, media and marketing campaigning. The early party adhered to an approach predicated on gaining maximum exposure through direct and mediated communications in an inter-war era that also witnessed limited but significant innovations in electioneering technique involving experimentation with film, advertising, radio, image projection. During this time Labour introduced its first logo and the party even began winning plaudits from pioneering American students of campaigning like Ralph Casey and Dean McHenry.[3] The early 1960s saw Labour embracing mediated electioneering through the use of public relations, market research and advertising expertise. Thereafter professionals would help to craft the party's message in each subsequent general election, albeit with varying degrees of influence. But it was only with the organisational and policy reforms of the mid to late 1980s that this tier of consultants finally emerged as the key source of strategic thinking. The result was that marketing concepts as well as personnel and techniques now informed everything the party did. This concluding discussion explores some of the key themes that have arisen from this study and assesses the continuities as well as changes in the way Labour has developed as an electoral organisation over the course of a century.

The eclipse of educationalism

Analysis of Labour's internal divisions has understandably focused on factional and ideological disputes. Less recognised are the tensions that have existed over political communication. Early campaigns were dominated by an 'educationalist' approach associated with Robert Blatchford, the ILP, the Socialist Sunday Schools and others who believed in 'making' socialists. It was their didactic methods and evangelical fervour that shaped Labour's early identity:

> (Its) policies... are of a special type; they presumably flow from a philosophical perspective which makes a critique of existing society and enunciates as a major objective the reconstruction of the social order. That the Labour Party is branded with a special stamp has more than once been indicated by Harold Wilson: '(It) is more than a political organisation; it is a crusade, or it would be better that it did not exist.'[4]

Educationalist orthodoxy encouraged inter-personal, fact-filled communication as a means of converting the public to the 'cause' in the hope of winning votes and countering the Conservatives and their media allies' frequently emotive appeals. This effort required a healthy grassroots network of local activists ready and able to proselytise on the party's behalf.

Universal suffrage led some organisers to challenge the efficacy of trying to make socialists and, influenced by ideas associated with

Graham Wallas, they began arguing it would be better to 'sell' socialism to a burgeoning electorate through the mass media and advertising. Wallas' fellow Fabian Sidney Webb urged campaigners to discriminate between voters and target certain groups. His advocacy of what he termed 'stratified electioneering' reinforced the persuasionalist case for making shorter-term appeals to what was perceived to be a largely apathetic public vulnerable to fear filled Tory overtures. To this end one agent suggested Labour adopt 'perpetual electioneering' while another championed the brand Bovril as a campaigning role model. The preoccupation with winning less committed voters encouraged Herbert Morrison to talk up the importance of cultivating non-traditional supporters like the middle-class 'brainworker'. Morrison promoted the value of professional publicity on Labour's National Executive although he failed to persuade colleagues to appoint an advertising agency in time for the 1935 campaign. The following election, held a decade later, appeared to vindicate the educationalist approach when a relatively unmediated, inter-personal campaign culminated with a famous victory.

The landslide triumph of 1945 rested on Labour's declared intention to rebuild the country through a collectivist welfare state designed to empower and emancipate the citizenry. The government's social democratic covenant pointedly identified 'ignorance' as one of the five 'giant' problems and resolved to combat this through a massive extension of state schooling. Educationalist thinking also continued to directly influence Labour's campaigning, most notably during the party's 1955 'penny farthing' inquiry into organisation. The 1959 defeat to a highly professional Conservative operation began a more urgent strategic re-evaluation and led a Fabian report to call for a 'permanent' campaign. Aneurin Bevan inspired the opposition in a debate that culminated with the once sceptical Hugh Gaitskell and Harold Wilson embracing mediated electioneering. Their actions provided an important rejoinder to the critiques of 'admass' politics that had previously dominated party thinking. Wilson, in particular, became a highly effective television performer and popularised soundbites such as the 'golden handshake' and 'white heat of technology'. Professionalism soon became something of a 'cargo cult' within the party and underlined how, in the words of one adviser: 'the managerial element in the party (had) won the argument and the theorists lost'.[5]

The leader's image and other presentational considerations dominated party campaigns whose primary purpose became 'winning votes not education'.[6] Like Tony Blair, Wilson used the 'New Britain' slogan, employed controversial spin-doctors such as T. Dan Smith and was compared to a charismatic Democratic President. But the earlier prime minister's career was soon beset with serious problems which contributed to the 1970 defeat, undermined Labour's unity and weakened the leader's authority. The ensuing shift to the left fostered the re-emergence of an educationalist coalition of radical activists and more conservative traditionalists keen on reasserting the importance of grass-roots' campaign initiatives. Wilson's successors James Callaghan and Michael Foot responded by promoting Labour as a virtuous party against the slick Conservatives and their high profile advertising agents Saatchi and Saatchi. Foot, like his mentor Bevan, was a living embodiment of the educationalist tradition and preferred addressing public meetings to taking part in studio interviews. His reticence to engage with the media created difficulties for strategists such as Johnny Wright & Partners, the first advertising agency formally retained by Labour during the 1983 election. The work of the firm and other advisers was hampered by an unresolved dilemma over what campaigning was for as one of the professionals involved later revealed: 'Electioneering is about persuasion not education (Labour, are you listening?)'.[7]

The educationalist critique of impersonal, image based electioneering transcended Labour's traditional factional divide by attracting support from across the movement. That said the most vocal proponents of the position tended to come from the left and is why the Greater London Council's (GLC's) campaign against abolition proved crucial in changing party attitudes towards marketing communication. The role of leading left-winger Ken Livingstone in this high profile venture promoted the benefits of advertising, public relations and market research to a sceptical internal audience. The GLC campaign helped new leader Neil Kinnock and his campaigns co-ordinator Robin Cook form an advisory 'breakfast' group of professional advisers which acted as the precursor to the Shadow Communications Agency (SCA). Cook was greatly influenced by the Conservative approach depicted in BBC Panorama documentary 'the Marketing of Margaret' although in many ways the leadership were picking up where Wilson had left off, albeit in a different political and media environment.

The eclipse of educationalism was symbolised in the way the Policy Review of the late 1980s began with the ill-conceived Labour Listens process, an exercise designed to appease traditionalists but which actually succeeded in misrepresenting their approach as outmoded, impractical and irrelevant. The later, and similarly hollow, Policy Forum and

Big Conversation exercises served a similar purpose by promoting the illusion of dialogue between the leadership and whomever they wanted to mollify. The kind of political culture fostered by the Review and the later pseudo consultations attracted criticism from within the party. As Ken Livingstone put it following the 1992 defeat, Labour had been turned into 'some sort of advertising agency'. It was a concern increasingly being voiced outside of the labour movement as *The Financial Times* demonstrated on the day the party was re-elected after 18 years out of office:

> It (the election) was a struggle between packaging and content, between politicians as soap powder and parties as vehicles for informed debate. Without question, the soap powder won... marketing was all that was left.[8]

The once influential belief in educationally based campaigning had become an alien concept to the contemporary party leadership. Chief marketing strategists Philip Gould admitted as much when he advised the by now Prime Minister Blair that Labour's 'contract' with voters was as 'emotional' as it was 'rational'. It was precisely this kind of sentiment that had earlier led former deputy leader Roy Hattersley to revisit Wilson's famous aphorism in concluding his party was now 'less of a moral crusade and more a marketing exercise'.[9]

Communication and control

The organisational and policy reforms that transformed Labour during the 1980s were anticipated by at least one commentator during the party's deep crisis at the beginning of that decade: '... the development of mass communications has accentuated the importance and autonomy of political leaderships over their actual followings. What is in effect political marketing, via opinion polls and television image, has become a principal instrument of political power, displacing the apparent importance of corporate attachment to unions or party membership- these may even appear to be liabilities'.[10] The relationship between intra-party power and bureaucracy had previously been explored in the work of Ostrogorski, Michels, Schumpeter and others. Michels' case material had been the European social democratic party and although the study did not explicitly examine Britain, it informed subsequent research on Labour. Far from being a peripheral exercise, electioneering came to be seen as increasingly crucial in defining strategic objectives as Schumpeter concluded: 'The psycho-technics of party management and party advertising, slogans and marching tunes, are not accessories. They are the essence of politics. *So is the political boss'*.[11]

Ironically the catalysts for Labour's post-1983 centralisation of power- leadership defections followed by a landslide defeat- had also been the motivating factors behind the reassertion of intra-party democracy half a century before. The traumatic 1931 election had led the party's extra-parliamentary wing to promote its collective influence and reign in the PLP leadership's authority. The National Executive's primacy in strategic and organisational matters was confirmed and the committee became less dependent on key individuals like Ramsay MacDonald and Arthur Henderson and more receptive to union and constituency affiliates. The reassertion of a participatory model of decision-making was one reason why London leader Herbert Morrison denied his educationalist inclined local party an effective role in the 1937 election because he feared they would veto the use of advertisers. Morrison's belief in professional advisers was not widely shared at a national headquarters distrustful of what Cole had termed 'clever' outsiders. The prevailing organisational culture meant experts only came to prominence after three successive election defeats in the 1950s and a protracted debate in which revisionists on Labour's right identified renewal of the party's image as a major issue. Their belief that mediated campaigning would enable the leadership to better co-ordinate and, by extension, control the message met firm opposition from left-wingers like Richard Crossman:

> A Left party, moreover is inevitably more concerned with policy than with image, just as a Right-wing party is inevitably more concerned with personality and image than with policy. A Left party is inevitably democratic in a way that a Right party is not.[12]

The pro-Gaitskell Campaign for Democratic Socialism (CDS) demonstrated the practical advantages of public relations when it covertly lobbied sympathetic journalists working for mainstream news organisations in a bid to counter the grassroots left. It was, however, former left-winger Harold Wilson who did most to augment the strategic influence of the post of leader. Wilson was characteristically presidential in both his image and party management and worked in close consultation with a kitchen cabinet of mainly unelected advisers. His aides co-ordinated a wider network of marketing and public relations consultants, one of whom later acknowledged their influence: 'As we translated policies into language that electors could understand, wrote ads and developed literature, not only the tone changed but the emphasis and relative weight of the policies did too'.[13] The arrangement underlined the relevance of Epstein's far-sighted 'contagion from the right' theory on the replacement, by stealth, of mass democratic parties by unelected professional experts. In effect Wilson's tenure served as a strategic 'half way house' between the parties of MacDonald and Blair and demonstrated the increased importance of electioneering as Rose noted: 'The activities of campaigning are less concerned with the flow of influence from voters to candidates than they are with the flow of influence within the political party themselves'.[14]

Party dissatisfaction with the Wilson government's performance found an outlet with the revival of serious factional disputes between the Labour right and left in the 1970s. The leader's power base was challenged by a more proactive and left-wing National Executive and General Secretary. Wilson's immediate successors both faced serious crises that made effective party management and use of marketing specialists difficult. Michael Foot supported the reassertion of National Executive authority and the replacement of Wilson's informal expert consultations by a more transparent committee based decision-making. Changing a campaign structure that had been fostered over twenty years created problems that were compounded by the recriminations that engulfed the 'very internalised' party that had emerged from the 1979 defeat.[15] Preparations for the subsequent general election of 1983 were paralysed before they started and the subsequent campaign was undermined by internal rivalries, unclear decision-making procedures and, most crucially, the absence of a network of aides and officials able to implement agreements.

Foot's successor Neil Kinnock invoked memories of the 1983 debacle in his mission to convince Labour as to the need for change. An unprecedented programme of organisational and policy reforms greatly enhanced the power and influence of his own aides, key officials, marketing consultants and specially recruited American political consultants. Collectively what Shaw terms the 'strategic community' subverted and then usurped the authority of the National Executive whilst simultaneously marginalising rival sources of advice from independent minded consultants such as occasional PR expert Lynne Franks and Labour's longstanding pollsters Market Opinion and Research International (MORI).[16]

Directing this process was head of Campaigns and Communications Peter Mandelson, a loyal Kinnock lieutenant and the contact person for the secretive Shadow Communications Agency. Ad hoc initiatives like Red Wedge were phased out in favour of a more tightly controlled and explicitly mediated approaches. Like his grandfather Herbert Morrison, Mandelson developed a formidable personal reputation and a keen interest in forging links between the party and its sympathisers in the marketing industry. Morrison's innovative London campaign and the Mandelson co-ordinated general election effort fifty years later were both lauded as groundbreaking efforts and parallels between the campaigns extended to their content, much of which revolved around promoting the leader's image. In the latter case the exposure Kinnock got helped him defy the conventional wisdom that losing elections necessarily weakened a politician.[17] Ultimately both campaigns demonstrated how the secretive cultivation of professional strategists, media contacts and wealthy donors could and would be used to subvert the party's democratic ethos and structures.

The 1987 defeat led to the Policy Review, an exercise whose value: '... lay as much in persuading the party of the need for change, as in persuading the public of Labour's electability'. According to one of the SCA advisers involved, the aim of the process was to create a synergy between Labour's substance and its now rejuvenated style.[18] Some left-wingers viewed the Review as a threat to the autonomy of the Annual Conference and National Executive and supported a leadership challenge in 1988. Kinnock's subsequent victory in that contest helped forge the highly centralised operation Tony Blair would eventually inherit. Blair also reassembled most of his predecessor's team. Philip Gould reoccupied his influential role as chief marketing strategist and advised Blair to pursue the 'unfinished revolution' by taking untrammelled control of campaigning. Yet as one practitioner observed, this was something the Review had already delivered:

> The things that were achieved were done by individual politicians, working with other individuals, bypassing the committees. This is the only way marketing can be carried out effectively by political parties: short lines of communication between leaders and the doors. That's the way the Tories operate; that's the way Labour now operates. It's the only way that works.[19]

Like other influential aides, Kinnock's former chief of staff Charles Clarke joined the Blair entourage before being eventually appointed to the new Cabinet post of Party Chairman after the 2001 election victory. Gaitskellites had first proposed such a portfolio; the fact it appropriated the title of its Conservative counterpart not to mention the name of the elected head of Labour's National Executive under-lined the degree to which the party could now be reorganised accord-ing to the leader's whim. The sidelining of the party's representative structures was encouraged by the introduction of more ad hoc forms of 'consultation' involving forums and ballots which, according to the foremost authorities on Labour membership, were hardly an effective substitute: 'Plebiscitary politics is really designed to legitimise decisions already taken by the leadership and is not in any meaningful sense a deliberative process involving grassroots party members. In this kind of politics a small group of people around the leadership decide which issues will be put to a vote of the members, and they decide on the framing and the wording of the questions'.[20]

The party's affiliated trade unions, collectively the most potent source of internal opposition, became increasingly reluctant to chal-lenge the leadership due to a combination of self-restraint, internal rivalries and policy divisions. Despite their role in sustaining Labour throughout its troublesome history the wider movement's involve-ment in intra as well as inter-party politics was routinely questioned in hostile media coverage. Just as the Conservative New Right benefited from the prejudiced and distorted reporting of the unions during the 1970s so did Labour's leadership twenty years later. The emasculation of party structures meant the Blair government sustained only one Conference defeat in its first term despite vigorous internal opposition to certain policies. A fast declining membership increasingly became of marginal influence in a series of debates over controversial measures such as single parent benefit cuts, public private partnerships and finance initiatives, foundation hospitals, student top-up fees and, most critically of all, the invasion of Iraq.

If the post-Review settlement diminished the importance of party members it simultaneously encouraged the growing myriad of policy entrepreneurs working for think tanks, lobbyists, pressure groups and assorted front organisations funded by corporate interests. They found a welcome audience in a leadership that was proud to proclaim Labour as 'the party of business' in a 1997 election broadcast. The private sector reciprocated by helping to finance a burgeoning tier of 'electoral professionals' undertaking capitally intense marketing activities aimed at the 'opinion electorate'.[21] Polling feedback and those responsible for collating it were now integral to the policy making process although there was a marked restriction on the flow of this kind of information within the party hierarchy. When Clare Short criticised the 'people in the dark' advising Blair, she made the arguably more revealing observation that National Executive members were denied access to Labour's own focus group findings under Blair (and Kinnock though not Smith). The admission confirmed that only a few trusted aides were in any position to make informed comments on the quality or implications of the polling. By contrast the rest of the party had to rely on key media 'auxiliaries' from those agenda-setting and Labour inclined newspapers like the *Guardian* to provide them with partial accounts of leaked researching findings.

The leadership approach of Kinnock and Blair was effortlessly reproduced in office when the party finally took over an already highly centralised system of government in 1997. Prime Ministerial Press Secretary Alistair Campbell, now supervising a public relations state inherited from Thatcher, did little to dispel Labour's reputation for ruthless news management. Campbell's reformed communication and information service was routinely subjected to the familiar charge that it was dominated by spin, the desire to be 'on message' and the kind of 'control freakery' associated with the party's Millbank headquarters. The image of a malign, manipulative government was reinforced during the so-called lobbygate saga in which Labour insider Derek Draper made various embarrassing claims including the plausible observation that a majority of the 17 most influential people in government were unelected aides not ministers.[22] The Prime Minister's allegiance to this burgeoning network of loyalist appointees was demonstrated in 2001 when ministerial spin-doctor Jo Moore sent a colleague an e-mail on the morning of September 11th suggesting it would be 'a good day to bury bad news'. Blair's failure to orchestrate the immediate removal of Moore led to more intensive questioning of Downing Street's media ethics during the government's second term. The resulting culture of mistrust was a contributory factor to Campbell's eventual departure from government in 2003.

The Completed Evolution: how the new right emasculated the Labour Party

In a compelling critique of Downs, Mauser argued conviction politicians could further their interests by adopting a positioning strategy designed to appeal to both core and less partisan voters alike. The success of Thatcher, Reagan and Mitterrand underlined how marketing professionalism was about more than responding to public opinion because, as Heath and his colleagues explained: 'Situating oneself close to the policy preferences of the median voter is neither a necessary nor a sufficient condition for electoral success'. Conservative dominance of an 'oligopolistic' political marketplace during the 1980s was based on a realisation that a minority vote share of between 40–45% was enough to comfortably guarantee office.[23] Thatcher's coalition building 'politics of support' was, however, only one dimension of a wider project involving what Gamble describes as a 'politics of power' intent on reshaping the political landscape in the furtherance of ideological objectives; and herein lies an important difference between electoral and more conventional marketing theory and practice: elected leaders are more readily able than individual commercial firms to shape their environment and most notably the institutions of state.[24]

Since its foundation Labour has been primarily engaged in forging a politics of support aided by extra-parliamentary sympathisers in the trade union and socialist movements. The party found itself operating in a state moulded by the innately conservative (if not Conservative) hierarchies of the church, monarchy, law, military, commerce and civil service. Collectively these institutions fostered a hostile climate where 'the best propaganda (was) completely unorganised'.[25] Blair's portrayal of Labour's failure in a 'Conservative Century' is based on a superficial historical analysis that neglects the underlying dynamics. Ultimately it took a most momentous event, the Second World War, to finally propel Labour into majority party status and a period of government in which it came nearest to embracing the politics of power through a massive extension of the public sector and Welfare State.

The Attlee governments forged a social democratic consensus that withstood thirty years until the New Right sponsored programme of economic liberalisation designed to enrich business entrepreneurs and enable some voters to buy their council houses and shares in publicly owned assets. As Tony Benn observed it was now Margaret Thatcher and the Conservatives, not Labour, who were pursuing something akin to an educationalist campaign in their promotion of market individualism. The resulting redistribution of income in favour of the wealthy also gave the burgeoning middle and skilled working-classes more modest but perceptible gains. Despite its electoral success, the Thatcherite project remained controversial, blighted by poor polling ratings and dependent on powerful allies in the City and 'Tory press'. Labour's ultimate response was, to use

Gould's phrase, 'concede and move on' through a Policy Review which downgraded its social democratic instincts and acquiesced to an emerging neo-liberal consensus.[26] The perception of electoral trends became as important as the trends themselves in a 'marketisation' of policy that eliminated apparently unpopular commitments but also succeeded in paralysing creative thinking:

> Unlike the revisionism of the 1950s, Kinnock's Policy Review was not so much a restatement of socialism (however flawed), as a cynical image-building capitulation to a seemingly hegemonic Thatcherism (which ironically, however, came too late, at a time when Thatcherism's own appeal and radicalism were waning)... Labour's philosophical bankruptcy became glaringly apparent. In the event, a party almost entirely concerned with image and media strategies failed to convince the electorate and lost its fourth consecutive general election.[27]

Though the Policy Review encouraged caution, it was a radical departure in its scope and status. Consequently the polling contained in the report *Labour and Britain in the 1990s* played a formal agenda-setting role denied *Must Labour Lose?* thirty years before. Similarly whereas qualitative methods had been used since the Wilson era, the Review ensured they now became an indispensable tool of voter analysis. The motive for using the increasingly ubiquitous focus group was likened to the Rousseau preoccupation with comprehending the General Will of 'the people'.[28] Selected findings from studies would be leaked by leadership acolytes to media contacts in a bid to convince the party of the need for further reform. Labour's potential strengths were consistently underplayed and all but one of its perceived weaknesses exposed to scrutiny. The exception was Neil Kinnock, a leader whose poor public standing had led the previous pollster to question the decision to presidentialise campaigning in the run up to the 1987 election. Political expediency meant this issue was repeatedly suppressed in the party's qualitative research and analysis as the strategist responsible later explained: 'It is true I presented without compromise all negatives about all other aspects of Labour but not about its leader. I went far, but not the whole way. I put loyalty to Neil first'.[29] The protection of Kinnock's reputation culminated with an orchestrated campaign to implicate the party union link as a major contributory factor to the 1992 defeat. This largely irrelevant issue dominated the post-mortem and focused attention away from the shortcomings of a 'new' (model)

Labour project that was, contrary to popular understandings, defeated in what was effectively its first electoral outing.

If the self-styled modernisers' coloured interpretations of focus group material continued to serve their own ideological purposes it also revealed the pervasive way these kinds of research findings were increasingly entering public debate at a time when traditional polling was being ridiculed for having 'failed' to predict the 1992 result. Given their trajectory the modernisers can, in spatial and historical terms, be more appropriately categorised as Labour's 'new right'. A defining characteristic of this group was the invaluable support it garnered from the national newspapers favoured by the membership as well as the initially sympathetic audience it received from the anti-left press and broadcasters whose impartiality was less rigid in covering intra-party affairs. Collectively these media uncritically accepted and framed debates in terms of 'moderniser' versus 'traditionalist' rather than the conventional left-right formula. The importance of journalistic agenda-setting was further demonstrated by the way it gave momentum to the new right's candidate for the leadership, Tony Blair, prior to the beginning of the formal contest in 1994. Similarly news coverage of the Clause Four debate reinforced Blair's claim that a 'new' party was emerging in place of 'old' Labour, a dubious concept that quickly became an accepted term for incompetence, extremism as well as an unlikely range of ideological rivals. If it meant anything 'new' Labour created the circumstances that gave rise to Blair rather than he it. Subsequent changes might be better characterised as a rebranding exercise designed to position the party further to the right on welfare, social and criminal justice policy matters in support of the leadership's pursuit of 'desperate respectability'. According to Naomi Klein this so-called 'triangulation' strategy closely imitated that of the 'new' Democrat strategist Dick Morris:

> Blair... took a page from the marketers of Revolution Soda and successfully changed the name of his party from the actual description of its loyalties and policy proclivities (that would be 'labour') to the brand-asset descriptor 'New Labour'.[30]

The disparity between the representation and reality of Labour's newness offered an early insight into why the Blair leadership would become synonymous with hyperbole and 'spin'. The claim for novelty formed an important dimension to an ongoing 'corporate populist' turn that was encouraged by advocates of a 'progressive' politics devoted to championing a 'revolution' in attitudes and practices and being more 'responsive' to 'the people' in delivering 'what works'. The combination of zealous pragmatism and managerial rhetoric reflected the neo-Marxist origins of leading new right Labour thinkers and their predilection for styling themselves as 'radicals' confronting 'the forces of conservatism' and 'elitists' within the party and beyond.[31] Like the new-old formula, such terminology downplayed the linear concept of left-right and promoted the leadership as dynamic and forward thinking. But actions were more instructive than words and Labour's sharp repositioning in the 'radical centre' in pursuit of a 'third way' underlined its attachment to rhetorics and stances more readily associated with the Conservatives. Contrary to the leadership's insistence on transcending traditional politics their activities actually confirmed the importance of a spatial view of party competition.

Labour's development was conditioned by, to borrow Miliband's phrase, a 'composite view' of floating voters as disillusioned and anxious Tories. Such a perception arose from and was reinforced by successive focus group research studies for and about the party's public standing. Like the New Right before it, the Labour new right project became highly attuned to certain strands of voter opinion as portrayed in polling studies.[32] The resulting crude Downsian motion, reinforced by populist newspaper reporting, rested on questionable assumptions about the electorate.[33] Nevertheless Philip Gould believed focus group studies about Labour, most of which he personally conducted and analysed, gave voice to a largely ignored strata of public opinion consisting of 'powerful autonomous' individuals. Self-proclaimed 'populist' Gould argued market research was integral to the forging of a 'new' politics and accused his left-wing detractors of 'progressive elitism', a charge previously levelled at GB Shaw for his contention that universal suffrage encouraged irrational political campaigning.[34] A less judgemental Fabian, Graham Wallas, came to similar conclusions in suggesting that politicians might benefit from making more short-term, image based 'persuasional' appeals aimed at what Philip Snowden termed 'matter-of-fact people' rather than 'higher intellectuals'. Wallas and Snowden were of course active in the early part of the 20th century but they were among the first to identify the apparent disconnection between Labour and wider public opinion. It was this theme that *Must Labour Lose?* returned to in the 1960s.

Following the 1979 election several commentators argued the party lost because of its poor reputation and described it as having a cloth cap image, being old fashioned, extremist and beholden to 'minorities'. One defeated MP attacked Labour as 'elitist' for wilfully ignoring popular sentiment as defined through opinion research evidence.[35] It was not long before this changed. From his earlier work for the party in 1985 onwards, Philip Gould promoted a broadly similar analysis to that offered by a dissenting minority after 1979; the difference was that his would soon become received wisdom. Despite its emancipatory pretensions, the reality of opinion research was that it encouraged a secretive, hierarchical culture within the party and an ideological conservatism antipathetic to spontaneity and transparency. The resulting caution was hardly surprising given marketing is a capitally intense function of strategic management rather than a participatory form of democratic dialogue. Labour's electoral professionals, like corporate executives working on commercial projects, determined who counted (and who did not) in their calculations and, by extension, the political public sphere. This trend was if anything exacerbated by focus groups because they, more than quantitative forms of polling, promoted the demographic as well as psychological characteristics of those voters increasingly seen as crucial in the pursuit of power. Yet here there was scope for misperception arising from widespread ignorance among the media and political elite as to the methodology, purpose and role of qualitative research. Even those responsible for the influential *Southern Discomfort* study appeared unaware that their sample of five seats included two that ranked among the top ten in terms of *Sun* readership levels. The consequence of the widespread ignorance about focus grouping could be seen in the way selected findings were inappropriately used to analyse the popularity or not of certain politicians, policies or proposals.

The aspirations of most of the voluntary party and core vote became increasingly marginal to a strategy that sought to align Labour with popular opinion on a range of salient domestic issues including tax, crime and the Euro. Blair's discourse of progressive politics was anything but on occasions and some policy initiatives appeared reactive if not downright reactionary in responding to populist right-wing press concerns over benefit claimants and asylum seekers. Strategic memos to the prime minister based on focus group analysis suggested media campaigns were having an impact on key voters who were interpreted as desiring what was euphemistically termed 'economic' and 'cultural stability'.[36] Blair's sensitivity to public opinion, particularly through feedback from qualitative research, became a recurrent theme in the reporting about his motives and actions. Underlying this type of commentary was a failure to appreciate how this kind of study was more concerned with the depth rather than breadth of public opinion on a given subject. Consequently sympathisers and critics alike interpreted the most significant crisis of the prime minister's career, Iraq, as the policy that finally undermined his image as a focus group obsessive.[37] Yet there is no necessary disparity between being a control freak and a politician highly conscious of polling research given the latter is malleable and lends itself to being formulated and interpreted according to the pre-existing bias of the former.

The Blair leadership's interest in pandering to broader public opinion has always been secondary to its preoccupation with the discreet targets within the electorate who have disproportionately populated the focus groups disclosed in journalistic reports. These are invariably the voters who have moved between the two major parties and whose loss to a rival is in effect worth double the value of any other defector or abstentionist. Given the defining characteristic of 'floaters' was their propensity to change allegiance, they were precisely the kinds of people likely to move from opposing to supporting the conflict in Iraq once hostilities had begun. The large movement of voters who swung behind the government position did so encouraged by a formidable coalition of the two main party leaderships and a vocal section of the agenda-setting press.[38] More fundamentally the real effect of political market research and analysis is not felt in relation to specific policies, no matter how important, nor from week to week or month to month. Rather the influence can be felt in the focus group evidence amassed and accumulated *over decades* and which has conditioned the Labour elite's thinking about voters' perceived prejudices and convinced them to jettison social democracy. That the original research programme began in earnest two decades ago at the height of the Thatcherite ascendancy helps put the Blair government's indulgence of neo-liberalism in context.[39]

The perils of stratified electioneering

The theory and practice of political marketing raises important questions about the nature of modern elections, participation and democratic accountability. Although it is claimed that opinion research represents the views of a silent majority who otherwise might be ignored this laudable ambition conflicts with the primary motives of those commissioning private polling: the desire to cultivate support, win votes and/or get elected.[40] The healthy functioning of democracy is a secondary consideration and, at most, something to be addressed once politicians are safely in office given: 'marketing tends to focus upon satisfying short-term customer wishes rather than long-term individual or group needs'. There is then no paradox, as has been suggested, between a political elite using unprecedented amounts of research to gauge the opinions of an increasingly disillusioned citizenry.[41] Where there is an irony it is in the way polling has placed a barrier between politicians and the wider electorate with discernible consequences for more complex matters of long-term public concern involving everything from civil rights and justice to health, education, transport or (not) joining the Euro.

At the core of Labour's politics of support is an approach preoccupied with the 'aspirational', owner occupiers, certain women, first time voters and those living in the English marginals of the South East, North West and West Midlands. This is because the modern application of stratified electioneering is devoted to understanding the groups seen as being 'key' to future electoral success, namely the 'new middle-class'.[42] The strategy has persistently disregarded those traditionally associated with the party such as the public sector workforce, committed partisans, blue-collar workers, ethnic minority communities, trade union members and the poor. By contrast the preoccupation with the security and aspirations of the new middle-class is reminiscent of the motivating factor behind *Must Labour Lose?* There is, however, a major difference between now and then in that whereas the 'revisionists had an ideological compass to steer by, Kinnock had opinion surveys'.[43] As Rita Hinden warned in her prescient conclusion to *Must Labour Lose?*, the party ought not to embark on an 'extreme' polling conscious strategy:

> ... the more (Labour) could fashion itself on the lines of the present-day Conservatives the more successful it would presumably be- for what the Conservatives are giving is, it seems, what the people want. This may be an inglorious path, but- so it is claimed- it is the path to power... (This meant) destroying the socialist inspiration of the Labour Party and the source of its vitality. The Labour Party has always been something more than a class party... the philosophy of socialism gave it its ideals and won for it the devotion of people of all classes. If it reduces itself now to an imitation of its rivals, its emotional strength will be disastrously undermined.[44]

Hinden's fears were realised decades later with the rise of what Galbraith termed a culture of contentment in which the increasingly vocal 'haves' threatened to limit the ability of social democrats to represent the 'have nots'. Shortly before becoming leader Tony Blair rejected Galbraith's thesis in a televised encounter between them in which the former argued the overriding goal for the left was winning office. The Policy Review ensured Blair's view had already become party orthodoxy and its image reinvented in a 'modern, managerial, middle-class guise' before he succeeded to the leadership.[45] Despite its professed desire to fashion a more 'inclusive' society, the Labour government would repeatedly alienate or ignore those who had traditionally formed its most loyal supporters. In contrast the Thatcherites engaged and mobilised core voters in formulating their party's strategic engagement in a politics of power. Labour's preoccupation with the least committed (or uncommitted) elements of its electoral base resulted in the leadership complaining about unrealistic demands from left partisans including a trade union movement that was told to expect 'fairness not favours'. Blair dismissed the unions as 'vested' interests, yet this is arguably a more fitting description for the various corporate bodies that continue to exert considerable influence over the political system. As former party insider Derek Draper put it, his ex-colleagues in commercial lobbying working on behalf of multinational corporations were in a better position to modify government legislation than even the exemplar '8 people drinking wine in a focus group in Kettering'.[46]

Draper's observation touches upon the way neo-liberalism increasingly subordinates the political to the economic and the democratic will to that of the market. If corporate interests have been the beneficiaries, the losers in this process have included the agencies of social democratic change on the orthodox left.[47] Both as and within parties these forces were denigrated by a 'market populism' that found particular resonance with the rise of the 'new economy' during the 1990s. Allied to this the 'new politics' movement championed alternative forms of public participation and accountability designed to bypass traditional debate. Predictably Draper's former employer Peter Mandelson became a prominent advocate for the new political economy and, in his most memorable speech as Secretary of State for Trade and Industry, pondered whether the era of representative democracy was about to be replaced by referenda and marketing based consultations involving focus groups and citizen juries. Mandelson's vision for Westminster reflected the kind of settlement that had already been imposed on his party. This is because, as Finlayson observes: 'New Labour doesn't like intermediate collective political institutions... that get in the way of the direct relations between individual citizen and their political market choice'.[48] This strategic focus undermined the importance of the collectivist perspective, a key tenet of social democracy.

The increasing marketisation of the political system and its evocation of the 'citizen-consumer' have subsequently placed greater emphasis on the value of economic activity as a form of public participation.[49] Despite some claims made of it, this process is not about democratisation, not least because those who form the core Conservative and Labour votes come from different social strata and resource backgrounds. The latter have been historically more dependent on their party and the public realm to safeguard and advance their material interests and is why the neo-liberal inspired promotion of 'depoliticisation' has had such a stark impact.[50] This registered most profoundly in 2001 with the director of the British Election Study describing the record near 40% of voters abstaining as 'a crisis of democratic politics in Britain'.[51] Previously Barry Cox, one of Blair's closest allies, had ventured to suggest a lack of political activity might actually be a sign of democratic stability and maturity. The 2001 turnout undermined this facile notion:

> Elections confer equal citizenship on all adults, as a counterweight to the inequalities of the market and natural endowment. In 2001 turnout fell to an exceptionally low level in the most deprived areas of Britain's cities. In 67 constituencies, all in such areas, the majority of the registered electorate failed to vote; in a few, under 40 per cent did so. The majority of the poor, the unemployed, the unqualified, single mothers on benefit and blacks disengaged from the election. The socially excluded felt politically excluded and so excluded themselves from the electoral process.[52]

Disquiet has rightly been expressed over the way the packaging of politics has led to debate being manipulated by spin doctoring and image making.[53] But marketing's colonisation of campaigning raises other, more fundamental concerns about the ends as well as the means of the democratic process and, more specifically, the way stratified electioneering devalues the importance and influence of the predominantly stable sections of the voting population. The logic of Dick Morris and Philip Gould's position is that it is actually counter-productive to have a fixed principled stance. This is 'political' marketing. To paraphrase George Orwell all voters may be created equal but some have become more equal than others. Blair, the supposed enemy of electoral complacency when it concerned floating voters, revealed the professionally sanctioned cynicism that had long informed party strategy when he calculated a section of his core vote would stay Labour because they had 'nowhere else to go'. The dramatic fall in turnout at the 2001 general election suggested otherwise.

Notes

Preface and Acknowledgements

1 Priestley, 1968. Reviewing a book on the latest American campaign techniques the same year, Labour agent Terry Pitt warned colleagues that politicians 'will be promoted and marketed like the latest model automobile' (*Labour Organiser* no. 558, December).
2 Palast, 2002, p. 161–69.
3 Editorial in *The Observer*, 18th August 1996.
4 The speech was made to the pro-business Institute of Directors, 'Mandelson: We sold Labour as news product', *The Guardian*, 30th April 1998.
5 Hughes and Wintour, 1990; Gould, 1998.
6 Cockett, 1994.

Introduction: Inside the Political Market

1 Coates, 1980; Minkin, 1980; Warde, 1982.
2 Hare, 1993; 'Top Consumer PR Campaigns of All Time', *PR Week* 29th March 2002. Of the other politicians featured the Suffragettes and Conservatives (1979) occupied the fifteenth and sixteenth places respectively.
3 Gould, 2002; Gould, 1998, p. 81.
4 Abrams and Rose with Hinden, 1960; Gould, 2002.
5 Mandelson and Liddle, 1996, p. 2; see also Wright, 1997. The Blair leadership, like most politicians, deny the extent to which they rely on professionals for strategic input and guidance (Mauser, 1989).
6 Interviewed on BBC1 'Breakfast with Frost', 14th January 1996, cited in Blair, 1996, p. 49. Blair regularly returns to this theme: in his 2003 Conference speech he attacked the interpretation of 'New Labour' as 'a clever piece of marketing, good at winning elections, but hollow where the heart should be' (*The Guardian*, 1st October 2003).
7 Driver and Martell, 1998, pp. 158–9.
8 Crompton and Lamb, 1986, p. 1.
9 Almond, 1990, p. 121. Kelley used the term in the following context: 'The team relies heavily but not entirely upon their own intuitive feel for providing political marketing conditions. They pride themselves on having "good average minds" that help them to see things as the average man sees them' (Kelley, 1956, p. 53).
10 Downs, 1957. For all of this work's popularity Peter Mandelson, the Labour practitioner most associated with putting its ideas into practice, admitted to his ignorance of the book when questioned in 1990 (Temple, 2000).
11 Wring, 1999.
12 Butler and Stokes, 1969; Denver, 1994.

13 Kotler and Levy, 1969; Rosenbloom, 1973.
14 Davidson, 1992, p. 78.
15 Gamble, 1974, p. 6. Schumpeter was an early advocate of the market analogy: 'Party and machine politicians are simply the response to the fact that the electoral mass is incapable of action other than a stampede, and they constitute an attempt to regulate political competition exactly similar to the corresponding practices of a trade association' (Schumpeter, 1943, p. 283).
16 Webb, 2000, p. 156. See also Palmer, 2002.
17 Wring, 1997a.
18 Farrell and Wortmann, 1987; Worcester, 1987.
19 Harrop, 1990; Newman, 1994.
20 Kotler, 1982. See also Mughan, 2000.
21 Denver, 1994.
22 Franklin, 1994.
23 Denver and Hands, 1997.
24 Niffenegger, 1989.
25 O'Keefe, 1989.
26 Kleinman, 1987; Smith and Saunders, 1990.
27 Mauser, 1983.
28 Keith, 1960; Shama, 1976. See also Smith and Saunders, 1990. The historical application of such terminology differs to Lees-Marshment's usage of similar concepts in her more explicitly contemporary analysis (Lees-Marshment, 2002).
29 Farrell, 1996; Norris, 1996, Wring, 1996.
30 Shama, 1976.
31 Qualter, 1985, p. 124.
32 Shama, 1976.
33 Harrop, 1990.
34 Shama, 1976; Kotler and Kotler, 1999.
35 For a useful comparative survey of trends see Mancini and Swanson, 1996.
36 Scammell usefully identifies the way in which political science, communication and management studies have all contributed to the emergence of political marketing as a lively field of research (Scammell, 1999).

1   To Educate or Persuade?

1 Wallas, 1948, p. 83.
2 Hamer, 1977, p. 318; Pulzer, 1967, p. 81.
3 Blewett, 1972, pp. 284 and 312; Gorman, 1985, p. 166.
4 *Labour Organiser* no. 63, 1926.
5 McKibbin, 1974, p. xiv and p. 124; McKenzie, 1955, pp. 559–61.
6 Cole, 1965, p. 228–32; Seyd and Whiteley, 1992, p. 14.
7 McLean, 1980.
8 One of whom suggested that Labour 'perhaps surpasses in effectiveness the most highly perfected American political machines sustained by spoils' (McHenry, 1938, p. 303; see also Casey, 1944).
9 Thorpe, 1991, p. 20.

10 McKenzie, 1955, p. 567. As Ramsay MacDonald's assistant in the Labour Representation Committee, Middleton was technically the party's first ever full-time employee (Morgan, 1992, pp. 231–38). Organisational politics was a feature of headquarters' life and changes were often greeted with suspicion by employees who suspected individuals were attempting to 'empire build': 'They feel there are already enough prima-donnas in the movement' (Stewart, 1974, p. 47).

11 Cambray, 1932.

12 Dalton had lost his seat in the 1931 election but remained influential (Pimlott, 1985, p. 204). Party headquarters have relocated around London a number of times: 1901–1905 saw the offices housed in MacDonald's flat at 3 Lincoln's Inn Fields; 1905–1914, 28 Victoria St; 1914–1918, 1 Victoria St; 1918–33, Eccleston Square; then Transport House in Smith Square (Hamilton, 1939, p. 51). In 1980 headquarters moved south of the Thames to Walworth Road. 1997 saw the organisation return to Westminster and a suite of offices at Millbank Tower. In 2002 the party occupied premises in Old Queen Street near parliament.

13 Morrison, 1920, p. 202.

14 Barker, 1972, pp. 60–61.

15 Jones, 1996, p. 15. For a wider discussion of the 'evangelical' socialist tradition within the party see Laybourn, 1997; and Weinbren, 1997, pp. 30–56.

16 Barker, 1972, p. 101. It was during this period that Walter Lippman and others began popularising the study of public opinion (Lippman, 1922).

17 Barker, 1972, pp. 95–96, and 121. Labour's gradualist approach also demarcated it from the vanguardist Social Democratic Federation and Communist Party (Barker, 1972, p. 275).

18 Hollins, 1981, pp. 126–130. Similar thinking informed the work of various organisations that flourished in the 1930s and 1940s including John Grierson's documentary film movement, the Army Bureau of Current Affairs (ABCA) and the Central Office of Information (COI) set up by the Attlee government (Wildy, 1985).

19 Ryan, 1986, p. 27 and p. 32.

20 *Labour Organiser* no. 182, 1936. Nearly fifty years later Sidney Blumenthal wrote an influential book, *The Permanent Campaign*, about this phenomenon (Blumenthal, 1982).

21 Wallas, 1948, p. 87; Qualter, 1985, p. 11.

22 Clarke, 1983, p. 11. The calm prognosis of some persuasionalist minded politicians led to them adopting an impassioned, even inflammatory rhetoric. This apparent paradox was noted by Kelley in his study into the increasing 'emotionalism, sentimentality, distortion and poverty of ideas' of many post-World War Two campaigns: 'the rational interests of the candidates and parties lead them to encourage irrationality in the electorate' (Kelley, 1960, p. 17 and p. 23).

23 Wallas, 1948, p. 84. On Wallas' enduring legacy see Bevir, 1997.

24 *Labour Organiser* no. 63, 1926. For a contemporary perspective on this point see McNair, 1999, pp. 23–4.

25 'Publicity in Politics', *The London News*, May 1937, p. 3.

26 *Labour Organiser* no. 171, 1935.

27 Hollins, 1981, p. 133.

28 New Fabian Research Bureau (1937).

29 Kornhauser, 1959.

30 *Labour Organiser* no. 126, 1931. See also comments by Dean McHenry, an author who had personal experience of emotive, mass mediated election-eering as an activist in Upton Sinclair's ill-fated 1934 'End Poverty In California' (EPIC) campaign for the governorship of California (McHenry, 1938; Mitchell, 1992, p. 76).

31 MacDonald, 1920, p. 53 cited in Hollins, 1981, p. 126.

32 *Labour Organiser* no. 23, 1922; *Labour Organiser* no. 34, 1923. Jennings, 1960, pp. 228–29. Jennings' propaganda analysis noted the importance of 'rank', 'nature of society', 'ruling few', 'class' and 'class and politics'.

33 Cockett, 1994; *Labour Organiser* no. 126, 1931.

34 Scammell, 1995, pp. 30–31.

35 In his pioneering study of the party Gamble identifies the Conservatives' motivation as the 'politics of power' rather than just the 'politics of support'. Thus whilst efforts were geared to influencing public opinion in the electoral market the Tories strove to condition the prevailing political environment by colonising the institutions of state (Gamble, 1974).

36 *Conservative Agents Journal*, August 1927, cited in Swaddle, 1990, p. 210.

37 Casey, 1939. Significant additional support was forthcoming from the right-wing 'Economic Leagues' formed by business interests in the 1920s, *Labour Organiser* no. 67, 1926.

38 Casey, 1944.

39 McKibbin, 1974, p. 124.

40 McHenry, 1938, p. 66; Hollins, 1981, p. 148.

41 Casey, 1944.

42 Cole, 1948, p. 124.

43 Seymour-Ure, 1996.

44 Matthews, 1987; Williams, 1980, p. 191; *Labour Organiser* no. 19, 1922.

45 Blewett, 1972, p. 308; McKibbin, 1974, p. 110.

46 Ferris and Bar-Joseph, 1993.

47 *Labour Organiser* no. 15, 1921.

48 Morrison, 1920, p. 202.

49 Antcliffe, 1984.

50 *Labour Organiser* no. 126, 1931. The allocations were 11 for the National parties, 3 for Labour, 1 Liberal. In 1935 the share was more equitable with 5 for the Nationals, 4 Labour and 3 Liberal. According to McHenry the pub-licity opportunity was squandered because Attlee and his colleagues' broad-casts employed a 'lecturing' style (McHenry, 1938, pp. 73–74; and p. 188).

51 Thorpe, 1991, pp. 216–17; *Labour Organiser* no. 143, 1933; *Labour Organiser* no. 193, 1937. Ironically Labour politicians became the most vocal op-ponents of post-war plans to allow privately owned, commercially funded broadcasting with Herbert Morrison denouncing Radio Luxembourg's advertising saturated service as 'sheer naked exploitation' despite its popu-larity with core Labour voters (Turner, 1952, p. 278; Fielding et al., 1995, p. 147).

52 Antcliffe, 1984; Attlee, 1954, p. 141; Pearce, 1997, p. 177.

53 Nicholas, 1951, p. 124; Butler, 1952, p. 69; Betteridge, 1995.

54 *Labour Organiser* no. 376, 1953.

55 Morgan, 1987, p. 26.
56 *Labour Organiser* no. 10, 1921, no. 30, 1923 and no. 105, 1930; McHenry, 1938, p. 76. During the 1920s the Labour Publishing Company helped promote socialist ideas and the Left Book Club did likewise during the following decade, Francis, 1984; Gorman, 1985, p. 53.
57 *Labour Organiser* no. 1, 1920, no. 48, 1924 and no. 76, 1927.
58 Curran, 1978; Richards, 1997.

2 The Challenge of Symbolic Communication

1 *Labour Organiser* no. 44, 1924, Ostrogorski, 1902. 'Propaganda' was sometimes used to distinguish a vocal appeal from its written equivalent 'publicity' and did not have the negative connotations it has subsequently acquired (*Labour Organiser* no. 33, 1923).
2 Butler, 1952, p. 30
3 Julian Amery, cited in Russell, 1973, p. 125.
4 McKibbin, 1974, p. 128.
5 Croft, 1945, p. 7.
6 Shinwell, 1981, pp. 97–101.
7 *Labour Organiser* no. 27, 1923; Hollins, 1981, p. 140.
8 Croft, 1945. The core method of canvassing altered little following innovations introduced during the 1950 Reading campaign. In devising the 'Reading pad', local MP Ian Mikardo's aim had been to identify and get the Labour vote out rather than convert people on the doorstep (Mikardo, 1988, p. 113).
9 *Labour Organiser* no. 34 and no. 37, 1923. Blewett, 1972, pp. 312–15. See also the later section of this chapter on 'stratified electioneering'.
10 The 1935 election also underlined the party's willingness to use more creative designs in publicity, notably in the major pamphlet 'What Socialism Will Really Mean to You' (Hollins, 1981, pp. 154–155, 158–62; McHenry, 1938, p. 52).
11 *Labour Organiser* no. 66, 1926 and no. 96, 1929; Gorman, 1985, pp. 23, 53 and 113; Hollins, 1981, p. 180.
12 Beattie, 1970, p. 504. Similarly Austen Chamberlain believed the name 'an excellent electioneering asset' (Hollins, 1981, p. 21).
13 *Labour Organiser* no. 42, 1924. The party conference apparently chose the winning logo by clapping loudest for their favourite design. The design was later known as the 'knife, fork and spoon' following its modification by party designer Jack Stoddart in the early 1970s (BBC 'Vote Race' unbroadcast interview with party official, 1991).
14 *Labour Organiser* no. 92, 1929; Jennings, 1960, p. 288.
15 Gorman, 1985, p. 142; Frow, 1999.
16 *Labour Organiser* no. 92, 1929.
17 *Labour Organiser* no. 23, 1922.
18 'Publicity in Politics', *The London News*, May 1937, p. 3.
19 Wallas, 1948, p. 87.
20 Pinto-Duschinsky, 1981, pp. 93–94.
21 *Labour Organiser* no. 41, 1924; no. 61, 1926; no. 175 and no. 176, 1936.

22 *Labour Organiser* no. 44, 1924. The phrase 'social advertising' foreshadowed the debate initiated by Philip Kotler and others over the appropriateness of applying marketing analysis to non-profit making activities (Kotler and Levy, 1969; Kotler and Zaltman, 1971).

23 *Labour Organiser* no. 43, 1924.

24 *Labour Organiser* no. 178, 1936.

25 Tunstall, 1964, p. 166; Hollins, 1981, p. 168.

26 Morrison, 1920, p. 201; Morrison, 1921; Donoughue and Jones, 1973, p. 96.

27 Donoughue and Jones, 1973, pp. 207–208.

28 Edelman, 1948, p. 30; Donoughue and Jones, 1973, p. 55. Edward Bernays popularised the term 'public relations' both as concept and practice from the mid-1920s onwards (Ewen, 1996).

29 Donoughue and Jones, 1973, p. 208.

30 Jones, 1973. Leslie had gained critical acclaim as the creator of the gas industry's 'Mr.Therm' logo. Later, in the Labour governments of the 1940s and 1960s, he worked advising ministers including Tony Benn (Toye, 2003, p. 221). A wealthy businessman, Wansborough was introduced to Morrison by Hugh Dalton and stood as a parliamentary candidate for Woolwich West. Fraser worked alongside Leslie at LPE before becoming Director-General of the Independent Television Authority after the war (Donoughue and Jones, 1973, p. 209). Following the war, the Exchange became the largest British owned agency in London and boasted several highly prestigious accounts including Ford motors (Pearson and Turner, 1965, pp. 13–44). LPE merged with Leo Burnett in the late 1960s.

31 *Daily Express*, 4th March 1937 *The London News*, January 1937; 'Mr Morrison calling London', *Daily Herald*, 25th February 1937; Donoughue and Jones, 1973, p. 209.

32 *Labour Organiser* no. 193, 1937; Casey, 1944.

33 Donoughue and Jones, 1973, p. 209. New Fabian Research Bureau (1937).

34 Morgan, 1992, p. 178 and p. 182. In government Morrison continued to take an interest in presentation and became a keen proponent of the new Central Office of Information (Rose, 1967, p. 61).

35 *Labour Organiser* no. 18, 1922 and no. 61, 1926; Hollins, 1981, p. 163; Gorman 1985, p. 166.

36 Hollins, 1981, p. 165.

37 Gorman, 1985, p. 168–69.

38 Attlee, 1954, p. 144.

39 Rosenbaum, 1997, p. 86.

40 Butler, 1995, p. 8.

41 Brooke, 1995.

42 Gorman, 1996; Pimlott, 1985, p. 320; Dalyell, 1989, p. 51.

43 *Labour Party National Executive Report*, 24th July 1945. Armstrong, an accomplished painter and commercial artist, worked with eminent people such as Alexander Korda and actress Elsa Lanchester, the star of *Bride of Frankenstein* (Gorman, 1996).

44 Mitchell, 1995.

45 The wartime Army Bureau of Current Affairs was held up as a model of this in action. ABCA organised political talks and education for service personnel and many of its instructors were sympathetic to the left although its

contribution to the 1945 victory is a contested one (Fielding et al., 1995, pp. 27–9).

46 Ryan, 1986, p. 3.
47 Hollins, 1981, p. 184; Hogenkamp, 1986, p. 18; Jones, 1987, p. 139. Francis Meynell's involvement is particularly significant given his background in publishing and design. In the 1930s Meynell became creative director for the leading London advertising firm that later took over the Conservatives' favoured agency to form Ogilvy Benson and Mather (Pigott, 1975, p. 40).
48 Hollins, 1981, p. 186; Ryan, 1986, p. 84 and p. 87; Jones, 1987, p. 140–44; *Labour Organiser* no. 160, 1934, no. 166, 1935.
49 *Labour Organiser* no. 162, 1934.
50 Lebas, 1995; Jones, 1987, p. 143.
51 Hollins, 1981, pp. 180 and 186; Thorpe, 1991, p. 180.
52 *Labour Organiser*, no. 166, 1935. Note that in 1930 the then Labour leader Ramsay MacDonald became the first premier to have a television installed at 10 Downing Street (Cockerell, 1989, p. 1).
53 Cited in McPherson, 1980, p. 153; Rotha, 1936; Hollins, 1981, p. 194; Hogenkamp, 1986, p. 180–1, and Jones, 1987, p. 144.
54 Bond, R. 1979; McHenry, 1938, p. 75.
55 Hogenkamp, 1986, p. 182; Burton, 1994, pp. 44–45.
56 Hollins, 1981, p. 206; Hogenkamp, 1986, p. 188; Hogenkamp, 2000, p. 33.
57 Berrington, 1992.
58 *Labour Organiser* no. 71, 1927. Such was the popularity of human science that Dr Lyster Jameson's National Council for Labour Colleges handbook, *An Outline of Psychology*, sold over 18,000 copies and was reprinted 10 times between the wars (Jameson, 1938).
59 *Labour Organiser*, no. 22, 1922.
60 *Labour Organiser* no. 81, 1928 and no. 108, 1930.
61 *Labour Organiser* no. 48, 1924 and no. 125, 1931.
62 *Labour Organiser* no. 126, 1931. See also New Fabian Research Bureau (1937).
63 *Labour Organiser* no. 25, 1922. Significantly stratified electioneering predates the popularisation of the mainstream market segmentation concept in the 1950s business literature.
64 *Labour Organiser* no. 89, 1929. Dean McHenry also acknowledged the important legacy of Webb's analysis in a book on the inter-war party unusual for its detailed attention to campaign organisation (McHenry, 1938, p. 99).
65 Croft, 1945, pp. 3–4 and 8.
66 *Labour Organiser* no. 54, 1925.
67 *Labour Organiser* no. 50, 1925.
68 *Labour Organiser* no. 16 and no. 19, 1922.
69 *Labour Organiser* no. 44, 1924; Croft, 1945.
70 Pelling, 1984, p. 26.
71 *Labour Organiser* no. 412, 1956. Over a decade later telling references were still being made to Webb's 'stratified electioneering' concept, notably in organiser Len Sims' review of the latest American campaign practices, *Labour Organiser* no. 531, 1967.
72 Jennings, 1960, pp. 228 and 249; McHenry, 1938, p. 303.
73 Labour Party, 1918; *Labour Organiser* no. 29, 1923; Berger, 1994, p. 63.
74 *Labour Organiser* no. 34, 1923.

75 Donoughue and Jones, 1973, p. 336; Madge, 1945, pp. 24–25.

76 NEC minutes, 23ʳᵈ January 1950; Berrington, 1992.

77 Beckett, 2000, p. 281.

78 *Labour Organiser* nos. 415 and 412, 1956. In the 1951 general election Labour attempted to appeal to non-traditional supporters with the slogan 'Fair Shares for All' (Jennings, 1960, p. 251). Similarly the columnist writing 'Quair's Page' in the party agents' journal recognised the success of 'Tory horror comics' in rousing the instrumental type 'Jimmy Green' voters during the 1955 campaign (*Labour Organiser* no. 398, 1955).

3 Admass Politics

1 McLuhan, 1964; Edelman, 1964.

2 Habermas, 1962; Qualter, 1962.

3 Wiener, 1980, p. 124. Priestley coined the term in a 1955 piece for the *New Statesman* on commercialism. See also the influential work by Hoggart, 1957; Packard, 1957; and Boorstin, 1962.

4 Williams, 1980, p. 184.

5 Galbraith, 1969, p. 134.

6 Kirchheimer, 1966. See also Rose, 1967, p. 22; Nimmo, 1970.

7 Epstein, 1967, pp. 257–60. The phrase inverted Duverger's 'contagion from the left', a description of the mass organisation favoured by European social democrats during the early twentieth century. Duverger himself acknowledged the possible emergence of a 'bureaucratic' or 'technocratic oligarchy' advising the 'Inner Circle' around party leaderships (Duverger, 1954, p. 155). See also Beer, 1965, pp. 416–8.

8 Seymour-Ure, 1974, p. 216.

9 Rogow, A. 1952; Wildy, 1985; Weinbren, 1997, p. 191. Despite widespread party animosity towards their industry some advertising agents still professed support for Labour (*Labour Organiser* no. 363, 1952).

10 Craig, 1982, pp. 178–79; NEC Policy and Publicity Sub-committee minutes, April 1955. Public relations techniques had been employed during the campaign courtesy of MPs with press expertise like Tom Driberg and Richard Crossman (NEC Policy and Publicity Sub-committee minutes, 15ᵗʰ November 1954).

11 Rose, 1963; Hattersley, 1966, p. 157; Teer and Spence, 1973, p. 167.

12 Teer and Spence, 1973, p. 165.

13 Howell, 1976, pp. 227–29.

14 Windlesham, 1966, pp. 83–84.

15 Fletcher, 1977; on the wider role of the CIA's Congress for Cultural Freedom see Stonor Saunders, 2000, and Wilford, 2003.

16 Roth, 1977, p. 233.

17 Rose, 1967, p. 62. Wring, 1997b.

18 Mort, 1990.

19 Butler and Rose, 1960, p. 20; Rose, 1967, pp. 36–43. The Conservatives' strategy was likened to the groundbreaking 1952 US Republican campaign, an election that Central Office's Head of Broadcasting John Profumo had observed at first hand (Tunstall, 1964, p. 168; Cockerell, 1989, p. 15). Talk

of detergent led one commentator to write of the parties competing as though they were Daz or Omo (Black, 203, p. 165).

20 Crosland, 1962, p. 161. Harold Wilson believed that CPV's efforts had contributed to Labour's defeat (Wilson, 1986, p. 170).

21 Street, 1992; Zweinger-Bargielowska, 1994.

22 Gamble, 1974, p. 15.

23 Butler and Rose, 1960, p. 17; Teer and Spence, 1973, p. 158. The psephological research that began appearing during the 1950s challenged a number of assumptions about electoral behaviour, notably the view that 'rational' voters were evenly distributed along a unilinear ideological spectrum. For 'heretics' such a distribution of opinions had long appeared an over-simplification (Jennings, 1960, p. 289; McLean, 1976, pp. 30–34).

24 Mayhew, 1969, pp. 96–97; Hogenkamp, 2000, pp. 36–7. As junior minister to Ernest Bevin in the Foreign Office, Mayhew had set up the Information Research Department having previously been a psychological warfare operative in the Second World War. The propaganda unit played a controversial role during the Cold War until its closure in 1977. Its associates included Labour's first head of publicity Herbert Tracey of the anti-communist union campaign Freedom First (Weiler, 1988, pp. 216–8).

25 Hogenkamp, 2000, p. 45.

26 Betteridge, 1997. Benn had observed the 1952 US presidential election and met Democratic candidate Stevenson on a trip that confirmed his belief in the electoral importance of television (Benn, 1995, p. 166). Professional advisers like Baverstock and Wheldon were routinely seconded from the BBC to help the parties produce their films. One of Baverstock's most successful PEBs, featuring journalists interviewing Herbert Morrison, was praised for appealing to 'floating voters' ('Report on Party Political Broadcasting', NEC minutes, 15th March 1955).

27 Adams, 1992, p. 142.

28 'Draft Plan for General Election Broadcasting', NEC Broadcasting Advisory Committee, 14th November 1958; Benn, 1994, p. 263.

29 Cockerell, 1989, pp. 59–60.

30 Milne, 1988, p. 25; Hogenkamp, 2000, p. 105. Other 'Tonight' broadcasters involved included Donald Baverstock and presenter Cliff Michelmore (Benn, 1994, pp. 295–96). The campaign post-mortem commended Milne as 'the key man in the operation' and noted the *Daily Mirror*'s commendation 'Labour Hits Television Jackpot' (*National Executive Report General Election Report 1959*). Similarly Leeds University's study of election broadcasting suggested the series had been effective (Trenamen and McQuail, 1961, p. 116).

31 Butler and Rose, 1960, p. 25–29.

32 *Labour Organiser* no. 416, 1957.

33 Butler and Rose, 1960, pp. 27 and 48.

34 Crane, 1959; Butler and King, 1965, pp. 61–65.

35 The Editorial prefaced Rowland, 1960.

36 Brivati and Wincott, 1993.

37 Rowland, 1960; Young Fabian Group, 1962. The party upgraded the Directorship of Publicity in 1962 although subsequent post-holders did not

gain the influence recommended by the Young Fabians. Their report's rec-ommendations were in effect implemented twenty years later when Robin Cook took up such a portfolio within the Shadow Cabinet as Campaigns Co-ordinator following the 1983 defeat (see Chapter Five).

38 *Socialist Commentary*, 1959; Mulley, 1961; Irving, 1962.

39 *Labour Organiser* no. 489, 1963.

40 Young Fabian Group, 1962. In the 1930s a Labour campaigner labelled this phenomenon as 'perpetual electioneering' (see Chapter One). The Group's use of the term 'permanent campaign pre-empted its popularisation twenty years later (Blumenthal, 1982).

41 Rowland, 1960.

42 Pearson and Turner, 1965, p. 258; Mitchell and Wienir, 1997, p. 38.

43 Butler and Rose, 1960, p. 25; Seymour-Ure, 1974, p. 215. Morgan Philips had originally joined headquarters in 1931 as Propaganda Officer.

44 Brivati and Wincott, 1993.

45 Brivati, 1992, pp. 132 and 149.

46 Windlesham, 1966, p. 102.

47 Jenkins, 1979, pp. 126–129.

48 See commentary by Patrick Seyd in Brivati and Wincott, 1993.

49 Brivati and Wincott, 1993.

50 Erwin Wasey, 1947.

51 'Notes on the Findings of the Public Opinion Polls', NEC Report on the 1950 General Election. 11th April 1950.

52 Teer and Spence, 1973, p. 166; Black, 2003, p. 176. Ginsburg's work was supported by several ex-ministers who had used survey research in government.

53 Gaitskell, 1955.

54 Labour Party, 1955.

55 Butler and King, 1965, p. 67.

56 Labour Party, 1959, pp. 108–114. See also Black, 2003.

57 Rowland, 1960. Aside from Abrams, other party research projects involved a candidate survey, analysis of Robert McKenzie's study into working-class Toryism and an assessment of the Leeds University evalua-tion of the election on television (NEC Home Policy Sub-committee minutes, 7th November 1959).

58 Fielding, 1993, p. 37; Worcester, 1991, p. 24.

59 Butler and King, 1965, p. 67. Abrams' four instalments were part of a series entitled 'Why Labour has lost elections' and appeared in successive issues of *Socialist Commentary* between May and August. The book reproduced Abrams' findings together with an appraisal of contemporary electoral politics by Rose, the academic and co-author of the 1959 Nuffield election study. Hinden, who is routinely left out when the text is cited, contributed an important section on the research finding's 'Lessons for Labour' (Abrams, Rose with Hinden, 1960). *Must Labour Lose?* also attracted Conservative inter-est and led to Abrams making a presentation to the party's influential Bow Group and producing analysis of the Tory working-class vote (Abrams, 1960).

60 Crosland, 1962; Crosland writing to Gaitskell, Black, 2003, p. 157. Crosland's growing awareness of the potential importance of the mass media is borne out in a letter written to Gaitskell in 1960 which isolated

Tony Benn's interest in this arena as a significant indicator of his broader political position in the party at that time: '... on the whole question of public relations, propaganda and reform of the machine... he holds quite enlightened views' (Crosland, 1983, pp. 104–5).

61 Rees, 1960; Abrams, Rose with Hinden, 1960, p. 100. Views like this led Gaitskellite MP Douglas Jay to suggest the party change its name (Forward, 16ᵗʰ October 1959).

62 Crane, 1969; Hattersley, 1966, p. 150–2.

63 Labour Party, 1960.

64 Butler and Rose, 1960, pp. 20 and 29.

65 His biographer did however note that Gaitskell 'did not neglect various electoral gimmicks' and made visits to 'old folks homes' (McDermott, 1972, pp. 170–71).

66 White, 1958; *Labour Organiser* no. 448, 1959.

67 Rose, 1967, p. 63; Challen, 1998, p. 60.

68 Abrams, 1964; Rose, 1965.

69 Black, 2003, p. 156.

70 Foot, 1973, p. 629.

71 Smith and Saunders, 1990; Black, 2003, p. 53. Although some began challenging the 'gospel' and 'Socialist Sunday School' approach to campaigning of Gaitskell's 'puritan' opponents, many agents remained hostile to 'glossy' television promotions ('How to Make Socialists', *Labour Organiser* no. 448, 1959; Hattersley, 1966, p. 41).

72 *Labour Organiser* no. 488, 1963.

73 Potter, 1960, p. 15; Black, 2003, p. 165.

74 Labour Party, 1961.

75 Tunstall, 1964, p. 235.

76 Morrison, 1960, p. 314; Hodder-Williams, 1970, p. 80. Similarly Bevan argued pollsters were an expensive irrelevance: 'We don't need to listen to this. I know what the working man thinks' (Rose, 1974, p. 76). For his part Richard Crossman was downright cynical: 'I am only completely convinced of the findings of the Gallup poll when they confirm my own impression of what the public is thinking' (Hodder-Williams, 1970, p. 80).

77 Benn, 1965, p. 35.

78 McQuail, 1960; Samuel et al., 1960; *Labour Organiser* no. 462, 1960 and no. 486, 1962.

79 Miliband, 1961, p. 347. See also Benson, 1978; Forester, 1976, pp. 20–23; and Black, 2003, p. 149–54. The 'embourgeoisement' thesis was later challenged by Essex University's influential affluent worker studies (Goldthorpe et al., 1968).

80 Abrams, 1964; Butler and King, 1965, p. 50–51.

81 Crossman, 1960. Similarly in a 1961 letter to Ralph Miliband, Crossman argued: 'What we should have concentrated on between elections was not propaganda to the apathetic voter, but the education of a cadre of active Socialists' (cited in Saville, 1996, p. 232). For other left-wingers like Michael Foot, Labour's challenge was stark: 'In order to win an election, we have to change the mood of the people in this country, to open their eyes to what an evil and disgraceful society it is' (Howell, 1976, p. 229).

82 Black, 2003, p. 173.

83 Samuel, 1960.

84 Miliband, 1961, p. 339.

4 Selling the Party

1 Butler and King, 1965, p. 64. Apart from the standing sub-committees of the Labour NEC (Organisation, Publicity, etc), ad hoc bodies were convened for specific purposes. The Campaign Committee, an example of the latter, consisted of party leader, deputy leader, party (NEC) chair, General Secretary (the headquarters' chief executive), national agent (head of organisation), and the chairs of NEC sub-committees on youth, finance, organisation and publicity. Other officials and representatives sat in when required.

2 Rowland, 1960; Cockerell, 1989, p. 89.

3 Dorril and Ramsay, 1992, pp. 32–3.

4 McKenzie, 1955, p. 568; NEC minutes, 24th January 1962; Howard and West, 1964, p. 129. The recruitment process was not without controversy as Barbara Castle voiced criticism of the way the posts were advertised (NEC Press and Publicity Sub-committee minutes, 15th February 1962; NEC minutes, 18th April 1962). The contenders for the Directorship included: Winston Fletcher, later an influential figure in advertising; Leif Mills, future leader of banking union BIFU; PR consultant Gerald Gulliver; and marketing executive Frank Green.

5 Pearson and Turner, 1965, p. 258. The important organisational role of both men's deputies should not be overlooked. Percy Clark, originally a candidate for Harris' job and party official since 1946, took the new Deputy Directorship of Publicity having previously worked as a journalist in north-west England and been a member of the *Tribune* editorial team (NEC minutes, 23rd May 1962; Pearson and Turner, 1965, p. 258). George Brown, elected deputy following his unsuccessful bid for the leadership against Wilson, was supportive of the polling research programme and helped establish links with advertising advisers like David Kingsley (NEC Publicity Sub-committee minutes, 15th February 1962; Altman, 1964).

6 Fielding, 1993; White, 1962.

7 Rose, 1967, p. 64; Worcester, 1991, p. 25.

8 Butler and King, 1965, p. 67–68; Howard and West, 1964, p. 130.

9 Howard and West, 1964, p. 130; Pearson and Turner, 1965, pp. 137 and 259; Rose, 1967, p. 72. Kingsley was briefly Prospective Parliamentary Candidate for East Grinstead prior to the 1964 election, the year in which he formed Kingsley Manton Palmer, a firm later renowned for its celebrated Salvation Army 1960s campaign 'For God's Sake Care' (Babaz, 1980).

10 *Labour Organiser* no. 492, 1964.

11 Mitchell and Wienir, 1997, pp. 38–9; Altman, 1964.

12 Teer and Spence, 1973, p. 169; Socialist Commentary, 1965, p. xix.

13 Abrams, 1964; Pearson and Turner, 1965, p. 260; and Hodder-Williams, 1970, p. 89. The research pinpointed 'wavering' and 'unattached electors' who needed 'systematically developed publicity' (NEC Campaign Committee minutes, 29th November 1962). Other aspects of the work focused on investigating the white-collar vote, notably the report 'Non-manual Workers and the Labour Party' (NEC Home Policy Committee minutes, January 1962).

14   Butler and King, 1965, pp. 68–71; Butler and King, 1966, p. 33.
15   Hattersley, 1966, pp. 159–60. Others enjoyed this kind of meeting. David
     Kingsley recalled how a May 1964 'sales conference' presentation to 1200
     officials, MPs, agents and candidates ended with a 'standing ovation',
     Kingsley, 1983.
16   Teer and Spence, 1973, p. 154.
17   Hodder-Williams, 1970, p. 86; Rose, 1967, pp. 75 and 80.
18   Rose, 1967, pp. 72 and 79.
19   Howard and West, 1964, p. 132. The original inspiration allegedly came
     from an advert devised for the SPD, Labour's West German sister party.
20   Howard and West, 1964, pp. 130–31.
21   Rose, 1967, p. 81.
22   Pearson and Turner, 1965, p. 261; Cockerell, 1989, p. 109. 'New Britain'
     provided the title of Wilson's own book of speeches (Wilson, 1964). Tony
     Benn recalls the role of his American wife and himself in getting Wilson to
     self-promote in this way (Mitchell and Wienir, 1997, pp. 35 and 40–1).
     Wilson was, however, careful to play down the importance of his own pres-
     idential style inner circle (Butler and King, 1965, p. 150).
23   Vig, 1968, pp. 37–38.
24   Mitchell and Wienir, 1997, pp. 62–3.
25   Pearson and Turner, 1965, pp. 258–59; Rose, 1967, p. 82; NEC Publicity
     Sub-committee minutes, 13th July 1962; NEC minutes, 23rd October 1962.
     Smith later gained public notoriety when he was imprisoned on corruption
     charges arising out of the Poulson affair during the 1970s (Wainwright,
     1987, p. 24). Smith, and his eventful life, formed the dramatic backdrop to
     BBC's critically acclaimed 1996 television series *Our Friends in the North*. His
     organisation gave PR advice to prospective candidates (see Peter Ward,
     'Press Relations', *Labour Organiser* no. 501, 1964).
26   NEC Broadcasting Advisory Committee minutes, April 1958; Babaz,
     1980, pp. 146–47; Mitchell and Wienir, 1997, p. 125. The ('senior')
     Broadcasting Committee, with overall control over output, contained
     politicians and was chaired by the Chief Whip, the person who tradition-
     ally represented the party on the official government body responsible
     for regulating and allocating PEB/PPB airtime. The ('junior') Broadcasting
     Advisory Committee headed by Tony Benn included politicians with
     technical expertise, journalists like George Ffitch and James Cameron,
     and the television dramatist and Ted Willis, the creator of 'Dixon of
     Dock Green'. In 1964 the functions of the senior committee were
     absorbed by the Campaign Committee to which Tony Benn, on behalf of
     his advisory group, attended whenever broadcasting strategy was dis-
     cussed (Butler and King, 1965, p. 68). The *Socialist Commentary* report on
     party organisation recommended handing over control to an advisory
     body of technical experts in an early attempt to prioritise presentational
     rather than purely political objectives in the material (Socialist
     Commentary, 1965).
27   Howard and West, 1964, p. 132–33. From October to July 1964 the team
     produced one 10, four 15 and one 20 minute PEBs for television and four of
     five and two of 10 minutes for the radio.
28   Butler and King, 1965, p. 177.

29 Socialist Commentary, 1965, p. iv. The 'Penny Farthing' report, co-ordinated by Jim Northcott, formed a key part of the so-called 'Plan for an Efficient Party' and proposed the creation of a new structure within head-quarters centred on three or four key officials or 'Directors', one of which would have responsibility for all party presentation. As the pamphlet pointed out 'a powerful Director with more people at his disposal should be able to co-ordinate all the elements of the Party's publicity' (Socialist Commentary, 1965, p. xx). Chapter Five discusses Kinnock's reforms.

30 Butler and King, 1966, p. 31.

31 Ibid, pp. 32–3. In 1966 Labour published the results of an inquiry into advertising. Chaired by Lord Reith since 1962, this relatively sympathetic investigation took soundings from experts including Brian Copland, Brian McCabe and party pollster Mark Abrams (Labour Party, 1966).

32 Interview with Robert Worcester. Clark became Director after the 1964 election and remained in post until 1979. Harris subsequently worked closely with Roy Jenkins as a peer, Home Office minister and prominent member of the SDP and Liberal Democrats.

33 *Labour Party Annual Conference Report*, 1966, p. 87; Butler and King, 1966, p. 32; Falkender, 1983, p. 144. If professional experts were becoming increasingly popular, the number of agents at local level had begun to decline. In 1951 there were 296 full-time organisers. By 1959 this figure had fallen to 243, was 193 by 1964 and only 128 in 1971. (Leonard, 1965; Leonard, 1975).

34 Butler and King, 1966, p. 180. The (in)famous 'kitchen cabinet' included aides and personal advisers such as political secretary Marcia Williams (later Lady Falkender), George Wigg MP, Gerald Kaufman (press secretary in the 1960s), Joe Haines (Kaufman's replacement in the 1970s), and Bernard Donoughue. The group, if not the exact same personnel, remained with Wilson for the rest of his leadership (Kavanagh, 1995, p. 78).

35 Howard, 1979, p. 395.

36 Williams, 1972, p. 294; Lees and Kimber, 1972, pp. 54–62.

37 Alexander and Watkins, 1970, p. 150. Ironically the party had originally planned to campaign on the major theme of 'Labour's Winning Team' (Butler and Pinto-Duschinsky, 1971, p. 133). Wilson's press secretary Joe Haines later blamed the 'massive miscalculation' of the presidential style campaign on Williams (Haines, 1977, p. 170–1).

38 *Labour Party National Executive Report*, 1970, pp. 29 and 155. Other personal-ities involved in the campaign included 'Callan' star Edward Woodward (ibid, p. 7).

39 *Labour Organiser* no. 556, 1969; *Labour Party Annual Conference Report*, 1969.

40 Alexander and Watkins, 1970, p. 155; Worcester, 1992.

41 Quoted in Francis Wheen, 'Well-suited to redder tones', *The Guardian*, 3rd April 1996.

42 *Labour Party National Executive Report*, 1970, p. 7; Butler and Pinto-Duschinsky, 1971, p. 133. The issue further embarrassed the Labour leadership when the BBC Panorama team made a post-election documentary on Wilson and his colleagues entitled 'Yesterday's Men' (Tracey, 1977).

43 Bing, 1971; Butler and Pinto-Duschinsky, 1971, pp. 56–57; Teer and Spence, 1973, pp. 171–72; Kavanagh, 1995, pp. 80 and p. 130. Jamieson went on to

work with those responsible for forming SRU, a company whose executives would begin helping Labour in the mid-1980s (see Chapter Five).

44   Worcester, 1991, p. 38.
45   Kavanagh, 1982.
46   Stewart, 1974, p. 48; Butler and Kavanagh, 1975, p. 253.
47   Stewart, 1974, p. 49; Babaz, 1980, p. 73. Former official Jim Parish remembered the haphazard approach to aspects of party presentation during this period and recalled how Percy Clark would canvass Publicity officials for ideas for Annual Conference slogans. The best of these was usually chosen without reference to politicians (Rosenbaum, 1997, p. 145).
48   Leonard, 1975; Butler and Kavanagh, 1975, p. 102; Worcester, 1991, pp. 43–44; Morgan, 1992, p. 460. Lyons was later knighted and Davis became Lord Lovell-Davis for their services to the party.
49   Rosenbaum, 1997, p. 12. Powell had been an ad hoc adviser to the party since 1971 and would later play a major role in the 1987, 1992 and 1997 elections (Powell, 2000).
50   Butler and Kavanagh, 1974, pp. 78–82, 112 and 200–2. They also noted: 'It is possible that all the manoeuvrings in Smith Square to which so much attention is given are of negligible importance, having at most only a random, effect on the outcome of the contest' (p. 248).
51   Leonard, 1975; Falkender, 1983, pp. 52–53.
52   Butler and Kavanagh, 1974, p. 158.
53   Worcester, 1991, pp. 49–51; Rosenbaum, 1997, p. 169. The findings were used to segment the electorate into distinct categories such as 'Old Fred' (Fallon and Worcester, 1992). Worcester later wrote how Ronald Reagan's consultant on psychographics Richard Wirthlin told him that the 'Red Book' MORI prepared for Labour prior to the 1974 campaign was 'ten years ahead of anything in America' (Worcester, 1996). Former LSE lecturer Bernard Donoughue helped assess and monitor the poll findings although the programme was dogged by a controversy surrounding payments made to fund it by Wilson associate and industrialist (later Lord) Harry Kissin (Morgan, 1992, p. 461).
54   Butler and Kavanagh, 1975, pp. 202 and 205; Worcester, 1991, p. 54. Worcester recalled how ex-statistician Wilson had 'a better memory for my data than I did' (Rosenbaum, 1997, p. 160). The former prime minister reflected on the value of polling not long after leaving office when he addressed the Market Research Society's Conference of 1978 (Wilson, 1978).
55   Falkender, 1983, p. 61. Wilson reportedly had particularly good working relationships with Director of Publicity Percy Clark and Broadcasting Officer Doreen Stainforth.
56   Rose, 1974, p. 81.
57   Butler and Kavanagh, 1980, p. 323–25; Johnson and Elebash, 1986; Cockerell, 1989, p. 248. Chancellor Denis Healey had earlier initiated the attack on the Saatchi brothers decision to 'sell Mrs.Thatcher as if she were a soap powder' (Labour Party Press and Publicity Department news release, 9th August 1978). Others, notably Michael Foot in his Conference speech that year, returned to this theme.
58   Butler and Kavanagh, 1980, p. 132; Delaney, 1982.
59   Leonard, 1981; Fletcher, 1984, p. 109. MORI input was supplemented by findings from Crewe's British Election Study, research which played a part

in Callaghan's fateful decision to delay going to the polls in Autumn 1978 prior to the 'Winter of Discontent' that undermined his government (Kavanagh, 1980).

60 Worcester, 1991, p. 71; Kavanagh, 1995, p. 132.

61 Johnson and Elebash, 1986.

62 Leonard, 1981. Leonard's piece, 'Labour and the Voters', formed part of a tribute to Anthony Crosland and urged the party to develop, adopting Crosland's phrase, a 'rapport' with the electorate. The former MP cited poll findings to argue in favour of the loosening of ties with the trade unions, for the party to be an enabling rather than bureaucratic force in government, and the abandonment of Clause Four and the policy of nationalisation. Leonard's sentiments were highly unfashionable and led him to leave Labour for the SDP.

63 Wheeler, 1979; Butler and Kavanagh, 1980, p. 134.

64 Butler and Kavanagh, 1980, p. 136; Fletcher, 1984, p. 109; Kavanagh, 1995, p. 89.

65 Wickham-Jones, 1996, p. 181.

66 Kogan and Kogan, 1983, p. 59; Innes, 1983.

67 *National Executive Report 1983*, pp. 55–58; Kellner, 1985. An insider suggested Bish's seniority led to an imbalance in campaign preparations, which favoured inputs from the Policy Department (Innes, 1983). Among the staff helping with press enquiries was Andrew Morton, future biographer of Princess Diana.

68 Butler and Kavanagh, 1984, p. 57–8; Wright, 1986; Johnson and Elebash, 1986. In addition a small advisory group of advertising experts was convened (Rosenbaum, 1997, pp. 22 and 161).

69 The 'Act Positive' clause was added as a compromise after objections, although General Secretary Jim Mortimer remained unhappy with the 'almost meaningless' slogan (Grant, 1986; Mortimer, 1998, p. 391).

70 Butler and Kavanagh, 1984, p. 57; Grant, 1986; Worcester and Mortimore, 1999, p. 12. Though electoral polling accounts for a fraction of the research company's overall business, firms tolerate awkward political clients because of the public relations opportunities that derive from such work (Blumler, Kavanagh and Nossiter, 1996).

71 *Labour Party Annual Conference Report 1983*, p. 45; Kellner, 1985; *Campaign*, 1st August 1986.

72 Butler and Kavanagh, 1984, pp. 56 and 64; Kellner, 1985.

73 Kellner, 1985. The party attempted to redress the deficiencies in Foot's public ratings by promoting Denis Healey, Peter Shore and Roy Hattersley at morning press conferences. General Secretary Jim Mortimer put Foot's own position on the agenda by admitting that the Campaign Committee had reaffirmed their faith in his leadership and thereby unwittingly suggested there had been serious discussions about the matter.

74 Interviewed on BBC1's Panorama 'The Marketing of Margaret', broadcast summer 1983. There was an important policy dimension to these beliefs given Shadow Home Secretary Roy Hattersley had previously denounced the advertising industry for creating an obsession with consumer durables and 'crude materialism'. Given Hattersley was on the Labour right, the stance underlined the continuing power of educationalist thought within

the party at the time. Such views were inevitably dismissed by professionals as 'an indulgence of the rich and the elite' (Fletcher, 1984, p. 122). Perhaps it was fitting that the executive who offered this rebuttal, Winston Fletcher, now advised the SDP having previously been an applicant for the Labour Publicity Directorship in the 1960s.

75 Mitchell, 1983. The Nuffield study attributes the 'longest suicide' phrase to Shadow Chancellor Peter Shore though others claim Gerald Kaufman first used the term (Butler and Kavanagh, 1984, p. 62).

5 Designer Labour

1 Hattersley et al., 1983; Whiteley, 1983; Harris, 1984. Kinnock's view was endorsed by NEC member Denis Howell who prefaced his submission to the electoral post-mortem: 'CAMPAIGN STRATEGY: There was none' (National Executive Committee minutes, July 1983). Similarly a former official commented: 'How dare we revel in our crude, brutally inefficient amateurism?' (Innes, 1983).

2 See the insightful piece by ex-SDP adviser Winston Fletcher 'What was the message?', *The Guardian*, 4th June 1990. See also Semetko, 1987 and Crewe and King, 1995.

3 Scammell, 1995, p. 272.

4 Kavanagh, 1995, p. 175.

5 Scammell, 1995, p. 76. See also Wendy Webster who draws attention to the complicity of the media in creating the Thatcher phenomenon (Webster, 1990, pp. 72–74).

6 Scammell, 1995, p. 105; Elebash, 1984.

7 Myers, 1986, pp. 115–6; Carvel, 1987, pp. 219–21.

8 Clark, 1986, p. 443.

9 Forrester et al., 1985, p. 80; Carvel, 1987, p. 233; Curran, 1987; Waller, 1988; Channon, 1989.

10 *Marketing Week*, 11th March 1988.

11 Kinnock, 1983.

12 *The Guardian*, 19th September 1991. See also 'The legacy of the GLC's pioneering publicity bid', *Campaign*, 28th March 1986; and comments by Publicity Director Nick Grant (*The Guardian*, 25th November 1985) and adviser Chris Powell (Powell, 2000).

13 *Tribune*, 25th April 1986.

14 *The Guardian*, 30th January 1985. The left's changing attitude towards advertising an consumption is discussed and articulated in Kathy Myers' book *Understains* (Myers, 1986). For a more critical perspective see Williamson, 1986.

15 *Labour Party Annual Conference Report 1983*, pp. 35–36, pp. 45–54; *Tribune*, 14th October 1983; Butler and Jowett, 1985, p. 63; Shaw, 1994, p. 54. MP Austin Mitchell applauded professionals for their 'sense of reality' (Mitchell, 1983, p. 127).

16 *Tribune*, 5th August 1983. Wise drew support from left-wing and conservative Executive members (see, for instance, 'No plans for propaganda', *New Statesman*, 15th July 1983). The same meeting saw Dennis

Skinner attacking proposals to hire an agency for the 1984 European elections.

17 Webb, 1992. By tradition the Chief Whip took responsibility for broadcasting. The CSC ended this and began using filmmakers like ex-BBC head of Current Affairs John Gau and performers like Prunella Scales (*National Executive Committee Report 1984*, pp. 51–55; Butler and Jowett, 1985, p. 64). Gau's restyled PPBs were modelled on the 1970s BBC news programme 'Nationwide' (*The Guardian*, 2nd October 1989). Gau continued his work until 1988 (*Campaign*, 12th February 1988).

18 Campaign Strategy Committee minutes, 29th November 1983; CSC minutes, 15th November 1983; *Tribune*, 2nd November 1984.

19 *Tribune*, 28th October 1983; *Tribune* diary, 11th May 1984; Shaw, 1994, p. 54. See also Webb, 1992. According to member Eric Heffer the Committee never met during the 1984–85 miners' strike (Heffer, 1986). The CSC was unlike most other European party campaign structures (Bowler and Farrell, 1992, p. 226).

20 Prior to 2001 the post of Labour Chain referred to the senior NEC member who presided over the Annual Conference and Executive meetings. After this time the title was appropriated by the leadership appointee charged with overseeing strategy.

21 Cockerell, 1983.

22 *The Guardian*, 3rd August 1984; *Tribune*, 5th July 1985.

23 Press and Publicity Sub-committee minutes, 19th July 1983. The Committee continued to be a largely compliant body under leadership ally Gwyneth Dunwoody (Press and Publicity Sub-committee minutes, 9th November 1984).

24 *The Guardian*, 25th April 1985; *The Guardian*, 22nd December 1986; *The Observer*, 17th May 1987.

25 Butler and Jowett, 1985, pp. 60–2; *Tribune*, 27th July 1984. Cook also applauded Livingstone: 'His campaign to save the GLC has not yielded an inch on the point of principle' (*The Guardian*, 3rd August 1984).

26 National Executive Committee minutes, 29th September 1983; Sackman, 1996; Sackman, 1998, pp. 210–213. Members of the group had informal discussions between themselves prior to this more formal launch (*The Guardian*, 2nd October 1989).

27 Kampfner, 1998, p. 67; Gould, 1998, p. 49; Sackman, 1998, pp. 210–213; *Campaign*, 10th October 1985.

28 *Tribune*, 14th June 1985; *PR Week*, 31st October 1985; PRWeek, 14th November 1985. Franks was reportedly the inspiration for character Edina in 1990s BBC sitcom 'Absolutely Fabulous'. On the television promotion of Kinnock during this period see Paterson, 1985.

29 Denselow, 1989, p. 218. Adviser Robert Elms caused controversy when he advocated 'Ditching the Drabbies', that is activists whose personal appearance presented Labour in an unfavourable light (*New Socialist*, June 1986; *The Times*, 31st October 1986).

30 *Tribune*, 31st January 1986; 7th February 1986; Denselow, 1989, p. 219. Polls taken at this time suggested an upturn in Labour's support (Worcester, 1991, p. 105).

31 *The Guardian*, 30th November 1984; *New Statesman*, 30th November 1984; *Tribune*, 22nd February 1985; *The Guardian*, 2nd April 1985; Shaw, 1994, p. 68.

32 *Tribune*, 31st May 1985; Heffernan and Marqusee, 1992, pp. 206–7. Socialist historian Raphael Samuel queried a Jobs and Industry campaign '... in which miners and their families might have been expected to have earned a privileged place. So far as Labour's public rhetoric is concerned, the miners' strike might never have taken place' (*The Guardian*, 10th June 1985).

33 Crick, 1986; Shaw, 1988.

34 Despite this effort the leader lost the Conference but won the NEC.

35 See Patrick Seyd, 'The dawn of the Left's new realists', *The Guardian*, 26th April 1985 as well as the same author's book (Seyd, 1987).

36 *Tribune*, 9th December 1983; 16th November 1984; 4th January 1985; 25th January 1985.

37 *Tribune*, 7th June 1985; see also *Tribune*, 1st February 1985.

38 The new structures resembled those first proposed by the Young Fabian Group and *Socialist Commentary* in the 1960s (see Chapters Three and Four).

39 *Tribune*, 27th September 1985; Heffernan and Marqusee, 1992, p. 209.

40 Hughes and Wintour, 1990, p. 13; McSmith, 1996, p. 255; Macintyre, 1999, p. 74. Following Mandelson's appointment as Director, James Naughtie jokingly reported 'Labour Party appoints Herbert Morrison' (*The Guardian*, 25th September 1985).

41 *The Guardian*, 25th November 1985; Sackman, 1993.

42 Shaw, 1994, p. 55 and p. 57.

43 Heffernan and Marqusee, 1992, p. 214; Hughes and Wintour, 1990, p. 56.

44 Shaw, 1994, p. 57; Macintyre, 1999, p. 217.

45 *PRWeek*, 28th May 1987; Routledge, 1999, p. 83. On Booth's plight, see *Tribune*, 31st October 1986, 14th November 1986. Franks was reportedly dismayed by Labour's failure to court Fleet Street editors.

46 Shaw, 1994, p. 62; Butler and Kavanagh, 1988, p. 62. The CMT was similar to the Office Action Group, a defunct forum that had planned the 1984 European campaign (Butler and Jowett, 1985, p. 62).

47 *National Executive Report*, 1987, p. 4; Shaw, 1994, p. 230; Butler and Kavanagh, 1988, p. 63. The unions' own campaign organisations, Trades Unions for a Labour Victory and the Trades Unions Co-ordinating Committee, merged in 1986 to form Trades Unions for Labour (TUFL) (*Tribune*, 4th April 1986). It promoted initiatives including 'Video International 86', a conference that drew in labour movement speakers and activists from around the world (*New Socialist*, September 1986).

48 *The Guardian*, 30th January 1985; *Labour Party Annual Conference Report 1985*; *PRWeek*, 14th November 1985.

49 Grant, 1986.

50 *Campaign*, 4th September 1987; Hughes and Wintour, 1990, p. 49.

51 Philip Gould, 'Communications Review', 22nd December 1985. See also Butler and Kavanagh, 1988, pp. 62–3; Hughes and Wintour, 1990, pp. 50–2; Kavanagh, 1995, pp. 62–3, and 93; Gould, 1998, pp. 54–56; Westlake, 2001, p. 348. For an alternative perspective to Gould's pessimistic analysis of Labour's predicament see Mann, 1985.

52 Hughes and Wintour, 1990, p. 53. The Tuesday Group was a collective of advertising and PR executives assembled to support Richard Nixon's successful 1968 presidential bid. The Conservatives adopted this type of campaign structure in the 1970 election (Bruce, 1992, p. 109).

53 *Campaign*, 30th May 1986.
54 Cook's proactive role was applauded by Colin Fisher, who subsequently became the SCA's secretary (Kampfner, 1998, p. 67).
55 Quoted in Macintyre, 1999, p. 88.
56 Hughes and Wintour, 1990, pp. 53–5; interviews.
57 Interviewed on Channel 4's 'The Parliament Programme', 5th February 1992. A single agency, Yellowhammer, had wanted the Labour contract for the 1987 election.
58 *PRWeek*, 9th October 1986.
59 Kavanagh, 1995, p. 93; interview. On the links between LPE and Labour see Chapter Two. For more on BMP see *Campaign*, 20th May 1988. Chris Powell, a longstanding supporter, belonged to an illustrious political family: his older brother Charles was foreign affairs adviser to premier Thatcher and younger sibling Jonathan became Blair's chief of staff soon after he won the leadership (*The Guardian*, 23rd July 1990; Rentoul, 1995, p. 446).
60 *Campaign*, 4th September 1987; Hughes and Wintour, 1990, p. 55.
61 *Financial Times*, 11th September 1991; unbroadcast interviews with BBC 'Vote Race' 1991; interviews; comments by Philip Gould at the UK Academy of Marketing Special Interest Group on Political Marketing Conference, Bournemouth University, September 1999. Hunter, a specialist filmmaker, had worked with Colombian President Oscar Arias and his Venezualan counterpart Jaime Lusinchi (O'Shaughnessy, 1990). Formal contact between Labour politicians and American consultants goes back at least as far as the 1975 Common Market referendum in which the services of Charles Guggenheim were retained (Sabato, 1981). See Chapter Six for more on the party's links with American consultants.
62 Macintyre, 1999, p. 138.
63 Gould, 1998, pp. 50–54. Most of the subsequent research for the party avoided the term 'race' and commonly referred to 'minorities'. The issue of voter racism is considered in more explicit detail by Fiona Devine (Devine, 1991; Devine, 1992).
64 Kinnock was particularly influenced by the historian's essay *The Forward March of Labour Halted?* (Hobsbawm and Jacques, 1981).
65 Gould, Herd and Powell, 1989. For a discussion of the research findings see Butler and Kavanagh, 1988, pp. 58 and 65–66. SRU built up a reputation for offering an idiosyncratic service to firms like Marks and Spencer, ICI and Unilever (*Financial Times*, 18th June 1990). Prior to his election as MP for Hartlepool in 1992 Peter Mandelson worked as a consultant with SRU (*Daily Telegraph*, 19th August 1990). Andrew McIntosh, briefly leader of the GLC and later a Labour minister, was also a partner in the agency. Many of those involved in the SRU had previously worked with Conrad Jamieson, the researcher who worked for the party in the 1960s and who nearly became Labour's pollster (see Chapter Four).
66 *The Guardian*, 25th November 1985.
67 *The Guardian*, 13th April 1986; *The Guardian*, 23rd April 1986; Grice, 1986. Nik Oakley Associates advised on the direct marketing of gifts and a book club (Marketing, 18th September 1986).
68 Julie Burchill, *Campaign*, 16th May 1986.

69   *PR Week*, 1ˢᵗ May 1986; *Labour Party Conference Guide 1986*, p. 22; *The Guardian*, 26ᵗʰ September 1986; Hughes and Wintour, 1990, p. 56; Macintyre, 1999, p. 106. Trevor Beattie went on to work for Labour in the 2001 general election.

70   Golding and Middleton, 1982, pp. 81–5.

71   Mandelson, 1988; Shaw, 1994, p. 69; Gould, 1998, pp. 49–50 and 122.

72   Benn, 1992, p. 442; *Tribune*, 17ᵗʰ October 1986; Heffernan and Marqusee, 1992, p. 211. See also Joe Napolitan's memo cited in Gould, 1998, p. 69. Labour strategists appeared reluctant to admit or examine voters' racist attitudes and preferred to dwell on the party's negative association with 'minorities'. Other researchers did, however, look at this issue (note 63 above).

73   Shaw, 1994, p. 63; Sackman, 1998, p. 298.

74   *The Guardian*, 20ᵗʰ May 1986.

75   *Tribune*, 5ᵗʰ December 1986, 19ᵗʰ December 1986.

76   Shaw, 1994, p. 232.

77   Hughes and Wintour, 1990, p. 16; memo from Joe Napolitan, 13ᵗʰ October 1986 cited in Sackman, 1998, p. 232; see also details of Napolitan's other pessimistic memos in Gould, 1998, p. 69.

78   *Marketing*, 26ᵗʰ March 1992. Prior to the red flag logo the party had used a modified version of the classic 1924 shovel, torch and quill emblem. Nicknamed the 'knife, fork and spoon', the silhouette version of the symbol was devised by party designer Jack Stoddart in the early 1970s (unbroadcast interview with party official, BBC 'Vote Race' 1992).

79   *Labour Party Conference Guide 1986*, p. 22; Hughes and Wintour, 1990, p. 53; Gould, 1998, pp. 62–3. Kinnock was particularly influenced by the use of the rose in the 1973 Swedish Social Democrat and 1981 French Socialist campaigns (London Weekend Television, 1993).

80   *Daily Telegraph*, 18ᵗʰ February 1987.

81   Hewitt and Mandelson, 1989; Harrop, 1990.

82   O'Shaughnessy, 1990, p. 2.

83   *New Statesman*, 13ᵗʰ March 1987; Wainwright, 1987, p. 291; Shaw, 1994, pp. 74–76; Hughes and Wintour, 1990, p. 19; Heffernan and Marqusee, 1992, p. 72.

84   Gould, Herd and Powell, 1989.

85   *The Guardian*, 20ᵗʰ May 1987.

86   Gould, Herd and Powell, 1989; Hughes and Wintour, 1990, p. 22.

87   *Campaign*, 8ᵗʰ May 1987; *Daily Telegraph*, 24ᵗʰ April 1987. Unlike the activists featured in the Saatchis' poster those who took part in Labour's shoot were actually unemployed.

88   Butler and Kavanagh, 1988, p. 69; Napolitan, 1976; *Sunday Times*, 22ⁿᵈ September 1991.

89   Hughes and Wintour, 1990, pp. 24–6; Macintyre, 1999, pp. 31 and 145. Mandelson later admitted the decision to promote Kinnock was influenced by intelligence from a Conservative Central Office contact warning of a forthcoming Tory attack on the Labour leader's credibility (*Independent*, 27ᵗʰ January 1989).

90   *National Executive Report*, 1987, pp. 4–6 and 36. Later, recalling his earlier role as a campaign strategist, Benn described himself as 'the Peter Mandelson-

Bryan Gould of the 1959 election. I fought a brilliant campaign and lost' (*The Guardian*, 11ᵗʰ July 1992).

91 Norris, 1987; BBC 'Vote Race' unbroadcast interview 1991.

92 The Saatchi commissioned demographic research suggesting Thatcher might be an electoral liability was challenged by Y & R's psychographic-based findings. Unsurprisingly the Conservative leader took particular interest in the latter's reports (Kleinman, 1987).

93 Tyler, 1987, p. 204 and pp. 247–8. Labour's efforts may not have impressed Thatcher but her PR adviser Tim Bell was sufficiently persuaded to offer Mandelson a job with his lobbying company (Today, 19ᵗʰ October 1987).

94 *The Spectator*, 20ᵗʰ June 1987; see also *Tribune*, 12ᵗʰ June 1987; Scammell, 1995, p. 156.

95 *Tribune*, 5ᵗʰ June 1987. Kinnock received the ultimate 'compliment' the following year when an American presidential hopeful, Democratic Senator Joe Biden, plagiarised one of his campaign speeches.

6 Market Research Socialism

1 Kaufman interviewed on 'Kinnock: the Inside Story' (London Weekend Television, 1993); Macintyre, 1999, p. 137. Pundit Peter Kellner agreed 'It wasn't the campaign, it was the product', *New Statesman*, 7ᵗʰ October 1987; similarly Harrop suggested Labour 'resembled an airline with a safety problem marketing itself on the quality of its in- flight meals' (Harrop, 1990).

2 Swindells and Jardine, 1990, p. viii; Mandelson, 1988. Similarly *The Times*, 27ᵗʰ July 1987 reported 'the product must be right before Labour could win'. An internal report by Mandelson claimed the party's presentation was 'so professional (it) risked being disqualified in the voters' minds'.

3 Shaw, 1994, p. x; *Tribune*, 14ᵗʰ November 1986; Hughes and Wintour, 1990, p. 42 and p. 46.

4 Hughes and Wintour, 1990, p. 173; *Tribune*, 2ⁿᵈ October 1987.

5 Gould on BBC Radio 4 'The World This Weekend', 5ᵗʰ July 1987, cited in Sopel, 1995, p. 95; Hughes and Wintour, 1990, p. 39; Hattersley was interviewed on Channel 4's 'A Week in Politics', 11ᵗʰ July 1987. The interview created media interest and greatly irritated Philip Gould (*The Guardian*, 13ᵗʰ July 1987; Gould, 1998, p. 85). When later questioned by Brian Walden as to whether the party had 'degenerated into marketing', the deputy leader was more conciliatory and defended Mandelson's 'enormously important' work (Cox, 1990, pp. 103–9).

6 Hughes and Wintour, 1990, p. 74.

7 Hughes and Wintour, 1990, p. 49; Butler and Kavanagh, 1992, p. 46; Shaw, 1994, p. 25; Gould, 1998, pp. 86–88.

8 Hughes and Wintour, 1990, pp. 59–61.

9 *Tribune*, 27ᵗʰ November 1987; *The Guardian*, 21ˢᵗ November 1987; *Sunday Telegraph*, 22ⁿᵈ November 1987; Hughes and Wintour, 1990, pp. 59–61.

10 Proposing 'reforms needed to bring Labour into the real world', Mitchell argued 'our organisation roots us to the past, to the declining sectors of society, the working class, the unions, the poor. It prevents us from changing

to the extent necessary to embrace the new, rising sections, the South, the new middle class; all the neighbours we no longer speak to because we're so preoccupied with ourselves' (*The Guardian*, 10th August 1987).

11 Hughes and Wintour, 1990. See also *The Guardian*, 23rd July 1987. On *Must Labour Lose?* see Chapter Three. Harrop and Shaw (1989) addressed similar themes to 'Labour and Britain in 1990s'. Their study *Can Labour Win* included a marketing analysis of the party's predicament as a 'service' organisation. *Labour and Britain in the 1990s* was eventually published (Labour Party, 1988). Though Philip Gould argues his research had 'enormous' influence on the Review he also suggested it did not have sufficient impact (Gould, 1998, pp. 86–90).

12 *The Independent*, 10th May 1989. See also *Tribune*, 15th January 1988; Hughes and Wintour, 1990, p. 46; see also *Tribune*, 26th February 1988; 22nd April 1988; Taylor, 1997, pp. 52–56.

13 Taylor, 1997, p. 12.

14 *The Times*, 6th December 1987; Macintyre, 1999, p. 74; see also Philip Gould's article on the aspirational working-classes (*New Statesman*, 4th December 1987) and reports of an internal inquiry into the surprise loss of marginal Battersea (*Tribune*, 8th January 1988).

15 *Tribune*, 26th February 1988; Hughes and Wintour, 1990, p. 46 and p. 102. The groups were 'Britain in a Modern World', 'Productive and Competitive Economy', 'Consumers and the Community', 'Democracy for the Individual and Community', 'Economic Equality', 'Physical and Social Environment', and 'People at Work' (*National Executive Report*, 1988, pp. 50–51). For more on the Policy Review in general see Smith and Spear, 1992; and Taylor, 1997.

16 Harman interviewed on 'Selling Socialism', The Media Show, 1990; Hughes and Wintour, 1990, pp. 137–38 and p. 153.

17 Golding and Middleton, 1982, pp. 91–95.

18 Mitchell, 1989, p. 128; Hughes and Wintour, 1990, pp. 109 and 127.

19 Shaw, 1994, pp. 99–101.

20 McSmith, 1994, p. 209. See also 'Labour changes its attitude: the Labour Party has shed its old animosity to the ad industry', *Campaign*, 8th November 1991.

21 Kinnock, 1994.

22 Tom Sawyer interviewed on ITV's 'Kinnock: the Inside Story' (London Weekend Television, 1993).

23 *Labour Party Annual Conference Report 1987*, p. 47; Hattersley interviewed on ITV's 'Kinnock: the Inside the Story', broadcast summer 1993.

24 *Tribune*, 14th October 1988; *Tribune*, 29th September 1989; Hughes and Wintour, 1990, p. 170; Temple, 2000. See also Butler and Kavanagh, 1992, p. 153. On accommodating and shaping voter preferences see Dunleavy, 1991.

25 *Sunday Telegraph*, 31st January 1988.

26 *Tribune*, 10th June 1988; *The Times*, 6th October 1988.

27 Rose, 1987; Gould, 1998, p. 93. On Kinnock's poor public standing see Foley, 2002, p. 88.

28 Todd also attacked the 'middle-class embarrassment' of the Labour hierarchy at being dependent on trade union support: 'They need out money

and our strength but they fear and resent our power' (*The Guardian*, 6th October 1988; Hughes and Wintour, 1990, p. 139). See also *Tribune*, 26th February 1988 and 22nd June 1990; *New Statesman*, 15th April 1988; Mitchell, 1990. *The Spectator* magazine parodied the *Review* as the 'marketing man's manifesto' (cited in Cox, 1990, p. 108).

29 Phil Kelly, *Tribune*, 13th May 1988. See also Anne Pettifor, *Tribune*, 26th January 1990; on 'Hard Labour' see *Tribune*, 28th October 1988.

30 Hughes and Wintour, 1990; Gould, 1998, p. 219.

31 Shaw, 1994, p. 112; Panitch and Leys, 1997, p. 219.

32 Hill, 1984.

33 Shaw, 1994, pp. 57–59.

34 Shaw, 1994, p. 62.

35 Minkin, 1992, p. 478; on union attitudes see, for instance, Tom Sawyer 'When New Realism can help the party activists: the new approach to trade unionism', *The Guardian*, 29th January 1987. Manning (1998) provides an extensive discussion of union communication strategies.

36 Webb, 1992; Shaw, 1994, p. 55 and pp. 215–16.

37 Bob Worcester interviewed in *Tribune*, 21st July 2000.

38 Worcester's initial problems with the party's 'principal spin doctor' arose from a dispute in 1986 over his research into Labour PEBs (Worcester, 1996; *Tribune*, 21st July 2000); Butler and Kavanagh, 1992, p. 60; Shaw, 1994, p. 147.

39 *PRWeek*, 19th March 1987; Di Giovanni, 1990. Gould also regularly worked on pro-European integration activities for the British Labour group at Strasbourg and its continental sister parties (*Campaign*, 25th March 1988; *Media Week*, 15th June 1990; *Independent*, 26th April 1993).

40 Larry Sabato interviewed by World in Action, 1992; BBC Vote Race unbroadcast interview 1992; Mellman and Lazarus also worked for Senator Al Gore and Russian President Boris Yeltsin (*The Financial Times*, 11th September 1991).

41 World in Action, 1992; *Independent on Sunday*, 28th July 1991; Rees, 1992, p. 91. Brendan Bruce claimed Doak and Shrum provided some of the creative inspiration for the acclaimed 1987 PEB 'Kinnock the Movie'. Bruce, 1992, pp. 111–12. Conservative Central Office and the Liberal Democrats also retained American consultants.

42 Shaw, 1994, p. 85; *The Guardian*, 22nd May 1989; *The Guardian*, 21st November 1989.

43 *Sunday Times*, 18th April 1991; *Financial Times*, 26th February 1992; Hughes and Wintour, 1990, p. 59.

44 Richards, 1989. See also *Sunday Times*, 15th May 1988; *The Guardian*, 22nd May 1989; *Campaign*, 22nd March 1991; *Sunday Times*, 22nd September 1991.

45 See, for example, *The Guardian*, 3rd April 1989 and a *New Socialist* article by Ed Richards (Richards, 1989). Journalists began to write of Labour MPs being 'Folletted', *The Guardian*, 6th April 1991; see also Hughes and Wintour, 1990, p. 59

46 *Sunday Times*, 9th June 1991; Jones, 1992.

47 *Marketing*, 13th June 1991; *Marketing*, 12th March 1992.

48 Heffernan and Marqusee, 1992, pp. 212 and 219; Shaw, 1994, p. 126.

49 Dennis Kavanagh, 'Keeping the lions away from the circus', *The Guardian*, 9th October 1990.

50 Comments made on 'Selling Socialism', The Media Show, 1990; *The Guardian*, 6th October 1990. The Labour leadership even criticised the dullness of a conference they had been so complicit in stage-managing for media consumption (Elliott, 1993, p. 144).

51 *The Times*, 24th June 1990.

52 Interviews on 'Selling Socialism', The Media Show, 1990. See also Hill, 1992, p. 61. Nick Moon, head of the NOP agency advising Labour, worried that if polling came to play an increasing role in policy rather than just helping with presentation then the system could become dominated by 'anodyne centre parties' (Interviewed on BBC1's 'The Vote Race', broadcast spring 1992).

53 *Tribune*, 20th April 1990.

54 *The Guardian*, 31st May 1990; *Tribune*, 8th June 1990. Barbara Castle criticised the 'wordy and anodyne' Review reports (Castle, 1993, p. 578). Her former Cabinet colleague Peter Shore described the outcome as a 'political vacuum' (Shore, 1993, p. 172). The LCC paper complained: 'No major company would simply leave its image in the hands of its PR director. The board would examine the research and determine the strategy, then leave it to the professionals to carry it out.' The LCC returned to this theme following the 1992 defeat (Thompson and Craven, 1992). Similarly *The Spectator* (26th May 1990) attacked the artificiality of 'Labour's Plastic Rose'.

55 *Financial Times*, 6th October 1989. During the same year there were other reports about off the record briefings: *Tribune*, 3rd March, 17th March, 28th April and 30th June 1989. See also Hugh Macpherson, *Tribune*, 15th February 1991; Shaw, 1994, p. 113; and Heffernan and Marqusee, 1992, p. 222.

56 Rees, 1992, p. 46; Mandelson would, for instance, selectively brief journalists on the proceedings of PLP and NEC meetings before the discussions had ended (Jones, 1995, p. 192).

57 *The Independent*, 1st July 1989. Mandelson was called 'descendant of Machiavelli' (*Today*, 6th November 1987), 'Labour's brilliant head of communications' (*The Guardian*, 6th October 1988), 'evil genius' and 'Kinnock's de facto deputy' (*The Independent*, 1st July 1989). Hugh Macpherson talked of the 'Mandelsonisation' of the Labour Party (*Tribune*, 20th May 1989). The recipient of this attention admitted: 'All I am prepared to say is that I am a political animal down to my fingertips' (*Today*, 4th October 1989). Mandelson has regularly featured in an apocryphal story in which he supposedly goes into a fish and chip shop during a campaign in northern England and orders a bowl of mushy peas in the belief that it is avocado dip. Needless to say the subject himself refutes the tale as do some of those who have written about him (*Sunday Telegraph*, 15th March 1992; McSmith, 1996).

58 *The Guardian*, 16th April 1992.

59 *The Guardian*, 6th March 1986.

60 Benn, 1992, p. 494.

61 *The Guardian*, 16th February 1990.

62 *Campaign*, 29th June 1990. On the controversy surrounding the Director's departure see *Tribune*, 1st December 1989; *The Independent*, 11th December 1989; *Tribune*, 26th January 1990; *Tribune*, 2nd February 1990; Heffernan and

Marqusee, 1992, p. 224. Before becoming MP for Hartlepool in 1992, Mandelson worked for SRU, a management consultancy with close links to Labour (*Daily Telegraph*, 19th August). He also became an adviser to the BBC, which reunited him with former LWT colleague John Birt (*The Guardian*, 3rd October 1990).

63 Comments by *Tribune* editor Phil Kelly interviewed in *PRWeek*, 5th July 1990. The same article ended prophetically: '(Underwood) could also have made himself one of the biggest political pawns within the fractious Labour Party'. See also *The Guardian*, 28th June 1990; *Tribune*, 6th July 1990; the new Campaigns Director was reportedly not Kinnock's first choice candidate (*The Guardian*, 25th February 1991).

64 *Campaign*, 28th September 1990.

65 *The Independent*, 7th June 1991. See also *The Guardian*, 6th June 1991; *The Times*, 7th June 1991; *PRWeek*, 13th June 1991. The matter of Underwood's replacement was deemed worthy of editorials in concerned titles (*The Guardian*, 7th June 1991; *PRWeek*, 4th July 1991). The candidates were David Hill, Jim Parrish and Andrew Fox (*The Times*, 9th July 1991).

66 Hughes and Wintour, 1990, p. 8. Many Labour politicians resented the leadership's control over the party. Shortly before his death MP Eric Heffer even compared Kinnock to Stalin (Heffer, 1991, p. 230).

67 Campaign, 21st February 1992; *PRWeek*, 19th March 1992.

68 Henley Centre Comment, *Marketing*, 20th December 1990; *Independent on Sunday*, 22nd September 1991; *Sunday Times*, 22nd September 1991; for a discussion of the impact of the change of Conservative leadership see Taylor, 1997, pp. 111–115.

69 Shaw, 1994, pp. 124; see also Butler and Kavanagh, 1992, p. 91; Rosenbaum, 1997, p. 264.

70 Composer Michael Kamen devised a special tune of the same name for the campaign. For more on the election, see Butler and Kavanagh, 1992; and King et al., 1992. Cook, 1995 and Hill, 1995 offer Labour's perspective. In his campaign memoir, David Hare noted party strategists' reluctance to engage with the Conservatives on tax and the economy because of Labour's perceived poor reputation on these issues (Hare, 1993, p. 183). Independent focus group analysis suggested the Tory bombshell attacks had resonated with voters unlikely to be touched by Labour's proposed changes but who nevertheless believed they would be liable to pay more. The electoral impact of the issue is doubted by the British Election Study authors (Morrison, 1992; Heath et al., 1994, pp. 292–4).

71 *Today*, 26th March 1992; *The Observer*, 12th April 1992; Harrop and Scammell, 1992; Rees, 1992, p. 119. Shadow Health Secretary Robin Cook later castigated the poor research for the Broadcast (Cook, 1995).

72 Hill, 1992, p. 69; Jones, 1992, p. 98; Kinnock's mentor Barbara Castle was particularly critical of this approach (Castle, 1993, p. 584). Similar sentiments formed the basis of an earlier article 'Marketing Mitterrand' by Phil Kelly that criticised attempts to package Kinnock 'as everything he is not' (*Tribune*, 13th May 1988). See also comments by Kinnock's press secretary Julie Hall (Hare, 1993, pp. 226–227).

73 Interviewed on Channel 4's 'A Week in Politics', 13th June 1992. As one marketing expert contended 'It seems so slick that to me it almost goes

against their positioning' (*Marketing*, 2nd April 1992). Those belonging to a leading trade journal's expert panel regularly expressed dismay over the nature and tactics employed by Labour and the other parties (see the 19th and 26th March, 2nd and 9th April 1992 editions of *Marketing*). The rally was ultimately more of symbolic mistake as it did not feature as a running news story (Gould, 1998, p. 148).

74 Thomas, 1998. Critics blamed advisers such as Patricia Hewitt for the tactical blunder on constitutional reform (*Sunday Times*, 21st June 1992; Hare, 1993, p. 240).

75 Interviewed on Channel 4's 'A Week in Politics', 13th June 1992; *The Guardian*, 25th May 1992; *Sunday Times*, 21st June 1992. MP Kim Howells was blunt: 'Mr Kinnock's kitchen cabinet – the so-called spin doctors, the party managers – should be sent packing back to the ad agencies which are their natural home. This absurd triumphalism and pompous music, all this glitz got in the way', *The Guardian*, 13th April 1992. Neil Stewart, a Kinnock aide, argued a strong Leader's Office had been necessary because of headquarters' perceived shortcomings (Hare, 1993, p. 189).

76 Butler and Kavanagh, 1992, p. 254; *Tribune*, 19th June 1992. National Executive member David Blunkett also called for greater accountability in the management of strategy, *Tribune*, 22nd May 1992. See also comments in *Campaign*, 3rd July 1992. Given those in charge of the campaign had doubled in number, some argued this inevitably weakened the ability of strategists to plan and execute initiatives. This point was picked up in a management consultants' evaluation of the party structure commissioned by John Smith (Pitt-Watson and Hay, 1993).

77 *Labour Party Annual Conference Report*, 1992, p. 68.

78 *Daily Telegraph*, 18th June 1992; Kinnock later said that if people had wanted excitement they should 'go to the circus', interviewed on 'Kinnock: the Inside Story' (London Weekend Television, 1993); see also Gould, 1998, pp. 155–57.

79 Rees, 1992, pp. 45–6.

80 Leys, 1990. Similarly Paul Foot argued: 'Labour Party policy is devised not by rational men and women with their own distinctive ideas, but by the opinion pollsters' (Foot, 1990, p. 79).

81 Shaw, 1994, p. 134.

82 Dunleavy, 1991. The discussion was part of a 1993 BBC2 programme, 'Fight Again', hosted by Roy Hattersley (Hattersley, 1993). In his book Galbraith's offers his view of modern democracy, expressing a fear that electoral participation is increasingly becoming the preserve of those with at least modest economic means to the exclusion of a substantial minority of poor citizens (Galbraith, 1992; see also Pimlott, 1988). For Blair's views see his article in the journal *Renewal* (Blair, 1993). Note the 1992 British Election Study doubts whether a post-Policy Review Labour party could have gained more votes from repositioning itself further to the right (Heath et al., 1994).

83 Hare, 1993; Shaw, 1994, pp. 175 and 130. See also Krieger, 1991; and Philo, 1993. In independent focus group research conducted during the election voters appeared to regard the Conservatives as having a superior technical ability to manage the economy (Morrison, 1992). For Lewis this was symptomatic of an underlying problem: 'The ahistorical influence of

TV news has been invaluable in the ideological process, leaving the left floundering in an attempt to re-establish the importance of social and economic causality' (Lewis, 1991, p. 204).

7   The New Right Ascendancy

1   Cohen, 1963; McCombs and Shaw, 1972; Lukes, 1974.
2   Minkin, 1980; Koelble, 1991.
3   Drucker, 1979.
4   Panebianco, 1988; Ostrogorski, 1902. See also Leys, 1996, pp. 241–43.
5   Michels, 1962; Panebianco, 1988.
6   *Tribune*, 2nd September 1988.
7   Minkin, 1992, p. 630. Critics began to regularly denounce these aides as conservative 'young fogeys'; see, for example, Hugh Macpherson, *Tribune*, 19th June 1992.
8   Webb, 1994.
9   Shaw, 1994, pp. 57–9; see also Heffernan and Stanyer, 1997. On the development of spin doctoring see Frank Johnson, 'Doctoring facts puts Labour in a spin', *Sunday Telegraph*, 29th March 1992.
10   On the organisational consequences of marketing for political parties see Shama, 1976; Kotler and Kotler, 1999.
11   Tiffen, 1989, p. 162.
12   Seyd and Whiteley, 1992, p. 37. The relationship between *The Guardian* and Labour during this period was examined in the left-wing satirical magazine *Casablanca* (1992). On this also see Hugh MacPherson's parliamentary column for *Tribune*; Heffernan and Marqusee, 1992, pp. 219–20; Shaw, 1994, p. 126. The relationship between the paper and party deteriorated following the appointment of Alan Rusbridger as editor in 1995. *The Mirror* had been a long time Labour supporter and even sponsored the party's official 'Red Rose' tour during the 1997 election.
13   In 1996 Labour MP and leadership sympathiser Geoffrey Robinson bought the *New Statesman* and *Society*. His re-titled *New Statesman* was initially more sympathetic to the Labour leadership's position.
14   Kavanagh, 1995, p. 145. For background on the development of focus group research from the 1940s onwards see Morrison, 1998; and Wilkinson, 1998.
15   Dionne, 1991, pp. 311–14. See also Jamieson, 1992.
16   Shaw, 1995a. Women voters became a particular concern (Hewitt and Mattinson, 1989; Smith and Spear, 1992).
17   Brivati, 1993.
18   Hain, 1993a.
19   Elliott, 1993.
20   A term used by *Tribune*, 21st July 1995.
21   Leys, 1996, p. 250. See also Thompson, 2002, pp. 24–7.
22   See, for instance, *Fabian Review*, May 1992.
23   Kinnock, 1994a.
24   Minkin, 1992, p. 678.
25   Koelble, 1991, pp. 126–7. See also Elliott, 1993, p. 127; and Shaw, 1995b.

26 *The Guardian*, 13th April 1992. Later another aide, Neil Stewart, publicly alleged unions affiliated to the party had purposely withheld up to £50 million from party coffers (*The Guardian*, 28th September 1992).

27 Glasgow University Media Group, 1976.

28 *The Independent*, 13th April 1992; *The Sunday Times*, 19th April 1992; *The Times*, 19th May 1992; *The Independent*, 19th May 1992; *The Independent*, 12th June 1992.

29 Minkin, 1992.

30 *The Independent on Sunday*, 3rd May 1992; *The Guardian*, 12th June 1992; *The Independent*, 18th June 1992; *The Financial Times*, 18th June 1992; *The Guardian*, 20th June 1992. At the behest of Philip Gould, political editor Alistair Campbell contributed a likeminded article to the *Daily Mirror* (Gould, 1998, p. 159).

31 *Daily Telegraph*, 22nd June 1992; Weir, 1992. Tory advertising (and press supporters) had briefly targeted the unions with copy like 'Labour In, Everybody Out' along with a picture of workers voting for strike action.

32 Gould, 1998, p. 144; see also the commentary by Thompson and Craven, 1992.

33 Gould, 1998, p. 158. This analysis was consistent with the SCA co-ordinator's first report for Labour in 1985 (Shaw, 1994, p. 174).

34 Labour Party, 1992. Similar figures were reported in the press following the NEC's post-mortem meeting on the campaign (*The Sunday Times*, 21st June 1992). The BES findings are contained in Heath et al., 1994.

35 *The Guardian*, 29th April 1994; Richards, 1996; Sackman, 1998, p. 306.

36 Andrew Grice, 'Plain John Smith?', *Sunday Times*, 22nd November 1992; Martin Kettle, 'Whatever is the matter with John Smith', *The Guardian*, 3rd December 1992. Journalist Peter Oborne claims aides of the leading Labour modernisers were particularly antagonistic towards John Smith's approach to leadership (Oborne, 1999, p. 96).

37 Raynsford, 1992. See also Thompson, 1994; and Wright, 1994.

38 Ferguson and Rogers, 1986, pp. 37–39. On 'special' versus 'national' interests see Herman and Chomsky, 1988, p. 331.

39 *Tribune*, 15th January 1993.

40 Philip Gould, 'The Politics of Victory', *The Guardian*, 6th November 1992.

41 Gould, 1998, p. 55. Similarly Peter Mandelson, observing the 1988 American presidential election at first hand, noted how the Democrats' major challenge was 'making sure that every one of the Bush attacks was factually rebutted', *The Guardian*, 7th October 1988.

42 Transport & General Workers' Union et al., 1993. The conference documentation struck something of a different note to most media reporting: it noted the importance of the United Auto Workers' union backed strike in associating the Democrats with organised labour (Transport & General Workers' Union et al., 1993).

43 *Independent on Sunday*, 3rd January 1993; *The Sunday Times*, 10th January 1993. Moderniser Mo Mowlam was particularly keen on embracing the 'New' Democrats as well as the middle-class (Mowlam, 1993).

44 Gould and Hewitt, 1993. On 1987 see, for example, comments the post-election analysis provided by the Fabian Society (Willman et al., 1987). The party agents' reports appear in Braggins et al., 1993. For alternative views on 'Clintonisation' from Lewis Minkin and others see Huw Richards,

'Reflections on the eye of an eagle', *Times Higher Education Supplement*, 22nd January 1993.

45 *The Guardian*, 16th December 1992; *Northern Echo*, 4th January 1993; *The Guardian*, 9th January 1993.

46 Blair, 1993.

47 Wybrow, R. (1992) 'The 1992 General Election and its Impact on the Image of Public Opinion Surveys', paper presented to the Political Studies Association Post-Election Conference, Essex University, September.

48 Radice, 1992. The seats were Gravesham, Harlow, Luton South, Slough and Stevenage. The other reports in the series appeared in successive years (Radice and Pollard, 1993; Radice and Pollard, 1994). Radice had been a leading intellectual supporter of Kinnock's modernisation strategy (Radice, 1989).

49 Gould Mattinson Associates, 1992.

50 See, for example, Peter Riddell 'Labour pulled both ways', *The Times*, 28th September 1992 and reports in the same day's *Guardian and Independent*. One the wider impact of the studies see, for example, Thompson, 1996, pp. 280–82; Taylor, 1997; Heath, Jowell and Curtice, 2001, p. 11.

51 Gould, 1998, p. 187; Macintyre, 1999, p. 240. Mandelson did, at the time of the leaks, claim that he had 'only the *Guardian* reports to go by' in commenting on the material, *The Guardian*, 6th January 1993.

52 *The Guardian*, 5th January 1993; *The Independent*, 6th January 1993.

53 *The Financial Times*, 11th January 1993.

54 Interviewed on 'Walden', broadcast on ITV, 24th January 1993.

55 *Tribune*, 15th January 1993.

56 Gould Mattinson Associates, 1992.

57 A notable exception was former SCA volunteer Steven Barnett, 'Polls apart, Labour must take its chance', letter to *The Guardian*, 12th January 1993. Former Director of Communications John Underwood argued the ensuing debate was somewhat flawed: 'Political vision does not come as an appendix to the latest batch of polling figures. It springs from political experience and political conviction' ('Labour party seeks the right vision', letter to *The Guardian*, 8th January 1993.)

58 *New Statesman*, 13th October 2003.

59 On the journalistic distortion of focus group findings see Mitofsky, 1996; and Worcester and Mortimore, 2001, pp. 298–300. Media usage of the method to gauge opinion during the 1997 election in the hope of anticipating the outcome failed to detect the impending landslide victory; instead the reports picked up voter ambivalence to politicians (see, for example, the *Daily Telegraph*, 22nd April 1997).

60 Kruegar, 1994, p. 36. For more general discussions of the methodology see Drayton et al., 1989; Morrison, 1998; Wilkinson, 1998; Lunt and Livingstone, 1996; and Barbour and Kitzinger, 1999. For a defence of the political applications of focus grouping see the piece by a researcher involved in the first *Southern Discomfort* study (Cooper, 1993) as well as Gould, 1998, pp. 326–33. For a more critical commentary see Gaber, 1996 and Gaber, 1997.

61 Devine, 1992. For differing perspectives on the reinforcement of 'individualism' in the market research process see Wainwright, 1987, p. 301; and Cooper, 1998.

62 Webber, 1993. Given the demographic profile of the other constituencies there is a strong likelihood that they too contained disproportionately large *Sun* readerships.

63 See Devine, 1991; Devine, 1992, pp. 189–99; and also the research by Morrison, 1992.

64 See, in particular, the methodological critique offered by Morrison, 1998 (especially pp. 166 and 186). Philip Gould, the strategist responsible for conducting most of Labour's focus groups, has himself admitted to being an interventionist moderator (Gould, 1998, pp. 327–28).

65 Ivo Dawney, *Financial Times*, 11th January 1993; *The Guardian*, 31st December 1992. Prescott also commented: 'I think the pollsters and the advisers are becoming the arch-priests in politics and the politicians are in danger of becoming the bit actors with their soundbites' (*The Guardian*, 6th January 1993).

66 Hain, 1993b (his fears about the party becoming a de-energised 'empty shell' are aired in Hain, 1994); *The Independent*, 11th January 1993. See also Seamus Milne, 'Death to the Modernisers', *Tribune*, 1st January 1993.

67 *The Guardian*, 30th November 1992.

68 Lovenduski and Norris, 1994; Alderman and Carter, 1994.

69 Sopel, 1995, pp. 59–62, and 92; see also Mandelson's comments in Gould, 1998, p. 197.

70 *The Guardian*, 1st March 1993.

71 Cited in Ali, 1994. The others included Trevor Kavanagh of *The Sun*, Simon Heffer in the *Daily Mail*, *News of the World* columnist Woodrow Wyatt, Martin Kettle of *The Guardian*, and Andrew Rawnsley in *The Observer*.

72 Richards, 1995, p. 23; *The Sunday Times*, 15th May 1994; and *Sunday Express*, 15th May 1994. John Curtice suggests Blair had a greater impact on commentators' perceptions rather than the public's opinion of Labour's electoral chances (Curtice, 1994).

73 Alderman, 1995.

74 Alderman and Carter, 1995. After the campaign there was some controversy when it emerged that ex-SDP member and supermarket owner David (later Lord) Sainsbury had been a major Blair benefactor. The fundraiser was Barry Cox and other donors included his former LWT colleagues Melvyn Bragg and Greg Dyke (Rentoul, 2001, pp. 359–60).

75 Franklin and Larsen, 1994. The nature and reasoning behind Brown's decision not to stand were the subject of renewed controversy following the publication of a biography of the Chancellor of the Exchequer (Routledge, 1998). The leadership contest ended the friendship of Brown and Mandelson (Rentoul, 1995, p. 379).

76 Jones, 1995, pp. 77–78, and 159–60; Rentoul, 1995, p. 389.

77 Whyte, 1988, notes the crucial function of leadership selection to a party's wider marketing strategy.

78 Interviewed on BBC1's *Breakfast with Frost*, broadcast 12th June 1994. On the importance of Clause Four to Labour see Bale, 1996; Kenny and Smith, 1997. For more on the campaign to change it see Wring, 1998.

79 Riddell, 1997.

80 *The Guardian*, 8th October 1994.

81 Tribune Group, 1994.

82 *The Guardian*, 26th January 1995; *Daily Telegraph*, 6th February 1995.

83 *Daily Mail*, 6th February 1995, cited in Philo, 1995.

84 Radice and Pollard, 1993; Radice and Pollard, 1994. Not surprisingly the Fabian Society's membership recruitment leaflet claimed these studies had 'prepared the way for the modernisation of Labour's Constitution and policies'.

85 *Tribune*, 3rd March 1995.

86 *Tribune*, 10th March 1995; Labour Co-ordinating Committee, 1995.

87 *The Guardian*, and *Daily Mirror*, 22nd April 1995.

88 *The Guardian*, 10th January 1995, and 12th January 1995. Little comment followed the advert's initial appearance in *Tribune* the previous November. Alex Falconer, one of the MEPs Blair targeted, contended the meeting had not as one-sided as reported, *Socialist Campaign Group News*, February 1995.

89 Levy, 1996.

90 *The Guardian*, 11th March, and 27th March 1995.

8   Brand 'New' Labour?

1 For more on this see Shaw, 1996, pp. 217–218; McKibbin, 1998; Bale, 1999; and Fielding, 2003, p. 209.

2 Radice, 1989, p. 55; Gould, 1998, p. 96; Kavanagh, 1990, p. 104.

3 Riddell, 1997. For the leadership perspective see Mandelson and Liddle, 1996, p. 211.

4 Leys, 1996, p. 243. On branding see Michael Hindley MEP 'Labour– just another brand name', *New Times*, 26th November 1994; Stern, 2000; Needham, 2001.

5 *The Observer*, 26th November 1995; Wright, 1997, p. 24.

6 Leys, 1996; Gould, 1998, p. 213.

7 *The Guardian*, 24th June 1995; Labour Party, 1996; Panitch and Leys, 1997, p. 241.

8 Freeden, 1999.

9 Blair, 1994; Mandelson and Liddle, 1996, p. 32; Anderson and Mann, 1997, pp. 243–49.

10 Editorial, *The Observer*, 9th July 1995. See also Anderson and Mann, 1997, pp. 256–58; Gould, 1998, p. 210.

11 Blair, 1995; Fielding, 1997b; *The Guardian*, 3rd October 1995.

12 A point made about Labour by Mark Steel in *Socialist Worker*, 5th March 1994 *before* Blair's leadership. His point was amplified with the publication of a *Harpers & Queens* piece featuring affluent party supporters (25th August 1994).

13 Panitch and Leys, 1997, p. 236.

14 On the political economy of 'new right' Labour see Thompson, 1996; Hay, 1999; and Heffernan, 2000.

15 *The Guardian*, 16th October 1994.

16 *The Guardian*, 19th August 1995; Kinnock, 1994a; Gould, 1996. The 'project' concept was originally popularised by revisionist journal *Marxism Today* during the 1980s (Rentoul, 1995, p. 232).

17 See *The Guardian*, 12th, 13th and 14th September 1995.

18 Oborne, 1999, p. 136.

19 Butler and Kavanagh, 1997, pp. 62–63.

20 Hugh Macpherson, 'No hats for this Trilby', *Tribune*, 8th September 1995; Mandelson and Liddle, 1996.

21 Butler and Kavanagh, 1997, p. 55; Panitch and Leys, 1997, p. 326.

22 Sawyer, 2000.

23 Butler and Kavanagh, 1997, pp. 62–63.

24 Pitt-Watson and Hay, 1993; Jones, 1997, pp. 25–26.

25 *The Observer*, 6th October 1996. The term was popularised by dissident Labour MPs like Ken Livingstone.

26 Heffernan and Stanyer, 1997; Heffernan, 1999, p. 53.

27 Butler and Kavanagh, 1997, pp. 57–58.

28 On this unfolding debate see *New Statesman*, 11th August 1995; *The Guardian*, 14th July 1995, 27th July 1995 and 10th September 1995.

29 McSmith, 1996, p. 283. Dromey's move was even endorsed in a *Guardian* editorial, a newspaper not generally thought of as required reading amongst the T&G's largely blue-collar membership (*The Guardian*, 30th May 1995).

30 Macintyre, 1999, p. 321; see also Gould, 1998, p. 258.

31 *The Guardian*, 13th September 1996; Davey, 1996, p. 84.

32 Butler and Kavanagh, 1997, p. 195.

33 Kelly, 1998. Ironically Davies' replacement was beset by problems albeit of a business rather than political nature.

34 Dispatches, broadcast Channel Four, 8th May 1997.

35 Seyd, 1998, p. 66.

36 *New Statesman*, 30th October 1998; see also Leys, 1996.

37 Richards, 1998, p. 36. On the self-contradictory notion of 'direct' party democracy see Lipow, 1996, pp. 6–7.

38 Short interviewed by Steve Richards, *New Statesman*, 9th August 1996. Blair cited in *The Observer*, 11th August 1996.

39 *The Sun*, 18th March 1997.

40 Gaber, 1998. BBC1's Panorama, for instance, had devoted an entire edition to Labour's spin-doctors, *The Guardian*, 27th September 1996.

41 *The Guardian*, 7th June 1997; Scammell, 1998.

42 Butler and Kavanagh, 1997, pp. 58–59. BMP had earlier replaced BDDH as the party's agency. A now Saatchiless Saatchi & Saatchi agency also helped Labour devise copy (Gould, 1998, p. 317).

43 Draper interviewed on BBC2 series *The Century of Self*, *The Observer*, 31st March 2002; Butler and Kavanagh, 1997, pp. 129–30. During the parliament NOP polls cost the party an estimated £500,000 and Philip Gould Associates work an additional £180,000. Other Americans consulted included new media specialist Phil Noble (http://www.pnoble.com).

44 Labour Party, 1997; Greenberg, 1997.

45 Gould, 1998, p. 267. The idea for the card came from a Californian referendum campaign.

46 Harrison, 1997, p. 152; Butler and Kavanagh, 1997, p. 132; Powell, 1998.

47 *Marketing*, 17th April 1997. A shadow minister identified the newspaper's female readership as a target audience (*The Guardian*, 17th January 1997). Worcester was a key target seat (*The Guardian*, 19th August 1996).

48 *The Guardian*, 22nd April 1997. See also Gould, 1998, pp. 144–45.

49 *The Times*, 21st April 1997. *Primary Colors* author Klein accompanied Blair during the early campaign.

50 *Daily Mail*, 26th March 1997; Labour Party, 1997; Anderson and Mann, 197, p. 301 and 386.

51 Jones, 1997, p. 12.

52 Crewe et al., 1998, p. xxi. See also King, 1998, p. 203; Worcester and Mortimore, 1999, pp. 4–5. Even those sympathetic to Blair admit 'Labour did not win as 'New Labour'. It won as "not the Tories"' (Lawson and Sherlock, 2001, p. 7).

53 Draper, 1997, pp. 8–10.

54 For a thorough analysis of the augmentation of the PR state under Thatcher see Deacon and Golding, 1994. The Conservatives denied it but they too were engaged in 'spin' throughout the 1980s (McNair, 2000, p. 137).

55 For more on the GICS see Franklin, 1998; Heffernan, 1999; Jones, 1999; Barnett and Gaber, 2001; Scammell, 2001; Seymour-Ure, 2002. The SCU was costing an annual £839, 440 by 2000 (*The Guardian*, 15th July 2000).

56 Franklin, 2001; see also Jones, 2001, pp. 143–8.

57 The caricature of on message Labour MPs waiting for leadership instructions to be sent to their pagers became a regular feature of journalistic attacks (see, for instance, Nick Cohen on the PLP's 'Stepford Wives', *The Observer*, 10th November 1997). This criticism was augmented when government MP Andrew Mackinlay admonished his own colleagues' 'soft' questioning of Blair (*The Guardian*, 13th June 1998). For an informed analysis see Cowley, 2002.

58 *The Guardian*, 16th September 1998

59 *The Guardian*, 19th October 1997.

60 *The Observer*, 2nd July 2000. For a fuller account see Cohen, 1999, pp. 149–57.

61 *The Observer*, 18th January 1998.

62 Barnett and Gaber, 2001, p. 96.

63 Jones, 2001, p. 92.

64 Oborne, 1999, p. 125; Scammell, 2001. The latter move followed injudicious remarks by Campbell about 'bog standard' comprehensives (*The Guardian*, 19th February 2001).

65 Jones, 2001, p. 89. By 1999 the 69 special advisers were costing £3.7 million per year (*The Guardian*, 20th August 1999). Most notoriously Jo Moore's infamous e-mail of September 11th 2001 suggested it 'was a good day to bury bad news'. The bad news was 'council expenses' and, almost as bizarre, her employer Stephen Byers stood by her. This incident even led Peter Mandelson to lament Labour's association with spin (Mandelson, 2002, p. xliv).

66 Hennessy, 1999.

67 Barnett, 2000.

68 *The Guardian*, 27th July 1997. On Blair's populist approach see Street, 2001, pp. 208–11.

69 Seymour-Ure, 2002, p. 131; Bunting, 2001; Short interviewed in *New Statesman*, 21st July 2003. See also Toynbee and Walker, 2001, p. 239. Blair's

own high profile denial of his reliance on soundbites was undermined during the Northern Ireland peace talks when he argued that it was not an appropriate time for them before uttering 'I feel the hand of history on my shoulder' (Franklin, 2001).

70 Seymour-Ure, 2002, p. 130; Scammell and Harrop, 2001, p. 162.

71 *Daily Mail*, 29th April 2000 – the comparison was made by the newspaper that broke the story i.e. *The Times*, 17th July 2000.

72 Scammell, 2001, p. 514.

73 For an early Blair criticism of the paper see *The Guardian*, 30th January 1998.

74 Butler and Kavanagh, 2002, p. 3. The Third Way is discussed by Blair, 1998; and Giddens, 1998. For left responses to Labour's neo-liberal rhetoric and policies see Hay, 1999, p. 135; Fairclough, 2000; and Leys, 2001. Basham, 2000, offers a New Right perspective.

75 See, for instance, Martin Ivens, 'Blair: the management will be the message', *Sunday Times*, 4th May 1997. Blair was particularly taken with Charles Leadbeater's applauding of the 'new economy' (Leadbeater, 1999).

76 Bayley, 1998; McGuigan, 2003.

77 See, for instance, 'Blair rules by market research' *Independent on Sunday*, 13th July 1997.

78 People's panels consist of members being re-interviewed over time. Government opinion research was costing an estimated £1 million a month by 1999 (*The Guardian*, 3rd September 1999). Deputy Prime Minister John Prescott was particularly dismissive of Philip Gould's focus group analysis for failing to appreciate the importance of transport as an issue (*The Observer*, 29th August 1999).

79 Draper, 1997, p. 72.

80 Rawnsley, 2000, p. 113. The newspaper's editorial was effusive about this matter ('Right Stuff', *Sun*, 12th December 1997).

81 *Sun*, 19th July 2000.

82 *The Sunday Times*, 11th June 2000. Public hostility to the currency was a marked feature of Gould's focus group work and featured in a leaked memo from December 1999, *The Times*, July 17th 2000. See also Rawnsley, 2000, p. 75.

83 *The Sunday Times*, 28th May and 11th June 2000; *Sun*, 17th July and 19th July 2000.

84 Morris used polling evidence to advise Clinton on everything from his choice of holidays to whether he ought to bomb a foreign country (Morris, 1999). The concept of 'triangulation' has obvious parallels with Downs (1957) and Dunleavy's notion of 'preference accommodation' (Dunleavy, 1991).

85 A comment about the party's ethnic minority voters attributed to Blair by Roy Hattersley, *The Guardian*, 6th December 1999.

86 *The Guardian*, 7th February 2000. See also Kilfoyle, 2000; and, for a leadership response, Diamond, 2000.

87 *The Guardian*, 16th March 1998; Goodhart and Tyrell, 1998. The desire for a new kind of political dialogue had been a recurrent theme in the work of Geoff Mulgan, founder of the think tank Demos turned Downing Street advisor (Scammell, 2001, pp. 528–29).

88 Marqusee, 1997; Seyd, 1999; Taylor, 1999; Jones, 2001, p. 27; Seyd, 2001.

89 Winstone, 1999; Black et al., 2001; Shaw, 2004.
90 Rawnsley, 2000, p. 355; Shaw, 2001; Needham, 2001. During the 1999 European selection process panels scrutinised candidates on their ability to deal with the media. The veracity and effectiveness of this controversial system was questioned when Kathleen Walker Shaw, the highest placed non-MEP on the Scottish list, was obliged to fight a by-election in an existing Euro constituency. She fared badly, came third and was subsequently dropped following a row during the campaign over her nationality to which she responded: 'It is all a misunderstanding, I was born in Stafford, but I was conceived in Aberdeen' (Wring et al., 2000).
91 Shaw, 1995b; and Shaw, 2000, discuss the evolving relationship between the Blair leadership and business. See also Barnett, 2000; Davies, 2001; and, on the 'institutionally corrupt' Blair government, Osler, 2002.
92 *The Observer*, 5th July 1998. See also Palast, 2002.
93 *The Guardian*, 21st June 1999; *The Guardian*, 8th January 2001.
94 During the Scottish campaign Alexander had written of the need to brand the regional party (Butler and Kavanagh, 2002, p. 35).
95 Seyd, 2001; Butler and Kavanagh, 2002, p. 128.
96 Seyd, 2001.
97 *The Economist*, 1st June 2002; *The Times*, 5th June 2002.
98 Lister, 2001; see also Dilnot, 2001.
99 Freedland, 2001.
100 Worcester and Mortimore, 2001, p. 96; Fielding, 2002, p. 38.
101 Gould, 2002.
102 *The Guardian*, 4th June 2001.
103 *The Guardian*, 13th December 1996, ISSN 0 267 257X–.
104 Peter Riddell, *The Times*, 9th May 2001.
105 Powell, 2001; see also comments by Peter Mandelson, *The Independent* 14th March 2001.
106 Cook, 2002.
107 Denver et al., 2002; Seyd, 2001.
108 Butler and Kavanagh, 2002, p. 128.
109 Butler and Kavanagh, 2002, p. 250
110 Harrop, 2001.

Conclusion: Everything Must Go

1 McKibbin, 1998; Marquand, 1999, p. 226.
2 Kotler, 1982; Fletcher, 1994.
3 McHenry, 1938; Casey, 1944.
4 Turner, 1978, p. 5.
5 Altman, 1964.
6 Bryan Murphy, 'The Purpose of Propaganda', *Labour Organiser*, no. 511, 1966. The author was a public relations adviser.
7 Worcester, 1985.
8 Livingstone interviewed on 'Kinnock: the Inside Story' (London Weekend Television, 1993); *Financial Times*, 1st May 1997.
9 *The Sun*, 19th July 2000; *The Observer*, 26th November 1995.

10 Rustin, 1981. Similarly there was a realisation among the party leadership that marketing 'required a diminution of internal party democracy in order to increase sensitivity to the electorate at large', Scammell, 1995, p. 12. See also Kavanagh, 1995, p. 94. Webb notes the leader now enjoyed 'an institutionalised battery of resources upon which he can draw to enhance his grip over the process of developing party policy and strategy' (Webb, 1994).

11 *Emphasis added.* Schumpeter, 1943, p. 283. Famously Michels commented 'he who says organisation says oligarchy' (Michels, 1962, p. 365). Drucker observed how Labour evolved formal, bureaucratic structures governed by codified rules as a guard against the centralisation of power evident in existing 'bourgeois' parties (Drucker, 1979).

12 Richard Crossman interviewed by David Butler in 1960, cited in Kavanagh, 1995, p. 79.

13 Mitchell and Wienir, 1997, p. 52.

14 Epstein, 1967; Brivati, 1997, p. 189; Rose, 1974, p. 90. Seymour-Ure also discussed the importance of political communication effects beyond voter persuasion (Seymour-Ure, 1974, pp. 62–63).

15 Wickham-Jones, 1996.

16 Shaw, 1994, pp. 57–9.

17 As one observer put it, 'the position of Labour leader- which, according to (Robert) McKenzie's criteria, should have been crippled by the party's heavy defeat in 1987 – was seemingly enhanced as a result, Kinnock using electoral rejection as the excuse for bracing internal reforms which, on the whole, boosted his own authority. For those students reared on the McKenzie thesis, the 1980s clearly left behind a series of perplexing questions' (Kelly, 1994).

18 Hughes and Wintour, 1990, p. 48; interview.

19 Winston Fletcher, *The Guardian*, 4th June 1990. The 'Unfinished Revolution' appeared in *The Guardian*, 12th September 1995 and became the title for Gould's memoirs (Gould, 1998).

20 Seyd and Whiteley, 2002.

21 Panebianco, 1988.

22 Draper's '17 people who count' were elected Cabinet members Blair, Gordon Brown, John Prescott, Jack Straw, Chief Secretary Alistair Darling and appointee Lord Derry Irvine. The only other elected politician was Minister without Portfolio Peter Mandelson. The appointees were strategist Philip Gould and Downing Street aides Alistair Campbell, David Miliband, Anji Hunter, Jonathan Powell, Geoffrey Norris, Sally Morgan and Roger Liddle plus two of Brown's advisers, Ed Balls and Charlie Whelan (*The Guardian*, 10th July 1998, *The Observer*, 12th July 1998).

23 Mauser, 1983; Heath et al., 2001, pp. 53–4, 156 and 166. See also Dunleavy, 1991 on politicians' preference shaping and accommodation strategies.

24 Gamble, 1974; Gamble, 1994.

25 Jennings, 1960.

26 Gould, 1998; Hay, 1999.

27 Desai, 1994, pp. 185–86; see also Anderson and Mann, 1997, pp. 384–5; and Taylor, 1997. On Labour's acceptance of people's capitalism and its perceived successes, see Heffernan, 2000, p. 166.

28 Cited in Lloyd, 1999; see Mair, 2000 on the significance of 'the people'.

29 Gould, 1998, p. 144. See also Barratt-Brown and Coates, 1996, p. 200.
30 Crouch, 2000, p. 66; Klein, 2001, p. 70.
31 Mandelson and Liddle, 1996; Barnett, 2000; Nick Cohen 'People's elite, *The Observer*, 31 August 2003. On the advisorial role of Charlie Leadbeater and Geoff Mulgan, see Frank, 2001, pp. 349–53.
32 Lewis 2001, p. 71; Miliband, 1961.
33 Norris, 2001.
34 Clarke, 1983; *Tribune*, 24th August 1999.
35 Leonard, 1981. See also commentaries from others on the Labour right, notably Mitchell, 1983; and Selbourne, 1984.
36 *The Sun*, 19th July 2000.
37 See, for instance, Matthew Taylor, 'Moral values and strategic thinking', *Inview*, the Institute for Public Policy Research newsletter, Spring 2003; and the editorial 'Listen Up', in *Progress*, January/February 2004.
38 It should be noted that Labour consistently led the Conservatives in all but one of the polls taken by MORI in 2003.
39 The Private Finance Initiative was arguably more complex and its popularity debatable if somewhat difficult to determine. For a critical perspective see Seamus Milne, *The Guardian*, 11th April 2001.
40 Those broadly sympathetic to the role of marketing in politics include: Harrop, 1990; Scammell, 1995; and Lees-Marshment, 2001.
41 Mauser, 1989, p. 44; Tyrell and Goodhart, 1998.
42 Gould, 1998, p. 397.
43 Marquand, 1999, p. 219.
44 Abrams and Rose with Hinden, 1960, pp. 101–2.
45 *New Statesman & Society*, 18th March 1994. The editorial was a response to the rise of anti-system politics on the far right.
46 Quote from the BBC2 documentary series *The Century of Self*, Nick Cohen, 'Primal Therapy', *The Observer*, 31st March 2002.
47 Mair, 2000.
48 Finlayson, 1999; and Finlayson, 2003, pp. 111–14. This picks up on the earlier work of Samuel, 1960; and Wainwright, 1987, p. 301.
49 Crouch, 2003; Needham, 2003; Marquand, 2004.
50 McKibbin 2000; Frank, 2001, p. xiv; Leys, 2001; Finlayson, 2003, pp. 208–12.
51 Whiteley, et al., 2001.
52 Crewe, 2002, p. 224; Cox, 2000.
53 Qualter, T. 1991; Franklin, 1994.

Bibliography

Abrams, M. (1960) New Roots of Working-class Conservatism, *Encounter*, 14:5, May, pp. 57–59.

Abrams, M. (1964) Public Opinion Polls and Party Propaganda, *Public Opinion Quarterly*, 28.

Abrams, M., Rose, R. with Hinden, R. (1960) *Must Labour Lose?* Harmondsworth: Penguin.

Adams, J. (1992) *Tony Benn*. London: Macmillan.

Alderman, K. and Carter, N. (1994) The Labour Party and Trades Unions: Loosening the Ties, *Parliamentary Affairs*, 47:3, pp. 321–37.

Alderman, K. and Carter, N. (1995) The Labour Party Leadership and Deputy Leadership Elections, *Parliamentary Affairs*, 48:3, pp. 438–55.

Alderman, K. (1995) Testing Party Democracy: The British Labour Party's Leadership Election 1994, *Representation*, 33:2, Summer/Autumn, pp. 51–57.

Alexander, A. and Watkins, A. (1970) *The Making of the Prime Minister 1970*. London: Macdonald.

Ali, T. (1994) The British Clinton, *New Statesman & Society*, 20th May, pp. 20–21.

Almond, G. (1990) *A Discipline Divided*. Newbury Park: Sage.

Altman, W. (1964) Selling the Labour Line, *Advertising Quarterly*, 2, Winter, pp. 7–10.

Anderson, P. and Mann, N. (1997) *Safety First: the Making of New Labour*. London: Granta.

Antcliffe, J. (1984) The Politics of the Airwave, *History Today*, March, pp. 4–10.

Attlee, C. (1954) *As it Happened*. William Heinemann.

Babaz, M. (1980) *Le Role de la Publicite dans les Campagnes Electorales Britanniques de 1964, 1966 et 1970*. Lille: University of Lille III.

Bale, T. (1996) '"The Death of the Past": Symbolic Politics and the Changing of Clause IV', in Farrell, D. et al. (eds) *British Parties and Elections Yearbook 1996*. London: Frank Cass.

Bale, T. (1999) The Logic of No Alternative? Political scientists, historians and the politics of Labour's past, *British Journal of Politics and International Relations*, 1:2, pp. 192–204.

Barbour, R. and Kitzinger, J. (1999) *Developing Focus Group Research*. London: Sage.

Barker, B. (1972) The Politics of Propaganda: a study in the theory of educational socialism and its role in the development of a national Labour Party. Unpublished M.Phil, York University.

Barnett, A. (2000) Corporate Populism and Partyless Democracy, *New Left Review*, 3.

Barnett, S. and Gaber, I. (2001) *Westminster Tales*. London: Continuum.

Barratt-Brown, M. and Coates, K. (1996) *The Blair Revelation*. Nottingham: Spokesman.

Bartle, J., Atkinson, S. and Mortimore, R. (eds) (2002) *Political Communications: the British General Election of 2001*. London: Frank Cass.

Basham, P. (2000) *The 'Third Way': Marketing Mirage or Trojan Horse*. Vancouver: Fraser Institute.

Bayley, S. (1998) *Labour Camp*. London: Batsford.

Beattie, A. (1970) *English Party Politics: Volume Two*. London: Weidenfeld & Nicolson.

Beckett, F. (2000) *Clem Attlee*. London: Politico's.

Beer, S. (1965) *Modern British Politics*. London: Faber & Faber.

Benn, T. (1965) 'Pollsters and Politics', in *The Regeneration of Britain*. London: Victor Gollancz.

Benn, T. (1992) *The End of an Era: Diaries 1980–90*. London: Hutchinson.

Benn, T. (1995) *Years of Hope: diaries, papers and letters, 1940–62*. London: Arrow.

Benson, L. (1978) *Proletarians and Parties*. London: Tavistock.

Berger, S. (1994) *The British Labour Party and the German Social Democrats, 1900–1931*. Oxford: Clarendon Press.

Berrington, H. (1992) 'Dialogue of the Deaf? The Elite and the Electorate in Mid-Century Britain', in Kavanagh, D. (ed.) *Electoral Politics*. Oxford: Oxford University Press.

Betteridge, J. (1997) 'Broadcasting the Post War Elections: Changing Media, Changing Rules, Changing Politics', paper presented to the Political Studies Association Annual Conference, Ulster University, April.

Bevir, M. (1997) Graham Wallas Today, *Political Quarterly*, 68:3, pp. 284–292.

Bing, I. et al. (eds) (1971) *The Labour Party: an organisational study*. Tract 407. London: Fabian Society.

Black, A. et al. (2001) *Reforming Labour*. Gloucestershire: Polemic.

Black, L. (2003) *The Political Culture of the Left in Affluent Britain 1951–64*. Hampshire: Macmillan Palgrave.

Blair, T. (1993) Why Modernisation Matters, *Renewal*, 1:4, October, pp. 4–11.

Blair, T. (1994) *Socialism*. Tract 565. London: Fabian Society.

Blair, T. (1995) *Face the Future: the 1945 anniversary lecture*. Tract 571. London: Fabian Society.

Blair, T. (1996) *New Britain: My Vision of a Young Country*. London: Fourth Estate.

Blair, T. (1998) *The Third Way*. London: Fabian Society.

Blewett, N. (1972) *The Peers, the Parties and the People: the General Elections of 1910*. London: Macmillan.

Blumenthal, S. (1982) *The Permanent Campaign*. New York: Simon & Schuster.

Blumler, J., Kavanagh, D. and Nossiter, T. (1996) 'Modern Communications versus Traditional Politics in Britain: Unstable Marriage of Convenience', in Swanson, D. and Mancini, P. (eds) *Politics, Media and Modern Democracy: An International Study of Innovations in Electoral Campaigning and Their Consequences*. Westport: Praeger.

Bond, R. (1979) 'Cinema in the Thirties', in Clark, J. (ed.) *Culture and Crisis in Britain in the Thirties*. London: Lawrence & Wishart.

Boorstin, D. (1962) *The Image, or What happened to the American dream*. London: Penguin.

Bowler, S. and Farrell, D. (eds) (1992) *Electoral Strategies and Political Marketing*. Hampshire: Macmillan.

Braggins, J., McDonagh, M. and Barnard, A. (1993) *The American Presidential Election 1992: What Can Labour Learn?* London: Labour Party.

Brivati, B. and Wincott, D. (1993) The Campaign for Democratic Socialism 1960–64, *Contemporary Record*, 7:2, Autumn, pp. 363–385.

Brivati, B. (1992) *The Campaign for Democratic Socialism*. Unpublished Ph.D, London University.

Brivati, B. (1993) Clause for Thought, *History Today*, 143, October, pp. 7–10.

Brivati, B. (1997) 'Earthquake or watershed? Conclusions on New Labour in Power', in Brivati, B. and Bale, T. (eds) *New Labour in Power: Precedents and Prospects*. London: Routledge.

Brooke, S. (1992) *Labour's War: The Labour party during the Second World War*. Oxford: Oxford University Press.

Bruce, B. (1992) *Images of Power*. London: Kogan Page.

Bunting, M. (2001) From Socialism to Starbucks: the decline of politics and the consumption of our inner self, *Renewal*, 9:2/3, summer.

Burton, A. (1994) *The People's Cinema: Film and the Co-operative Movement*. London: British Film Institute.

Butler, D. and Jowett, P. (1985) *Party Strategies in Britain*. London: Macmillan.

Butler, D. and Kavanagh, D. (1974) *The British General Election of February 1974*. Hampshire: Macmillan.

Butler, D. and Kavanagh, D. (1975) *The British General Election of October 1974*. London: Macmillan.

Butler, D. and Kavanagh, D. (1980) *The British General Election of 1979*. London: Macmillan.

Butler, D. and Kavanagh, D. (1984) *The British General Election of 1983*. London: Macmillan.

Butler, D. and Kavanagh, D. (1988) *The British General Election of 1987*. Hampshire: Macmillan.

Butler, D. and Kavanagh, D. (1992) *The British General Election of 1992*. Hampshire: Macmillan.

Butler, D. and Kavanagh, D. (1997) *The British General Election of 1997*. Hampshire: Macmillan.

Butler, D. and Kavanagh, D. (2002) *The British General Election of 2001*. Hampshire: Macmillan Palgrave.

Butler, D. and King, A. (1965) *The British General Election of 1964*. London: Macmillan.

Butler, D. and King, A. (1966) *The British General Election of 1966*. London: Macmillan.

Butler, D. and Pinto-Duschinsky, P. (1971) *The British General Election of 1970*, London: Macmillan.

Butler, D. and Rose, R. (1960) *The British General Election of 1959*. London: Macmillan.

Butler, D. and Stokes, D. (1969) *Electoral Change in Britain*. London: Macmillan.

Butler, D. (1952) *The British General Election of 1951*. London: Macmillan.

Butler, D. (1995) *British General Elections since 1945*. Oxford: Blackwell. Second Edition.

Carvel, J. (1987) *Citizen Ken*. London: Hogarth.

Casablanca (1992) Who guards the Guardian: part 2, *Casablanca*, 1, October/November, p. 7.

Casey, R. (1939) The National Publicity Bureau and British Party Propaganda, *Public Opinion Quarterly*, October, pp. 623–634.

Casey, R. (1944) British Politics: Some Lessons in Campaign Propaganda, *Public Opinion Quarterly*, Spring, pp. 72–83.

Castle, B. (1993) *Fighting All the Way*. Hampshire: Macmillan.

Challen, C. (1998) *Price of Power: the Secret Funding of the Tory Party*. London: Vision.

Channon, C. (1989) 'The GLC's Anti-Paving Bill: Advancing the Science of Political Issue Advertising', in Channon, C. (ed.) *Twenty Advertising Case Histories*. London: Cassell.

Clark, E. (1986) *The Want Makers*. Kent: Coronet.

Clarke, P. (1983) 'The Social Democratic Theory of the Class Struggle', in Winter, J. (ed.) *The Working Class in Modern British History*. Cambridge: Cambridge University Press.

Coates, D. (1980) *Labour in Power?: a study of the Labour government 1974–1979*. London: Longman.

Cockerell, M. (1983) 'The Marketing of Margaret', *The Listener*, 16th June.

Cockerell, M. (1989) *Live From Number 10: The Inside Story of Prime Ministers and Television*. London: Faber & Faber.

Cockett, R. (1994) 'The Party, Publicity and the Media', in Seldon, A. and Ball, S. (eds) *Conservative Century*. Oxford: Oxford University Press.

Cohen, B. (1963) *The Press and Foreign Policy*. New Jersey: Princeton University Press.

Cohen, N. (1999) *Cruel Britannia*. London: Verso.

Cole, G.D.H. (1948) *A History of the Labour Party from 1914*. London: Routledge & Kegan Paul.

Cole, G.D.H. (1965) *British Working Class Politics, 1832–1914*. London: Routledge & Kegan Paul.

Cook, R. (1995) 'The Labour Campaign' in Crewe, I. and Gosschalk, B. (eds) *Political Communications: the British General Election Campaign of 1992*.

Cook, G. (2002) 'The Labour Campaign', in Bartle, J., Atkinson, S. and Mortimore, R. (eds) *Political Communications: the British General Election of 2001*. London: Frank Cass.

Cooper, P. (1993) Blaming Messengers, *Fabian Review*, 105:6, December, pp. 10–11.

Cooper, P. (1998) 'Market Research and Democracy', in Macdonald, C. (eds) *ESOMAR Handbook of Market Research*. Amsterdam: Esomar.

Cowley, P. (2002) *Revolts and Rebellions: parliamentary voting under Blair*. London: Politicos.

Cox, B. (2000) Defending Apathy, *Prospect*, August/September.

Cox, D. (ed.) (1990) *The Walden Interviews*. London: Boxtree.

Craig, F.W.S. (ed.) (1982) *Conservative and Labour Party Conference Decisions, 1945–81*. Chichester: Parliamentary Research Services.

Crane, P. (1959) What's in a Party Image, *Political Quarterly*, 30.

Crewe, I. and Gosschalk, B. (eds) (1995) *Political Communications: the General Election Campaign of 1992*. Cambridge: Cambridge University Press.

Crewe, I. and Harrop, M. (eds) (1986) *Political Communications: the General Election Campaign of 1983*. Cambridge: Cambridge University Press.

Crewe, I. and Harrop, M. (eds) (1989) *Political Communications: the General Election Campaign of 1987*. Cambridge: Cambridge University Press.

Crewe, I. and King, A. (1995) *SDP: the Birth, Life and Death of the Social Democratic Party*. Oxford: Oxford University Press.

Crewe, I. (2002) 'A New Political Hegemony?', in King, A. (ed.) *Britain at the Polls 2001*. London: Chatham House.

Crewe, I., Gosschalk, B. and Bartle, J. (1998) *Political Communications: Why Labour Won the General Election of 1997*. London: Frank Cass.

Crick, M. (1986) *The March of Militant*. London: Harmondsworth.

Croft, H. (1945) *Conduct of Parliamentary Elections*. London: Labour Party. Second Edition.

Crompton, J. and Lamb, C. (1986) *Marketing Government and Social Services*. New York: John Wiley.

Crosland, A. (1956) *The Future of Socialism*. London: Jonathan Cape.

Crosland, A. (1962) 'Can Labour Win?', in *The Conservative Enemy*. London: Jonathan Cape.

Crosland, S. (1983) *Tony Crosland*. London: Coronet.

Crossman, R. (1960) *Labour and the Affluent Society*. London: Fabian Society Tract 325.

Crouch, C. (2000) *Coping with Post-democracy*. Fabian Society Tract 598.

Crouch, C. (2003) *Commercialisation or Citizenship*. London: Fabian Society Tract 606.

Curran, J. (1978) 'Advertising and the Press', in Curran, J. (ed.) *The British Press*. London: Macmillan.

Curran, J. (1987) 'The Boomerang Effect: the Press and the Battle for London 1981–86', in Curran, J. et al. (eds) *Impacts and Influences*. London: Methuen.

Curtice, J. (1994) 'What the Polls Really Say About Blair', *Parliamentary Brief*, October, p. 52.

Dalyell, T. (1989) *Dick Crossman*. London: Weidenfeld & Nicolson.

Davey, K. (1996) 'The Impermanence of New Labour', in Perryman, M. (ed.) *The Blair Agenda*. London: Lawrence & Wishart.

Davidson, M. (1992) *The Consumerist Manifesto*. London: Comedia/Routledge.

Davies, L. (2001) *Through the Looking Glass: A Dissenter Inside New Labour*. London: Verso.

Deacon, D. and Golding, P. (1994) *Taxation and Representation: the Media, Political Communication and the Poll Tax*. London: John Libbey.

Delaney, T. (1982) 'Labour's Advertising Campaign', in Worcester, R. & Harrop, M. (eds) *Political Communications: the British General Election of 1979*. London: Methuen.

Denselow, R. (1989) *When the Music's Over: The Story of Political Pop*. London: Faber & Faber.

Denver, D. (1994) *Elections and Voting Behaviour in Britain*. Hemel Hempstead: Harvester Wheatsheaf. Second Edition.

Denver, D. and Hands, G. (1997) *Modern Constituency Electioneering: Local Campaigning in the 1992 General Election*. London: Frank Cass.

Denver, D. et al. (2002) 'The Impact of Constituency Campaigning in the 2001 General Election', in Bennie, L. et al. (ed.) *British Elections and Parties Review 12*. London: Frank Cass, pp. 80–94.

Desai, R. (1994) *Intellectuals and Socialism: 'Social Democrats' and the Labour Party*. London: Lawrence & Wishart.

Devine, F. (1991) 'Working-class evaluations of the Labour Party', in Crewe, I. et al. (eds) *British Elections and Parties Yearbook 1991*. New York: Harvester Wheatsheaf.

Devine, F. (1992) *Affluent Workers Revisited: Privatism and the Working-class.* Edinburgh: Edinburgh University Press.

Di Giovanni, J. (1990) Shadow Boxer, *Harpers & Queens*, November.

Diamond, P. (2000) *Must Labour Choose?* London: Progress.

Dilnot, A. (2001) Our Unequal Society, *The Guardian*, 2nd June.

Dionne, E.J. (1991) *Why Americans Hate Politics.* New York: Simon & Schuster.

Donoughue, B. and Jones, G. (1973) *Herbert Morrison: Portrait of a Politician.* London: Weidenfeld & Nicolson.

Dorril, S. and Ramsay, R. (1992) *Smear! Wilson and the Secret State.* London: Grafton.

Downs, A. (1957) *An Economic Theory of Democracy.* New York: Harper and Row.

Draper, D. (1997) *Blair's Hundred Days.* London: Faber & Faber.

Drayton, J., Farhad, G. and Tynan, C. (1989) The Focus Group: A Controversial Research Technique, *Graduate Management Review*, Winter, pp. 34–51.

Driver, S. and Martell, L. (1998) *New Labour.* Oxford: Polity.

Drucker, H. (1979) *Doctrine and Ethos in the Labour Party.* London: George Allen & Unwin.

Dunleavy, P. (1991) *Democracy, Bureaucracy and Public Choice.* Hemel Hempstead: Harvester Wheatsheaf.

Duverger, M. (1954) *Political Parties.* London: Methuen.

Edelman, M. (1948) *Herbert Morrison.* London: Lincolns Prager.

Edelman, M. (1964) *The Symbolic Uses of Politics.* Urbana: University of Illinois Press.

Elebash, C. (1984) The Americanisation of British Political Communication, *Journal of Advertising*, 13:3.

Elliott, G. (1993) *Labourism and the English Genius.* London: Verso.

Epstein, L. (1967) *Political Parties in Western Democracies.* London: Pall Mall Press.

Erwin Wasey (1947) Preliminary Report of Sociological Survey to Assess the Present State of Political Opinion. Unpublished paper, Erwin Wasey & Co Ltd, London, April–May.

Ewen, S. (1996) *PR! A Social History of Spin.* New York: Basic Books.

Fairclough, N. (2000) *New Labour, New Language?* London: Routledge.

Falkender, Lady (1983) *Downing Street in Perspective.* London: Weidenfeld and Nicolson.

Fallon, I. and Worcester, R. (1992) 'The Uses of Panel Studies in British General Elections, paper presented at the Political Studies Association Post-Election Conference, Essex University, September 1992.

Farrell, D. (1996) 'Campaign Strategies and Tactics', in LeDuc, L. et al. (eds) *Comparing Democracies: Elections and Voting in Global Perspective.* London: Sage.

Farrell, D. and Wortmann, M. (1987) Parties strategies in the electoral market: Political marketing in West Germany, Britain and Ireland, *European Journal of Political Research*, 15.

Ferguson, T. and Rogers, J. (1986) *Right Turn.* New York: Farrar, Straus and Giroux.

Ferris, J. and Bar-Joseph, U. (1993) Getting Marlowe to Hold His Tongue: The Conservative Party, the Intelligence Services and the Zinoviev Letter, *Intelligence and National Security*, 8:4, pp. 100–137.

Fielding, S. (1993) '"White Heat" and white collars': The Evolution of 'Wilsonism', in Coopey, R., Fielding, S. and Tiratsoo, N. (eds) *The Wilson Governments 1964–70*. London: Pinter.

Fielding, S. (1997a) *The Labour Party 'Socialism' and Society since 1951*. Manchester: Manchester University Press.

Fielding, S. (1997b) 'Labour's path to power', in Geddes, A. and Tonge, J. (eds) *Labour's Landslide: the British General Election 1997*.

Fielding, S. (2002) 'No one else to vote for? The Labour campaign', in Geddes, A. and Tonge, J. (eds) *Labour's Second Landslide*. Manchester: Manchester University Press.

Fielding, S. (2003) *The Labour Party*. Hampshire: Macmillan.

Fielding, S., Thompson, P. and Tiratsoo, N. (1995) *England Arise!: The Labour Party and Popular Politics in 1940s Britain*. Manchester: Manchester University Press.

Finlayson, A. (1999) 'New Labour and the Third Way: Re-visioning the economic', *Renewal*, 7:2, pp. 42–51.

Finlayson, A. (2003) *Making Sense of New Labour* London: Lawrence and Wishart.

Fletcher, R. (1977) 'Who Were They Travelling With?', in Hirsch, F. and Fletcher, R., *The CIA and the Labour Movement*. Nottingham: Spokesman.

Fletcher, W. (1984) *Commercial Breaks: insights into advertising and marketing*. London: Advertising Press.

Fletcher, W. (1994) *How to Capture the Advertising High Ground*. London: Century.

Foley, M. (2002) *John Major, Tony Blair and a conflict of leadership*. Manchester: Manchester UP.

Foot, M. (1973) *Aneurin Bevan*. London: Davis-Poynter.

Foot, P. (1990) *The Case for Socialism*. London: Socialist Worker Party.

Forester, T. (1976) *The Labour Party and the Working Class*. London: Heinemann.

Forrester, A., Lansley, A. and Pauley, R. (1985) *Beyond Our Ken*. London: Fourth Estate.

Francis, P. (1984) The Labour Publishing Company 1920–9. *History Workshop*, 18, pp. 115–123.

Frank, T. (2001) *One Market Under God*. London: Secker and Warburg.

Franklin, B. (1998) *Tough on Soundbites, Tough on the Causes of Soundbites: New Labour and news management*. London: Catalyst Trust.

Franklin, B. (2001) 'The Hand of History', in Ludlam, S. and Smith, M. (eds) *New Labour in Government*. Hampshire: Macmillan Palgrave.

Franklin, B. and Larsen, G. (1994) Kingmaking in the Labour leadership contest, *British Journalism Review*, 5:4, pp. 63–70.

Franklin, R. (1994) *Packaging Politics: Political Communications in Britain's Media Democracy*. London: Edward Arnold.

Freeden, M. (1999) 'The Ideology of New Labour', *Political Quarterly*, 70:1, January–March, pp. 42–51.

Freedland, J. (2001) Labour listens and learns from Gore's great mistake, *The Guardian*, 4th June.

Frow, R. (1999) White Cockade–Tannenbaum or Maryland, *Working Class Movement Library Newsletter*, 9, pp. 22–23.

Gaber, I. (1996) Hocus-pocus Polling, *New Statesman*, 10th August.

Gaber, I. (1998) 'New Labour and the New Information Order: the view from the television newsroom', in Dobson, A. and Stanyer, J. (eds) *Contemporary Political Studies*. Keele: UK Political Studies Association.

Gaitskell, H. (1955) Understanding the Electorate, *Socialist Commentary*, July, pp. 203–206.

Galbraith, J.K. (1969) *The Affluent Society*. Harmondsworth: Penguin.

Galbraith, J.K. (1992) *The Culture of Contentment*. New York: Sinclair-Stevenson.

Gamble, A. (1974) *The Conservative Nation*. London: Routledge & Kegan Paul.

Gamble, A. (1994) *The Free Economy and the Strong State: the Politics of Thatcherism*. Hampshire: Macmillan.

Giddens, A. (1998) *The Third Way*. Cambridge: Polity.

Glasgow University Media Group (1976) *Bad News*. London: Routledge & Kegan Paul.

Golding, P. and Middleton, S. (1982) *Images of Welfare. Press and Public Attitudes to Poverty*. Oxford: Martin Robertson.

Goldthorpe, J. et al. (1968) *The Affluent Worker: Political Attitudes and Behaviour*. Cambridge: Cambridge University Press.

Gorman, J. (1985) *Images of Labour*. London: Scorpion.

Gorman, J. (1996) The Labour Party's Election Posters in 1945, *Labour History Review*, 61:3, Winter, pp. 299–308.

Gould Mattinson Associates (1992) *Qualitative Research Amongst Waverers in Labour's Southern Target Seats*. London: Fabian Society.

Gould, B. (1996) *Goodbye To All That*. Hampshire: Macmillan.

Gould, P. and Hewitt, P. (1993) Lessons from America, *Renewal*, 1:1, January, pp. 45–51.

Gould, P. (1998) *The Unfinished Revolution: How the Modernisers Saved the Labour Party*. London: Little Brown.

Gould, P., Herd, P. and Powell, C. (1989) 'The Labour Party's Campaign Communications', in Crewe, I. and Harrop, M. (eds) *Political Communications: the General Election Campaign of 1987*.

Gould, P. (2002) 'Labour Party Strategy', in Bartle, J., Atkinson, S. and Mortimore, R. (eds) *Political Communications: the British General Election of 2001*. London: Frank Cass.

Grant, N. (1986) 'A Comment on Labour's Campaign', in Crewe, I. and Harrop, M. (eds) *Political Communications: the General Election Campaign of 1983*.

Greenberg, S. (1997) The Mythology of Centrism, *American Prospect*, 24, September, pp. 42–44.

Grice, A. (1986) Political Advertising: how Labour staged a marketing revolution, *Campaign*, 30th May.

Habermas, J. (1962) *The Structural Transformation of the Public Sphere*. Republished by Oxford: Polity in 1989.

Hain, P. (1993a) Neither mod nor trad, *Fabian Review*, 105:4.

Hain, P. (1993b) *What's Left*. London: Tribune publications.

Hain, P. (1994) Labour's Empty Shell, *New Statesman & Society*, 8th December.

Haines, J. (1977) *The Politics of Power*. London: Coronet.

Hamer, D. (1977) *The Politics of Electoral Pressure*. Sussex: Harvester.

Hamilton, M.A. (1939) *The Labour Party Today*. London: Labour Book Service.

Hare, D. (1993) *Asking Around: Background to the David Hare Trilogy*. London: Faber & Faber.

Hare, D. (1994) 'Don't they know what a play is?', *Fabian Review*, 106:1.

Harris, R. (1984) *The Making of Neil Kinnock*. London: Faber & Faber.

Harrison, M. (1992) 'Politics on the Air', in Butler, D. and Kavanagh, D. *The British General Election of 1992.*

Harrison, M. (1997) 'Politics on the Air', in Butler, D. and Kavanagh, D. *The British General Election of 1997.*

Harrop, M. and Scammell, M. (1992) 'A Tabloid War', in Butler, D. and Kavanagh, D. *The British General Election of 1992.*

Harrop, M. and Shaw, A. (1989) *Can Labour Win?* London: Fabian Society/ Unwin.

Harrop, M. (1990) Political Marketing, *Parliamentary Affairs*, 43:3, pp. 277–291.

Harrop, M. (2001) An Apathetic Landslide: the British General Election of 2001, *Government and Opposition*, 63, pp. 295–313.

Hattersley, R. (1966) 'New Blood', in Kaufman, G. (ed.) *The Left*. London: Anthony Blond.

Hattersley, R. et al. (1983) *Labour's Choices*. Tract 489. London: Fabian Society.

Hattersley, R. (1993) 'Fight Again', broadcast on BBC2 (in three parts), May.

Hay, C. (1999) *The Political Economy of New Labour: Labouring Under False Pretences?* Manchester: Manchester University Press.

Heath, A. et al. (eds) (1994) *Labour's Last Chance? The 1992 Election and Beyond.* London: Dartmouth.

Heath, A., Jowell, R. and Curtice, J. (1985) *How Britain Votes*. Oxford: Pergamon.

Heath, A., Jowell, R. and Curtice, J. (2001) *The Rise of New Labour: Party Policies and Voter Choices*. Oxford: Oxford University Press.

Heffer, E. (1986) *Labour's Future: Socialist or SDP Mark Two?* London: Verso.

Heffer, E. (1991) *Never a Yes Man: the Politics of an Adopted Liverpudlian*. London: Verso.

Heffernan, R. (1999) Labour's Transformation: A Staged Process with No Single Point of Origin, *Politics*, 18:2, pp. 101–106.

Heffernan, R. (1999) 'Media Management: Labour's Political Communications Strategy', in Taylor, G. (ed.) *The Impact of New Labour*. Hampshire: Macmillan.

Heffernan, R. (2000) *New Labour and Thatcherism*. Hampshire: Macmillan.

Heffernan, R. and Marqusee, M. (1992) *Defeat from the Jaws of Victory: Inside Kinnock's Labour Party*. London: Verso.

Heffernan, R. and Stanyer, J. (1997) 'The Enhancement of Leadership Power: The Labour Party and the Impact of Political Communications', in Pattie, C. et al. (eds) *British Parties and Elections Review Volume 7.*

Hennessy, P. (1999) *The Blair Centre: a question of command and control?* London: Public Management Foundation.

Herman, E. and Chomsky, N. (1988) *Manufacturing Consent*. New York: Pantheon.

Hewitt, P. and Mandelson, P. (1989) 'The Labour Campaign', in Crewe, I. and Harrop, M. (eds) *Political Communication: the General Election Campaign of 1987.*

Hewitt, P. and Mattinson, D. (1989) *Women's Votes: the Key to Winning*. Research Series no.353. London: Fabian Society.

Hill, D. (1984) Political Campaigns and Madison Avenue: A Wavering Partnership, *Journal of Advertising*, 13:3, pp. 21–26.

Hill, D. (1992) *Out for the Count*. London: Macmillan.

Hill, D. (1995) 'The Labour Campaign', in Crewe, I. and Gosschalk, B. (eds) *Political Communications: the General Election Campaign of 1992.*

Hobsbawm, E. and Jacques, M. (eds) (1981) *The Forward March of Labour Halted?* London: Verso.

Hodder-Williams, R. (1970) *Public Opinion Polls and British Politics*. London: Routledge & Kegan Paul.

Hogenkamp, B. (2000) *Film, Television and the Left 1950–1970*. London: Lawrence & Wishart.

Hogenkamp, B. (1986) *Deadly Parallels: Film and the Left In Britain, 1929–1939*. London: Lawrence & Wishart.

Hoggart, R. (1957) *The Uses of Literacy*. London: Chatto & Windus.

Hollins, T.J. (1981) The Presentation of Politics: The Place of Party Publicity, Broadcasting and Film in British Politics. Unpublished Ph.D, Leeds University.

Howard, A. and West, R. (1964) *The Making of the Prime Minister*. London: Jonathan Cape.

Howard, A. (1979) *The Crossman Diaries: selections from the diaries of a Cabinet Minister, 1964–70*. London: Mandarin.

Howell, D. (1976) *British Social Democracy*. London: Croom Helm.

Hughes, C. and Wintour, P. (1990) *Labour Rebuilt: the New Model Party*. London: Fourth Estate.

Innes, J. (1983) The inside story of Labour's Press machine, *The Journalist*, July, pp. 8–9.

Irving, S. (1962) Party Propaganda, *Socialist Commentary*, February, pp. 8–10.

Jameson, H. (1938) *An Outline of Psychology*. London: National Council of Labour Colleges. Tenth Edition.

Jamieson, K.H. (1992) *Dirty Politics: deception, distraction, and democracy*. New York: Oxford University Press.

Jenkins, M. (1979) *Bevanism: Labour's High Tide*. Nottingham: Spokesman.

Jennings, I. (1960) *Party Politics, Volume One: Appeal to the People*. Cambridge: Cambridge University Press.

Johnson, K. and Elebash, C. (1986) 'The Contagion from the Right: The Americanization of British Politics', in Kaid, L. et al. (eds) *New Perspectives on Political Advertising*.

Jones, G. (1973) Political Leadership in Local Government: How Herbert Morrison Governed London 1934–1940, *Local Government Studies*, June, pp. 1–11.

Jones, N. (1992) *Election '92*. London: BBC.

Jones, N. (1995) *Soundbites and Spin Doctors: How politicians manipulate the media- and vice versa*. London: Cassell.

Jones, N. (1997) *Campaign 1997: How the General Election was Won and Lost*. London: Indigo.

Jones, N. (1999) *Sultans of Spin*. London: Victor Gollancz.

Jones, N. (2001) *The Control Freaks*. London: Politico's.

Jones, S. (1987) *The British Labour Movement and Film, 1918–1939*. London: Routledge Kegan & Paul.

Jones, T. (1996) *Remaking the Labour Party: From Gaitskell to Blair*. London: Routledge.

Kampfner, J. (1998) *Robin Cook*. London: Victor Gollancz.

Kavanagh, D. (1982) 'Political Parties and Private Polls', in Worcester, R. and Harrop, M. (eds) *Political Communications: the General Election of 1979*.

Kavanagh, D. (ed.) (1982) *The Politics of the Labour Party*. London: George Allen & Unwin.

Kavanagh, D. (1990) *Politics and Personalities*. London: Macmillan.

Kavanagh, D. (1995) *Election Campaigning: The New Marketing of Politics*. Oxford: Blackwell.

Keith, R. (1960) The Marketing Revolution, *Journal of Marketing*, January, pp. 35–38.

Kelley, S. (1956) *Professional Public Relations and Political Power*. Baltimore: John Hopkins Press.

Kelley, S. (1960) *Election Campaigning*. Washington: Brookings Institute.

Kellner, P. (1985) 'The Labour Campaign', in Ranney, A. (ed.) *Britain at the Polls 1983*.

Kelly, R. (1994) 'Power and leadership in the major parties', in Robins, L. et al. (eds) *Britain's Changing Party System*. London: Leicester University Press.

Kelly, R. (1998) The Blair Effect: Power in the Labour Party, *Politics Review*, November, pp. 2–6.

Kenny, M. and Smith, M. (1997) 'Discourses of Modernisation: Comparing Blair and Gaitskell', in Pattie, C. et al. (eds) *British Parties and Elections Review Volume 7*.

Kilfoyle, P. (2000) *Left Behind*. London: Politico's.

King, A. et al. (1992) *Britain at the Polls*. New Jersey: Chatham House.

King, A. et al. (1998) *New Labour Triumphs: Britain at the Polls*. London: Chatham House.

King, A. (1998) 'Why Labour Won – At Last', in King, A. et al., *New Labour Triumphs*.

Kingsley, D. (1983) 'Photography and the Election', *Creative Camera*, July–August, pp. 1056–59.

Kinnock, N. (1983) 'John Macintosh Memorial Lecture', unpublished transcript, June.

Kinnock, N. (1994a) Reforming the Labour Party, *Contemporary Record*, 8:3, winter, pp. 535–554.

Kinnock, N. (1994b) 'Tomorrow's socialism' (part two: rethinking the future), broadcast on BBC2, 11th February.

Kirchheimer, O. (1966) 'The Transformation of the Western European Party System', in LaPalombra, J. and Weiner M. (eds) *Political Parties and Political Development*. New Jersey: Princeton University Press.

Klein, N. (2001) *No Logo*. London: Flamingo.

Kleinman, P. (1987) The Research Market: Did psychographics win the General Election?, *Admap*, September, pp. 16–18.

Koelble, T. (1991) *The Left Unravelled: social democracy and the new left challenge in Britain and West Germany*. Durham, NC: Duke University Press.

Kogan, D. and Kogan, M. (1983) *The Battle for the Labour Party*. London: Kogan Page.

Kornhauser, W. (1959) *The Politics of Mass Society*. London: Routledge.

Kotler, P. and Kotler, N. (1999) 'Political Marketing: Generating Effective Candidates, Campaigns, and Causes', in Newman, B. (ed.) *Handbook of Political Marketing*.

Kotler, P. and Levy, S.J. (1969) Broadening the Concept of Marketing, *Journal of Marketing*, 33:1, January, pp. 10–15.

Kotler, P. and Zaltman, G. (1971) Social Marketing: An Approach to Planned Social Change, *Journal of Marketing*, July 35:3, pp. 3–12.

Kotler, P. (1982) 'Voter Marketing, Attracting Votes', in Kotler, P. *Marketing for Non-profit Organisations*. New Jersey: Prentice Hall.

Krieger, J. (1991) 'Class, Consumption and Collectivism: Perspectives on the Labour Party and Electoral Competition in Britain', in Piven, F.F. (ed.) *Labor Parties in Postindustrial Societies*. Cambridge: Cambridge University Press.

Kruegar, R. (1994) *Focus Groups*. California: Sage.

Labour Co-ordinating Committee (1995) *Labour Activist*, 29th April, special Clause Four conference edition.

Labour Party (1918) *Why Brainworkers Should Join the Labour Party*. London: Labour Party.

Labour Party (1955) *Take it from here: a policy for the Young People who think for themselves*. London: Labour Party.

Labour Party (1959) *Labour Party Annual Conference Report*. London: Labour Party.

Labour Party (1960) *Labour in the Sixties*. London: Labour Party.

Labour Party (1961) *First Things Last?* London: Labour Party.

Labour Party (1966) *Report of the Party Commission on Advertising*. London: Labour Party.

Labour Party (1988) *Labour and Britain in the 1990s*. London: Labour Party.

Labour Party (1996) *New Labour, New Britain the Guide*. London: Labour Party.

Labour Party (1997) 'War Book Version 3: Two Futures – A Future of Hope for New Labour, A Future of Fear with the Conservatives', unpublished strategy paper.

Labour Party (various) Campaign Strategy Committee minutes, Labour Party Archive, Manchester.

Labour Party (various) *Labour Party Annual Conference Reports*. London: Labour Party.

Labour Party (various) National Executive Committee minutes, Labour Party Archive, Manchester.

Labour Party (various) Press and Publicity Sub-committee minutes, Labour Party Archive, Manchester.

Labour Party (various) *Report of the National Executive Committee*. London: Labour Party.

Lawson, N. and Sherlock, N. (2001) 'The Progressive Century: Ours to Make', in Lawson, N. and Sherlock, N. (eds), *The Progressive Century: the Future of the Centre-Left in Britain*. Hampshire: Palgrave.

Laybourn, K. (1997) *The Rise of Socialism in Britain c1881–1951*. Stroud: Sutton.

Leadbeater, C. (1999) *Living on Thin Air*. London: Viking.

Lebas, E. (1995) "When Every Street Became a Cinema" – The Film Work of Bermondsey Borough Council's Public Health Department 1923–1953, *History Workshop Journal*, 39.

Lees, J.D. and Kimber, R. (eds) (1972) *Political parties in modern Britain*. Routledge & Kegan Paul.

Lees-Marshment, J. (2001) *Political Marketing and British Political Parties*. Manchester: Manchester University Press.

Leonard, D. (1975) 'The Labour Campaign', in Penniman, H. (ed.) *Britain at the Polls*. Washington: American Enterprise Institute.

Leonard, D. (1981) 'Labour and the Voters', in Leonard, D. and Lipsey, D. (eds) *The Socialist Agenda*. London: Jonathan Cape.

Leonard, R. (1965) 'Labour's Agents', *Plebs*, 57:10, October.

Levy, M. (1996) 'Modernisation and Clause Four Reform', in Farrell, D. (eds) *British Elections and Parties Yearbook 1996*. London: Frank Cass.

Lewis, J. (1991) *The Ideological Octopus: An Exploration of Television and its Audience*. London: Routledge.

Lewis, J. (2001) *Constructing Public Opinion*. New York: Columbia University Press.

Leys, C. (1990) Still a Question of Hegemony, *New Left Review*, 181, pp. 119–128.

Leys, C. (1996) 'The British Labour Party's Transition from Socialism to Capitalism', in Panitch, L. (ed.) *Socialist Register*. London: Merlin.

Leys, C. (2001) *Market-Driven Politics*. London: Verso.

Lipow, A. (1996) *Political Parties and Democracy: Explorations in History and Theory*. London: Pluto.

Lippman, W. (1922) *Public Opinion*. New York: Macmillan.

Lister, R. (2001) Social cost of the Middle England ethos, *The Guardian*, 25th May.

Lloyd, J. (1999) Falling Out, *Prospect*, October, pp. 22–27.

London Weekend Television (1993) 'Kinnock: the Inside Story', broadcast on ITV (four parts), July–August.

Lovenduski, J. and Norris, P. (1994) Labour and the Unions: After the Brighton Conference, *Government and Opposition*, 29:2.

Lukes, S. (1974) *Power: A Radical View*. London: Macmillan.

Lunt, P. and Livingstone, S. (1996) Rethinking the Focus Group in Media and Communications Research, *Journal of Communication*, 46:2, pp. 79–98.

MacDonald, J.R. (1920) *A Policy for the Labour Party*. London: Labour Party.

Macintyre, D. (1999) *Mandelson: The Biography*. London: Harper Collins.

Madge, C. (ed.) (1945) *Pilot Guide to the General Election*. London: Pilot Press.

Mair, P. (2000) Partyless Democracy: Solving the Paradox of New Labour?, *New Left Review*, 2, March/April, pp. 21–35.

Mandelson, P. (2002) *The Blair Revolution Revisited*. London: Politico's.

Mandelson, P. and Liddle, R. (1996) *The Blair Revolution: Can New Labour Deliver?* London: Faber & Faber.

Mandelson, P. (1988) Marketing Labour: Personal Reflections and Experience, *Contemporary Record*, Winter.

Mann, M. (1985) *Socialism can Survive: Social Change and the Labour Party*. Tract 502. London: Fabian Society.

Manning, P. (1998) *Spinning for Labour: Trades Unions and the New Media Environment*. Hampshire: Ashgate.

Marquand, D. (1999) *The Progressive Dilemma: from Lloyd George to Blair*. London: Phoenix. Second Edition.

Marquand, D. (2004) *The Decline of the Public*. Cambridge: Polity.

Marqusee, M. (1997) New Labour and Its Discontents, *New Left Review*, 224, pp. 127–42.

Marwick, A. (1982) *British Society since 1945*. Harmondsworth: Penguin.

Matthew, H.C.G. (1987) 'Rhetoric and Politics in Great Britain, 1860–1950', in Waller, P.J. (ed.) *Politics and Social Change in Modern Britain*. Sussex: Harvester.

Mauser, G. (1983) *Political Marketing: an approach to campaign strategy*. New York: Praegar.

Mauser, G. (1989) 'Marketing and Political Campaigning: Strategies and Limits', in Margolis, M. and Mauser, G. (eds) *Manipulating Public Opinion*, Pacific Grove, California: Brooks Cole.

Mayhew, C. (1969) *Party Games*. London: Hutchinson.

McCombs, M. and Shaw, D. (1972) The agenda-setting function of mass media, *Public Opinion Quarterly*, 36, pp. 176–187.

McDermott, G. (1972) *Leader Lost: A Biography of Hugh Gaitskell*. London: Leslie Frewin.

McGuigan, J. (1998) National Government and the Cultural Public Sphere, *Media International Australia*, 87, pp. 68–83.

McGuigan, J. (2003) The Social Construction of a Cultural Disaster: New Labour's Millennium Experience, *Cultural Studies*, 17:6, winter.

McHenry, D. (1938) *The Labour Party in Transition 1931–38*. London: George Routledge & Sons.

McKenzie, R. (1955) *British Political Parties*. London: Heinemann.

McKibbin, R. (1974) *The Evolution of the Labour Party 1910–24*. Oxford: Oxford University Press.

McKibbin, R. (1998) Third Way, Old Hat, *London Review of Books*, 20:17, 3rd September.

McKibbin, R. (2000) Corporate Populism and Partyless Democracy, *New Left Review*, 3, pp. 80–89.

McLean, I. (1976) *Elections*. London: Longman.

McLean, I. (1980) 'Party Organisation', in Cook, C. and Taylor, I. (eds) *The Labour Party*. London: Longman.

McLuhan, M. (1964) *Understanding the Media*. London: Routledge & Kegan Paul.

McNair, B. (1999) *An Introduction to Political Communication*. London: Routledge.

McPherson, D. (1980) *Traditions of Independence: British Cinema in the Thirties*. London: British Film Institute.

McQuail, D. (1960) untitled correspondence, *Socialist Commentary*, August, pp. 25–6.

McSmith, A. (1994) *John Smith*. London: Mandarin.

McSmith, A. (1996) *Faces of Labour: The Inside Story*. London: Verso.

Michels, R. (1962) *Political Parties*. New York: Free Press. First published in 1915.

Mikardo, I. (1988) *Backbencher*. London: Weidenfeld & Nicolson.

Miliband, R. (1961) *Parliamentary Socialism: A Study in the Politics of Labour*. London: George Allen and Unwin.

Miller, W. et al. (1990) *How Voters Change: the 1987 British election campaign in perspective*. Oxford: Clarendon.

Milne, A. (1988) *DG: the Memoirs of a British Broadcaster*. London: Hodder and Stoughton.

Minkin, L. (1978) *The Labour Party Conference*. London: Allen Lane.

Minkin, L. (1980) *The Labour Party Conference*. Manchester: Manchester University Press. Revised Edition.

Minkin, L. (1992) *The Contentious Alliance: Trade Unions and the Labour Party*. Edinburgh: Edinburgh University Press.

Mitchell, A. and Wienir, D. (1997) *Last Time: Labour's Lessons from the Sixties*. London: Bellew.

Mitchell, A. (1983) *Four Years in the Death of the Labour Party*. London: Methuen.

Mitchell, A. (1989) *Beyond the Blue Horizon*. London: Bellew/Fabian Society.

Mitchell, A. (1990) The Labour Party: Back from the Brink, *Wroxton Papers in Politics*, series A: paper A11.

Mitchell, A. (ed.) (1995) *Election '45: Reflections on the Revolution in Britain.* London: Bellew/Fabian Society.

Mitchell, G. (1992) *The Campaign of the Century: Upton Sinclair's race for governor of California and the birth of media politics.* New York: Random House.

Mitofsky, W. (1996) Focus Groups: Uses, Abuses and Misuses, *Harvard International Journal of Press/Politics*, 1:2, pp. 111–15.

Morgan, K. (1987) *Labour People.* Oxford: Oxford University Press.

Morgan, K. (1992) *Labour People.* Oxford: Oxford University Press. Revised Edition.

Morris, D. (1999) *Behind the Oval Office.* Los Angeles: Renaissance.

Morrison, D. (1992) 'Conversations with Voters: the 1992 General Election', unpublished paper, Leeds University Institute of Communication Studies.

Morrison, D. (1998) *The Search for a Method: Focus Groups and the Development of Mass Communication Research.* Luton: John Libbey Press.

Morrison, H. (1920) 'On the fighting of a Municipal Election', in *The Labour Party Handbook of Local Government.* London: George Allen & Unwin.

Morrison, H. (1921) *The Citizen's Charter.* London: Labour Party.

Morrison, H. (1960) *An Autobiography.* London: Odhams.

Mort, F. (1990) 'The Politics of Consumption', in Hall, S. and Jacques, M. (ed.) *New Times.* London: Lawrence & Wishart.

Mortimer, J. (1998) *A Life on the Left.* Sussex: Book Guild

Mowlam, M. (1993) What's wrong with being middle-class?, *Fabian Review*, 104:5, January–February, pp. 4–6.

Mughan, A. (2000) *Media and the Presidentialisation of Parliamentary Elections.* Hampshire: Macmillan.

Mulley, F. (1961) Do We Want to Win? *Socialist Commentary*, December, pp. 8–10.

Myers, K. (1986) *Understains: the Sense and Seduction of Advertising.* London: Comedia.

Napolitan, J. (1976) 'Media Costs and Effects in Political Campaigns', *Annals of the American Academy*, 427, September, pp. 114–124.

Needham, C. (2001) New and Improved? New Labour's Brand Values, *Renewal*, 9:2, pp. 106–114.

Needham, C. (2003) *Citizen-consumers.* London: Catalyst Forum.

New Fabian Research Bureau (1937) Selling Socialism Conference Report, October. London: Fabian Society.

Newman, B. (1994) *Marketing the President: Political Marketing as Campaign Strategy.* London: Sage.

Nicholas, H. (1951) *The British General Election of 1950.* London: Macmillan.

Niffenegger, P. (1989) Strategies for success from the political marketers, *Journal of Consumer Marketing*, Winter, 6:1, pp. 45–51.

Nimmo, D. (1970) *The Political Persuaders: the Techniques of Modern Election Campaigns.* New Jersey: Prentice Hall.

Norris, P. (1987) Four weeks of sound and fury... the 1987 British general election campaign, *Parliamentary Affairs*, 4:4, pp. 458–67.

Norris, P. (1996) *Electoral Change since 1996.* Oxford: Blackwell.

Norris, P. (2001) 'New Labour and Public Opinion', in White, S. (ed.) *New Labour.* Hampshire: Macmillan Palgrave.

Oborne, P. (1999) *Alastair Campbell*. London: Aurum.

O'Keefe, G.J. (1989) 'Political Campaigns: Strategies and Tactics', in Salmon, C.T. (ed.) *Information Campaigns*. Newbury Park: Sage.

O'Shaughnessy, N.J. (1990) *The Phenomenon of Political Marketing*. Hampshire: Macmillan.

Osler, D. (2001) *Labour Party PLC*. London: Mainstream.

Ostrogorski, M. (1902) *Democracy and the Organisation of Political Parties*. Chicago: Quadrangle.

Packard, V. (1957) *The Hidden Persuaders*. London: Longmans, Green & Co.

Palast, G. (2002) *The Best Democracy Money Can Buy*. London: Pluto.

Palmer, J. (2002) Smoke and mirrors: is that the way it is? Themes in political marketing, *Media Culture and Society*, 24, pp. 345–63.

Panebianco, A. (1988) *Political Parties: Organisation and Power*. Cambridge: Cambridge University Press.

Panitch, L. and Leys, C. (1997) *The End of Parliamentary Socialism: From New Labour to New Left*. London: Verso.

Paterson, R. (1985) 'Fragments of Neil: Entertainment and Political Leadership', in Masterman, L. (ed.) *Television Mythologies: Stars, Shows and Signs*. London: Comedia.

Pearce, R. (1997) *Attlee*. Essex: Longman.

Pearson, J. and Turner, G. (1965) *The Persuasion Industry: British Advertising and Public Relations in Action*. London: Eyre & Spottiswoode.

Pelling, H. (1984) *The Labour Governments 1945–51*. Hampshire: Macmillan.

Philo, G. (1993) Political Advertising, Popular Belief and the 1992 General Election, *Media, Culture and Society*, 15, pp. 407–18.

Philo, G. (1995) 'Political Advertising and Popular Belief', in Philo, G. (ed.) *Glasgow Media Group Reader, Volume Two*. London: Routledge.

Pigott, S. (1975) *OBM*. London: Ogilvy Benson and Mather.

Pimlott, B. (1985) *Hugh Dalton*. London: Jonathan Cape.

Pimlott, B. (1988) 'The Future of the Left', in Skidelsky, R. (ed.) *Thatcherism*. London: Chatto & Windus.

Pimlott, B. (1994) 'Occupying Office or Using It?', *Fabian Review*, 106:1, January, pp. 4–5.

Pinto-Duschinsky, M. (1981) *British Political Finance 1830–1980*. Washington: American Enterprise Institute.

Pitt-Watson, D. and Hay, A. (1993) There is more to politics than winning: a management report on Labour, *Renewal*, 1:4, October, pp. 12–14.

Potter, D. (1960) *The Glittering Coffin*. London: Victor Gollancz.

Powell, C. (1998) ' The role of Labour's advertising in the 1997 general election', in Crewe, I. et al. (eds) *Political Communications: the British General Election of 1997*.

Powell, C. (2000) *How the Left Learned to Love Advertising: social and political advertising by BMP 1970–2000*. London: BMP DDB.

Powell, C. (2001) Time for a little old style fervour, *The Observer*, 20th May.

Priestley, J.B. (1968) *The Image Men*. London: William Heinemann.

Pulzer, P. (1967) *Political Representation and Elections in Britain*. London: George Allen & Unwin.

Qualter, T. (1962) *Propaganda and Psychological Warfare*. New York: Random House.

Qualter, T. (1985) *Opinion Control in the Democracies*. Hampshire: Macmillan.

Qualter, T. (1991) *Advertising and Democracy in the Mass Age*. London: Macmillan.

Radice, G. and Pollard, S. (1993) *More Southern Discomfort: a year on – taxing and spending*. Tract 560. London: Fabian Society.

Radice, G. and Pollard, S. (1994) *Any Southern Comfort?* Tract 568. London: Fabian Society.

Radice, G. (1989) *Labour's Path to Power: The New Revisionism*. Hampshire: Macmillan.

Radice, G. (1992) *Southern Discomfort*. Tract 555. London: Fabian Society.

Rawnsley, A. (2000) *Servants of the People*. London: Hamish Hamilton.

Raynsford, N. (1992) 'Sleepwalking to Oblivion?', *Fabian Review*, 104:6, November.

Rees, L. (1992) *Selling Politics*. London: BBC.

Rees, M. (1960) The Social Setting, *Political Quarterly*, 31, July, pp. 285–99.

Rentoul, J. (1995) *Tony Blair*. London: Little Brown.

Rentoul, J. (2001) *Tony Blair*. London: Little Brown.

Richards, E. (1989) Marketing the Labour Party, *New Socialist*, April/May.

Richards, H. (1997) *The Bloody Circus: the Daily Herald and the Left*. London: Pluto.

Richards, P. (1998) 'The Permanent Revolution of New Labour', in Coddington, A. and Perryman, M. (eds) *The Moderniser's Dilemma: Radical Politics in the Age of Blair*. London: Lawrence & Wishart.

Richards, S. (1995) Soundbite Politics, *Reuter Foundation Papers*, no. 14, Green College, Oxford.

Richards, S. (1996) Interview: Clare Short, *New Statesman*, 9th August.

Riddell, P. (1997) The End of Clause IV 1994–95, *Contemporary British History*, 11:2, summer, pp. 24–49.

Rogow, A. (1952) Public Relations and the Labour Government, *Public Opinion Quarterly*, Summer, 16, pp. 201–224.

Rose, R. (1963) The Professional of Politics, *New Society*, 45, 8th August.

Rose, R. (1965) 'Pre-Election Public Relations and Advertising', Butler, D. and King, A. (eds) *The British General Election Campaign of 1964*.

Rose, R. (1967) *Influencing Voters: A Study of Campaign Rationality*. London: Faber & Faber.

Rose, R. (1974) *The Problem of Party Government*. London: Macmillan.

Rose, R. (1987) Labour C'est Moi, *The Spectator*, 20th June.

Rosenbaum, M. (1997) *From Soapbox to Soundbite: Party Political Campaigning in Britain since 1945*. Hampshire: Macmillan.

Rosenbloom, D. (1973) *The Election Men: Professional Campaign Managers and American Democracy*. New York: Quadrangle.

Roth, A. (1977) *Harold Wilson: Yorkshire's Walter Mitty*. London: Macdonald and Jane's.

Rotha, P. (1936) *Film and the Labour Party*. London: Labour Party.

Routledge, P. (1998) *Gordon Brown: The Biography*. London: Simon & Schuster.

Routledge, P. (1999) *Mandy: The Unauthorised Biography of Peter Mandelson*. London: Simon & Schuster.

Rowland, C. (1960) Labour Publicity, *Political Quarterly*, 31, July.

Russell, A.K. (1973) *Liberal Landslide: The General Election of 1906*. Newton Abbott: David & Charles.

Rustin, M. (1981) Different Conceptions of Party: Labour's Constitutional Debates, *New Left Review*, 126, March–April, pp. 17–42.

Ryan, T. (1986) Labour and the Media in Britain 1929–39. Unpublished Ph.D, Leeds University.

Sabato, L. (1981) *The Rise of Political Consultants: new ways of winning elections.* New York: Basic Books.

Sackman, A. (1993) 'Managers and Professionals in Neil Kinnock's Labour Party 1983–87: A Case Study of Campaign Management', paper presented at the European Consortium for Political Research, Leiden University, April.

Sackman, A. (1996) The learning curve towards New Labour: Neil Kinnock's corporate party 1983–1992, *European Journal of Marketing*, 30:10/11, pp. 147–158.

Sackman, A. (1998) Political Marketing and the Labour Party: The Development of Campaign Strategy 1983–1992. Unpublished PhD, Manchester University.

Samuel, R. et al (1960) The Abrams Survey, *Socialist Commentary*, September.

Samuel, R. (1960) Dr. Abrams and the End of Politics, *New Left Review*, 5, September, pp. 2–9.

Saville, J. (1996) 'Parliamentary Socialism Revisited', in Panitch, L. (ed.) *The Socialist Register 1995*. London: Merlin.

Sawyer, T. (2000) *The Politics of Leadership*. London: Progress.

Scammell, M. (1995) *Designer Politics: How Elections Are Won*. Hampshire: Macmillan.

Scammell, M. (1998) The Wisdom of the War Room, *Media, Culture & Society*, 20:2, April, pp. 251–75.

Scammell, M. (1999) Political Marketing: Lessons for Political Science, *Political Studies*, 47, pp. 718–39.

Scammell, M. (2001) 'The Media and Media Management', in Seldon, A. (ed.) *The Blair Effect*. London: Little Brown.

Scammell, M. and Harrop, M. (2002) 'The Press Disarmed', in Butler, D. and Kavanagh, D. (2002) *The British General Election of 2001*. Hampshire: Macmillan Palgrave.

Schumpeter, J. (1943) *Capitalism, Socialism and Democracy*. London: Urwin.

Selbourne, D. (1984) *Against Socialist Illusion*. Hampshire: Macmillan.

Semetko, H. (1987) Political Communications and Party Development in Britain: The Social Democratic Party from Its Origins to General Election Campaign of 1983. Unpublished PhD: LSE.

Seyd, P. and Whiteley, P. (1992) *Labour's Grassroots: the Politics of Party Membership*. Oxford: Clarendon Press.

Seyd, P. and Whiteley, P. (2002) *New Labour's Grassroots: the Transformation of the Labour Party Membership*. Hampshire: Palgrave Macmillan.

Seyd, P. (1987) *The Rise and Fall of the Labour Left*. Hampshire: Macmillan.

Seyd, P. (1998) 'Tony Blair and New Labour', in King, A. et al., *New Labour Triumphs: Britain at the Polls*.

Seyd, P. (1999) New Parties/New Politics? A Case Study of the British Labour Party, *Party Politics*, 5:3, July, pp. 383–405.

Seyd, P. (2001) The Labour Campaign, *Parliamentary Affairs*, 54:4, October, pp. 607–23.

Seymour-Ure, C. (1974) *The Political Impact of the Mass Media*. London: Constable.

Seymour-Ure, C. (1996) *The British Press and Broadcasting since 1945*. Oxford: Blackwell. Second Edition.

Seymour-Ure, C. (2002) 'New Labour and the Media', in King, A. (ed.) *Britain at the Polls 2001*. London: Chatham House.

Shama, A. (1976) The Marketing of Political Candidates, *Journal of the Academy of Marketing Sciences*, 4:4, pp. 764–777.

Shaw, E. (1988) *Discipline and Discord in the Labour Party*. Manchester: Manchester University Press.

Shaw, E. (1994) *The Labour Party Since 1979: Crisis and Transformation*, London, Routledge.

Shaw, E. (1995a) 'Programmatic Change in the Labour Party 1984–94', paper presented at the Party Politics Conference, Manchester University, January.

Shaw, E. (1995b) 'Old Labour, New Labour', paper presented at the Political Studies Association Elections Public Opinion and Parties Group Conference, London Guildhall University, September.

Shaw, E. (1996) *The Labour Party since 1945*. Oxford: Blackwell.

Shaw, E. (2000) 'New Labour, New Democratic Centralism?', paper presented at the Political Studies Association Annual Conference, London School of Economics, April.

Shaw, E. (2001) New Labour: Pathways to Parliament, *Parliamentary Affairs*, 54, pp. 35–53.

Shinwell, E. (1981) *Lead with the Left*. London: Cassell.

Shore, P. (1993) *Leading the Left*. London: Weidenfeld & Nicolson.

Smith, G. and Saunders, J. (1990) The Application of Marketing to British Politics, *Journal of Marketing Management*, 5:3.

Smith, M. and Spear, J. (eds) (1992) *The Changing Labour Party*. London: Routledge.

Socialist Commentary (1959) Rapier: A peep at Transport House, *Socialist Commentary*, September, pp. 15–16.

Socialist Commentary (1962) Editorial: Professionalism in Politics, *Socialist Commentary*, April, pp. 3–5.

Socialist Commentary (1965) Our Penny-Farthing Machine, *Socialist Commentary*, October supplement.

Sopel, J. (1995) *Tony Blair: The Moderniser*. London: Michael Joseph.

Stern, S. (2000) Brand on the run, *Tribune*, 14th July.

Stewart, M. (1974) *Protest or Power?* London: George Allen & Unwin.

Stonor Saunders, F. (2000) *Who Paid the Piper? The CIA and the Cultural Cold War*. London: Granta.

Street, J. (2001) *Mass Media, Politics and Democracy*. Hampshire: Macmillan Palgrave.

Street, S. (1992) The Conservative Party Archive, *Twentieth Century British History*, 3:1, pp. 103–11.

Swaddle, K. (1990) Coping with a Mass Electorate. Unpublished Ph.D, Oxford University.

Swanson, D. and Mancini, P. (eds) (1996) *Politics, Media and Modern Democracy: An International Study of Innovations in Electoral Campaigning and Their Consequences*. Westport: Praeger.

Swindells, J. and Jardine, L. (1990) *What's Left: Women in Culture and the Labour Movement*. London: Routledge.

Taylor, G. (1997) *Labour's Renewal? The Policy Review and Beyond.* Hampshire: Macmillan.

Taylor, G. (1999) 'Power in the Party', in Taylor, G. (ed.) *New Labour in Power.* Hampshire: Macmillan.

Teer, F. and Spence, J.D. (1973) *Political Opinion Polls.* London: Hutchinson.

Temple, M. (2000) 'New Labour's Third Way: pragmatism and governance', *British Journal of Politics and International Relations*, 2:3, October, pp. 302–25.

The Media Show (1990) 'Selling Socialism', broadcast on Channel Four, 7th October.

Thomas, J. (1998) 'Labour, the Tabloids, and the 1992 General Election', *Contemporary British History*, 12:2, summer, pp. 80–104.

Thompson, N. (1996) *Political Economy and the Labour Party.* London: UCL Press.

Thompson, N. (2002) *Left in the Wilderness: the Political Economy of British Democratic Socialism since 1979.* London: Acumen.

Thompson, P. and Craven, M. (1992) *Beyond Defeat: Labour's road to renewal.* London: Labour Co-ordinating Committee.

Thompson, P. (1994) Editorial commentary: Labour's year of not living dangerously, *Renewal*, 2:1, January.

Thorpe, A. (1991) *The British General Election of 1931.* Oxford: Oxford University Press.

Tiffen, R. (1989) *News and Power.* North Sydney: Allen & Unwin.

Toye, R. (2003) *The Labour Party and the Planned Economy 1931–1951.* Suffolk: Boydell.

Toynbee, P. and Walker, D. (2001) *Did Things Get Better?* London: Penguin.

Tracey, M. (1977) Yesterday's Men – a case study in political communication. In Curran, Gurevitch & Woolacott (eds) *Mass Communication and Society*, London: Edward Arnold.

Transport & General Workers' Union (1993) *Clinton Economics: a First Summary*, report of the TGWU conference in association with *The Guardian* and European Policy Institute, 9th January.

Trenamen, J. and McQuail, D. (1961) *Television and the Political Image: A Study of the Impact of Television on the 1959 General Election.* London: Methuen.

Tribune Group (1994) *Beyond Clause Four.* London: Tribune Group of MPs.

Tunstall, J. (1964) *The Advertising Man.* London: Chapman & Hall.

Turner, E.S. (1952) *The Shocking History of Advertising.* Middlesex: Penguin.

Turner, J.E. (1978) *Labour's Doorstep Politics in London.* London: Macmillan.

Tyler, R. (1987) *Campaign! The Selling of the Prime Minister.* London: Grafton.

Tyrell, R. and Goodhart, D. (1998) Opinion poll democracy, *Prospect*, October, pp. 50–54.

Vig, N. (1968) *Science and Technology in British Politics.* Oxford: Pergamon.

Wainwright, H. (1987) *Labour: A Tale of Two Parties.* London: Hogarth.

Wallas, G. (1948) *Human Nature in Politics.* London: Constable. Fourth Edition.

Waller, R. (1988) *Moulding Public Opinion.* London: Croom Helm.

Warde, A. (1982) *Consensus and Beyond: the Development of Labour Party Strategy since the Second World War.* Manchester: Manchester University Press.

Webb, P. (1992) Election campaigning, organisational transformation and the professionalisation of the Labour Party. *European Journal of Political Research*, 21, pp. 267–288.

Webb, P. (1994) 'Party Organisational Change: the Iron Law of Centralisation?', in Katz, R. and Mair, P. (eds) *How Parties Organise*. London: Sage.

Webb, P. (2000) *The Modern British Party System*. London: Sage.

Webber, R. (1993) 'The 1992 General Election: constituency results and local patterns of national newspaper readership', in Denver, D. et al. (eds) *British Elections and Parties Yearbook 1993*. Hemel Hempstead: Harvester Wheatsheaf.

Webster, W. (1990) *Not to a Man to Match Her: the Marketing of a Prime Minister*. London: The Women's Press.

Weiler, P. (1988) *British Labour and the Cold War*. Stanford: Stanford University Press.

Weinbren, D. (1997) *Generating Socialism: Recollections of Life in the Labour Party*. Sutton Publishing.

Weir, S. (1992) 'Operation Scapegoat', *New Statesman and Society*, 4th September, pp. 15–16.

Westlake, M. (2001) *Kinnock*. London: Little Brown.

Wheeler, D. (1979) Campaign 79, *The Listener*, 3rd May.

White, E. (1958) Putting Ourselves Across, *Fabian Journal*, 26, November.

White, T. (1962) *The Making of the President 1960*. London: Jonathan Cape.

Whiteley, P. et al. (2001) 'Turnout', *Parliamentary Affairs*, 54:4, pp. 775–788.

Whiteley, P. (1983) *The Labour Party in Crisis*. London: Methuen.

Whyte, J. (1988) 'Organisation, person and idea marketing exchanges', in Thomas, M. and Waite, N. (eds) *The Marketing Digest*. London: Heinemann.

Wickham-Jones, M. (1996) *Economic Strategy and the Labour Party: Politics and Policy-making, 1970–83*. Hampshire: Macmillan.

Wiener, M. (1980) *English Culture and the Decline of the Industrial Spirit, 1850–1980*. Cambridge: Cambridge University Press.

Wildy, T. (1985) Propaganda and Social Policy in Britain 1945–51: publicity for the social legislation of the Labour Government. Unpublished Ph.D, Leeds University.

Wilford, H. (2003) *The CIA, the British Left and the Cold War: Calling the Tune?* London: Frank Cass.

Wilkinson, S. (1998) Focus Group Methodology: a review, *International Journal of Social Research Methodology*, 1:3, pp. 181–203.

Williams, M. (1972) *Inside No 10*. London: Weidenfield & Nicolson.

Williams, R. (1980) 'Advertising: the Magic System', in *Problems in Materialism and Culture*. London: Verso.

Williamson, J. (1986) *Consuming Passions*. London: Marion Boyers.

Willman, J. et al. (1987) *Labour's next moves forward*. Tract 521. London: Fabian Society.

Wilson, H. (1964) *The New Britain: Labour's Plan Outlined by Harold Wilson*. London: Penguin.

Wilson, H. (1978) Market research in the private and public sectors, *Journal of the Market Research Society*, 20:3.

Wilson, H. (1986) *Memoirs*. London: Weidenfeld & Nicolson and Michael Joseph.

Windlesham, Lord (1966) *Communication and Political Power*. London: Jonathan Cape.

Winstone, M. (1999) Filtering out Democracy, *Red Pepper*, October, pp. 25–27.

Worcester, R. and Harrop, M. (eds) (1982) *Political Communication: the General Election of 1979*. London: George Allen & Unwin.

Worcester, R. and Mortimore, R. (1999) *Explaining Labour's Landslide*. London: Politico's.

Worcester, R. and Mortimore, R. (2001) *Explaining Labour's Second Landslide*. London: Politico's.

Worcester, R. (1985) Review of Himmelweit, H et al., 1985, *How Voters Decide*. London: Open University Press; in *Journal of the Market Research Society*, 27:3, pp. 205–208.

Worcester, R. (1991) *British Public Opinion*. Oxford: Blackwell.

Worcester, R. (1996) 'Political Marketing: the Application of Market Research Instruments for Political Marketing', paper presented at the Political Marketing Conference, Cambridge University, March 1996.

World in Action (1992) 'The Dirty War', broadcast on ITV, 2nd March.

Wright, J. (1986) 'Advertising the Labour Party', in Crewe, I. and Harrop, M. (eds) *Political Communications: the General Election Campaign of 1983*.

Wright, T. (1994) What new politics? *Renewal*, 2:2, April.

Wright, T. (1997) *Why Vote Labour?* London: Penguin.

Wring, D. (1996) 'From Mass Propaganda to Political Marketing: the Transformation of Labour Party Election Campaigning', in Rallings, C., Broughton, D., Denver, D. & Farrell, D. (eds) *British Parties and Elections Yearbook 1995*, Hampshire: Frank Cass, pp. 105–124.

Wring, D. (1996) 'Political Marketing and Party Development in Britain: A "Secret" History', *European Journal of Marketing*, 30:10/11, pp. 92–103.

Wring, D. (1997a) 'Reconciling Marketing with Political Science: Theories of Political Marketing', *Journal of Marketing Management*, 13:7, pp. 651–663.

Wring, D. (1997b) 'Soundbites versus Socialism: the Changing Campaign Philosophy of the British Labour Party', *Javnost/The Public*, 4:3, pp. 59–68.

Wring, D. (1997c) 'Political Marketing and the Labour Party'. Unpublished PhD, Cambridge University.

Wring, D. (1998) 'The Media and Intra-Party Democracy: "New" Labour and the Clause Four Debate', *Democratization*, 5:2, pp. 42–61.

Wring, D. (1999) 'The Marketing Colonisation of Political Campaigning', in Newman, B. (ed.) *A Handbook of Political Marketing*, London: Sage, pp. 41–53.

Wring, D. (2001) '"Selling Socialism": the marketing of the "very old" British Labour Party', *European Journal of Marketing*, 35:9/10, pp. 1038–46.

Wring, D. (2001) 'Labouring the Point: Operation Victory and the Battle for a Second Term', *Journal of Marketing Management*, 17:9–10, pp. 913–27.

Wring, D., Baker, D. and Seawright, D. (2000) 'Panelism in Action: Labour's 1999 European Parliamentary Candidate Selections', *Political Quarterly*, 71:2, pp. 234–45.

Wybrow, R. (1992) 'The 1992 General Election and its Impact on the Image of Public Opinion Surveys', paper presented to the Political Studies Association Post-Election Conference, Essex University, September.

Young Fabian Group (1962) *The Mechanics of Victory*, February.

Zweinger-Bargielowska, I. (1994) Rationality, Austerity and the Conservative Party Recovery after 1945, *The Historical Journal*, 37:1, March, pp. 173–97.

Index